The Battle for
Hearts and Minds

A WASHINGTON QUARTERLY READER

The Battle for Hearts and Minds

USING SOFT POWER TO UNDERMINE TERRORIST NETWORKS

EDITED BY
ALEXANDER T. J. LENNON

THE MIT PRESS
Cambridge, Massachusetts
London, England

CONTENTS

vii Introduction: The Battle for Hearts and Minds ▪
Alexander T. J. Lennon

PROLOGUE: THE ROLE OF MILITARY POWER

3 The Limits of Military Power ▪ *Rob de Wijk*

29 The Future of International Coalitions: How Useful?
How Manageable? ▪ *Paul Dibb*

45 Forging an Indirect Strategy in Southeast Asia ▪
Barry Desker and Kumar Ramakrishna ˙

65 The Imbalance of Terror ▪ *Thérèse Delpech*

PART I: STATE FAILURE AND NATION BUILDING

79 The New Nature of Nation-State Failure ▪ *Robert I. Rotberg*

94 Do Terrorist Networks Need a Home? ▪ *Ray Takeyh and
Nikolas Gvosdev*

108 Democracy by Force: A Renewed Commitment to Nation
Building ▪ *Karin von Hippel*

130 Strategic Democracy Building: How U.S. States Can Help ▪
Bill Owens and Troy A. Eid

150 Sierra Leone: The State That Came Back from the Dead ▪
Michael Chege

PART II: POSTCONFLICT RECONSTRUCTION

169 Toward Postconflict Reconstruction ▪ *John J. Hamre and
Gordon R. Sullivan*

184 Building Better Foundations: Security in Postconflict
Reconstruction ▪ *Scott Feil*

200   Dealing with Demons: Justice and Reconciliation ▪
      Michèle Flournoy and Michael Pan

215   Achieving Socioeconomic Well-Being in Postconflict
      Settings ▪ *Johanna Mendelson Forman*

232   Governing When Chaos Rules: Enhancing Governance and
      Participation ▪ *Robert Orr*

PART III: PUBLIC DIPLOMACY

251   Public Diplomacy Comes of Age ▪ *Christopher Ross*

262   Deeds Speak Louder Than Words ▪ *Lamis Andoni*

282   Winning the War of Ideas ▪ *Antony J. Blinken*

299   A Broadcasting Strategy to Win Media Wars ▪
      Edward Kaufman

PART IV: TRANSFORMING FOREIGN ASSISTANCE

317   Compassionate Conservatism Confronts Global Poverty ▪
      Lael Brainard

342   Will the Millennium Challenge Account Be Different? ▪
      Steve Radelet

362   Promoting Democratization Can Combat Terrorism ▪
      Jennifer L. Windsor

381   Lessons and New Directions for Foreign Assistance ▪
      Jim Kolbe

Alexander T. J. Lennon

Introduction: The Battle for Hearts and Minds

The image on the cover of this book was chosen intentionally. Most obviously, the Pentagon was the building in Washington, D.C., that was successfully attacked by the Al Qaeda terrorist network on September 11, 2001. But the authors in *The Battle for Hearts and Minds* look outside the Pentagon to debate the utility of nonmilitary responses to the threat from terrorist networks. Military operations—because they are tangible, increasingly short, and produce dramatic television images—generate tremendous attention and analysis.

Yet the tools being used and considered to undermine terrorist networks extend well beyond military operations. Some of those tools include improving intelligence collection and cooperation, law enforcement, and ways to undermine terrorist financing. There are still others, as the authors of the 2002 U.S. National Security Strategy wrote:

> We will also wage a war of ideas to win the battle against international terrorism. This includes:
>
> - using the full influence of the United States, and working closely with allies and friends, to make clear that all acts of terrorism are illegitimate so that terrorism will be viewed in the same

Alexander T. J. Lennon is editor-in-chief of *The Washington Quarterly* and is pursuing his Ph.D. in policy studies, part-time, at the University of Maryland's School of Public Affairs.

light as slavery, piracy, or genocide: behavior that no respectable government can condone or support and all must oppose;

- supporting moderate and modern government, especially in the Muslim world, to ensure that the conditions and ideologies that promote terrorism do not find fertile ground in any nation;

- diminishing the underlying conditions that span terrorism by enlisting the international community to focus its efforts and resources on areas most at risk; and

- using effective public diplomacy to promote the free flow of information and ideas to kindle the hopes and aspirations of freedom of those in societies ruled by the sponsors of global terrorism.[1]

As a group, these tools are the "soft power" that Joseph Nye first defined in 1990.[2] Unlike hard power, which involves ordering or compelling others, soft power is the ability to co-opt or persuade other countries or actors to follow the original country or to want what it wants. In hard-power language, it may be analogous to preparing the diplomatic battlefield. As Nye wrote, "it is just as important to set the agenda and structure the situations in world politics as to get others to change."[3]

To set the stage of *The Battle for Hearts and Minds: Using Soft Power to Undermine Terrorist Networks*, four authors from around the world discuss the challenges and limits of hard power, or military force, to combat terrorism. In this extensive prologue, they do not argue that military operations are always useless or counterproductive against terrorist networks, but they do advise that they are not a panacea.

Rob de Wijk from the Netherlands argues that Western military forces—shaped by concepts such as collateral damage, proportionality, and coercive diplomacy—are particularly not well equipped for unconventional battles against terrorists. He analyzes the experiences in Afghanistan and elsewhere to conclude that these formative concepts provide little practical utility for the battles ahead. Paul Dibb from

Australia questions the sustainability of an international coalition when only the United States has suffered a severe attack. Beyond these challenges, Barry Desker and Kumar Ramakrishna from Singapore write that in Southeast Asia—which they argue is becoming the center of gravity of the global battle against terrorist networks after Afghanistan—political, economic, and ideological measures are necessary to defeat terrorism. Finally, Thérèse Delpech from France outlines the implications of terrorism for global order, including both the limited value of deterrence and defense as well as the strategic challenge of failed states.

State failure, along with the traditional notion of nation building, is the subject of part one of this book. Ray Takeyh and Nikolas Gvosdev discuss the utility that terrorist networks derive from the anarchy and lawlessness of failed states. Robert I. Rotberg then presents the conditions, based on his research, that have historically preceded state failure.

The prologue and these two preliminary chapters define the problems faced. What to do about terrorists, given the potential benefit they get from state failure and the limited ability of military power to address the threat, is the subject of the rest of the book. Of the four objectives cited from the national security strategy at the beginning of this introduction, the first can be called the international norm "to make clear that all acts of terrorism are illegitimate." The second, supporting moderate governments, can involve a vast array of tools such as foreign assistance or diplomatic support. In this book, authors first address the most extreme challenges to moderate governance presented by state failure and ways to address them.

In the concluding three chapters of part one, the authors review the historical success of different, but not necessarily exclusive, approaches to combating state failure. Karin von Hippel examines the lessons the United States learned from interventions for nation building in the 1990s. Colorado governor Bill Owens and his chief of staff, Troy A. Eid, then discuss how, through the State Partnership Program and similar efforts, strategic democracy building can be enhanced through bipartisan federal-state partnerships. To compliment those U.S. policy lessons,

Sierra Leone provides a case study of the transition from anarchy to tentative reconstruction, which Michael Chege dissects.

In part two, authors focus on one particular strategy in depth: post-conflict reconstruction. In the opening chapter, John J. Hamre and Gordon R. Sullivan distinguish it from nation building in three ways: post-conflict reconstruction uses local actors more; relies less on the military; and can be initiated before conflict has ceased entirely. The other four chapters in this section then delve in detail into the four pillars of post-conflict reconstruction. Security, Scott Feil contends, is the foundation on which progress rests, identifying areas for the United States to better develop, access, organize, and focus its efforts and international capabilities to meet security needs. Beyond security, justice and reconciliation represent a second pillar, which Michèle Flournoy and Michael Pan maintain helps post-conflict societies address past, and prevent future, lawlessness, corruption, and crime. Third, socio-economic well-being can be restored through strategies, outlined by Johanna Mendelson Forman, to promote economic hope and opportunity. Finally, Robert Orr develops measures to assist governance and participation activities, the fourth pillar of post-conflict reconstruction and the last chapter of part two.

Part three tackles a third measure outlined in the national security strategy: public diplomacy, which is described in the opening chapter by Ambassador Christopher Ross, the U.S. special coordinator for public diplomacy. Subsequent chapters by a policymaker, former NSC staffer Antony J. Blinken, and a media executive, Edward Kaufman, propose how to help bridge the perception gap between U.S. policies and the way they are understood overseas. Yet Lamis Andoni, a journalist with extensive experience in the Middle East, contends that simply changing U.S. messages will not address the resentment that, she argues, U.S. policies have caused in the Arab and Muslim world.

The other policy tool outlined in the national security strategy, and the final part of this book, addresses foreign assistance as a soft power tool to undermine terrorist networks. The extensive debate about whether poverty causes terrorism is not tackled thoroughly in this volume; that subject has been covered elsewhere. The authors here debate the efficacy of the administration's new development assistance strategy and program, the Millennium Challenge Account, to improve foreign assistance. Regardless of how directly or indirectly poverty may contribute to terrorism, as President Bush himself announced when he unveiled the program, "we fight against poverty because hope is an answer to terror."[4]

Beyond describing the program and how it improves U.S. foreign assistance, both Lael Brainard and Steve Radelet, former members of a Democratic and Republican administration, respectively, argue that additional decisions need to be made about both the program and a broader strategy for foreign assistance than the Millennium Challenge Account currently provides. Beyond development assistance, foreign assistance can help combat terrorism in other ways. Jennifer Windsor contends that assisting democratization abroad can also address the causes of frustration that arguably lead to terrorist and nihilist acts. Based on his decades of experience, the chairman of the House Foreign Operations Subcommittee, James Kolbe, draws broad foreign assistance lessons to help countries achieve broad-based economic growth and integrate them into the global economy, in this book's final chapter.

Together, the purpose of the authors in *The Battle for Hearts and Minds* is not to argue that military power has no role in combating terrorism; it clearly does. The goal of these chapters is to raise the profile of debates over other potential means to combat terrorism that do not generate stunning images or brief stories in the broadcast or print media. The purpose is to stimulate you, as a reader, to learn from the authors' insights, to challenge their thoughts, and to continue the debates yourselves (whether in a classroom, online, in the halls of power around the world, in the media itself, or elsewhere).

This book intends to stimulate you to ask critical questions, such as: In the long run, what contributions, if any, can soft power tools such as post-conflict reconstruction, public diplomacy, and foreign assistance make to dry up the recruiting grounds that failed states provide terrorist networks? Military power may win wars against terrorists, but how important are soft power tools to win hearts and minds and, ultimately, to undermine those terrorist networks themselves and secure peace? The authors in the following pages provide some initial answers, but what we really want is to develop what you think....

Notes

1. *The National Security Strategy of the United States of America* (Washington, D.C.: The White House, September 2002), p. 6.

2. Joseph S. Nye Jr., "Soft Power," *Foreign Policy* 80 (F all 1990): 153-171.

3. *Ibid.*, p. 166.

4. George W. Bush, remarks to the United Nations Conference on Financing for Development, Monterrey, Mexico, March 22, 2002.

The Battle for Hearts and Minds

Prologue

The Role of Military Power

Rob de Wijk

The Limits of Military Power

Defense planning had only fleetingly dealt with the threat of apocalyptic terrorism prior to September 11. If the hastily revised U.S. quadrennial defense guidelines give any insight, the basis of defense planning will now shift from a threat-based model, analyzing whom the adversary might be, to capability-based planning, which focuses more on how an adversary might fight. Adopting this model is a great step forward, but the review itself offers little insight into the question of how an adversary might actually fight and what forces are needed to fight and win future wars.[1] The events of September 11 clarified the urgent need to refocus and restructure the way the United States and its allies think about and plan for a military campaign.

- The West's armed forces are fundamentally flawed. Conceptually, the focus is still on conventional warfare, but the new wars will be unconventional.

- Contemporary concepts, such as limited collateral damage and proportionality, have little value when preparing for the new wars.

Rob de Wijk is professor of international relations and strategic studies at the Clingendael Institute for International Relations, Royal Military Academy, and Leiden University.

This article originally appeared in slightly modified form in *The Washington Quarterly* • 25:1 pp. 75–92.

- How concepts such as coercive diplomacy and coercion can be used effectively is unclear.

In sum, the United States and its allies face significant practical as well as conceptual challenges. The September 11 attacks demonstrated that terrorism no longer can be considered a tactical or local challenge, requiring cooperation between the national intelligence services and the police. The new terrorism is a strategic or international challenge, requiring international cooperation between intelligence services and armed forces. Meeting the challenge requires a new approach as well as new assets.

'Savage Warfare'

Western armed forces demonstrated their superiority clearly during the Persian Gulf War in 1991 when, after the extensive use of airpower, U.S. ground forces gained a decisive victory over Iraq within 100 hours. In contrast to conventional warfare, which relies on technological capabilities—manned arms and standoff weaponry—to engage the enemy, terrorists fight unconventionally. Technology plays a supporting role at best, for personal protection, communications, and targeting. In the final analysis, however, successes depend on old-fashioned fighting skills and the use of knives or small-caliber arms in search-and-destroy operations.

In conventional warfare, armies take and hold ground, air forces conduct strategic bombing operations and engage the enemy, and navies support land forces by conducting offshore attacks and cutting off lines of supply. This method of operation is the Western way of waging war. The new wars on terrorism, however, will have to deal with irregular forces that practice guerrilla tactics, instill panic, and retaliate asymmetrically—when, where, and how they choose.

Actually, referring to the military campaign now under way as the "new" war demonstrates little understanding of the history of warfare. In 1898, in *Lockhart's Advance through Tirah*, Capt. L. J. Shadwell wrote about "savage warfare" (that is, non-European warfare) "that differs from that of civilized people." Some areas in the world have not changed much since Shadwell's time.

> A frontier tribesman can live for days on the grain he carries with him, and other savages on a few dates; consequently no necessity exists for them to cover a line of communications. So nimble of foot, too, are they in their grass shoes, and so conversant with every goat-track in their mountains that they can retreat in any direction. This extraordinary mobility enables them to attack from any direction quite unexpectedly, and to disperse and disappear as rapidly as they came. For this reason, the rear of a European force is as much exposed to attack as its front or flanks.[2]

In Afghanistan today, the biggest change is that army boots or Nikes have replaced grass shoes. Furthermore, local fighters possess limited numbers of modern weapons systems, such as Stinger antiaircraft missiles, which were acquired during the 1980s when the United States considered Afghans to be freedom fighters who needed support in their struggle against Soviet occupation. The basic Afghani weapons platform is the pickup truck, which carries fighters armed with guns; in mountainous regions, the mule is still the most important mode of transportation.

In most Western countries, irregular warfare has always been considered "savage warfare," for which there is no preparation. Historically, the British and the Dutch, in particular, fought insurgents quite successfully in their colonies. With the loss of Indonesia in the 1950s, the Dutch lost not only all their experience in waging this kind of war but also their mental preparedness for such action.

The Dutch army is now preparing a new field manual on counterinsurgency and counterterrorism. In drafting the manual, the army's staff utilized the old manuals that General Johannes van Heutsz used during the early twentieth century when he was combating insurgents and terrorists in what is now the Republic of Indonesia. Van Heutsz also reorganized his conventional ground forces to confront the insurgents, creating small units of a dozen armed men to carry out search-and-destroy missions. This military action led to an episode that the Dutch do not want to repeat. To-day, that army's counterinsurgency operations could be perceived as war crimes. Because no distinction could be made between com-batants and noncombatants, the Dutch burnt down entire villages in order to eliminate fighters' bases. For this reason, U.S. secretary of defense Donald Rumsfeld argued that direct attacks on terrorists are useless; forces are required to "drain the swamp they live in."[3]

In addition to consulting Van Heutsz's tactics, the Dutch used the British counterinsurgency manual, which is still considered the most detailed manual for this type of warfare. Of the former colonial powers, only the British have not given up their military skills; at the same time, British forces have maintained the mental preparedness needed to carry out counterinsurgency operations.

The West needs special forces to confront irregular fighters such as terrorists, and these forces are not available in large quantities. A dis-tinction should be made between special operations forces (SOF), which are used for covert or clandestine action, and specialized forces, which carry out specialized overt missions. The most famous of all SOF, Great Britain's Special Air Service (SAS), conceived by Captain David Stirling, has existed since 1941. Most SOF—such as Australia's Special Air Service Regiment; Holland's Bijzondere Bijstands Eenheid (BBE); France's new joint Commandement des Operation Speciale (COS) units; Germany's Grenzschutzgruppe (GSG)-9; Israel's Sayeret Matkal/ Unit 269; and the U.S. Army 1st Special Forces Operational Detach-ment, Delta Force, and Naval Special Warfare Development Group— were established in the 1970s as a direct response to terrorist incidents.

When radical supporters of Iran's revolution captured 53 staff mem-bers and guards at the U.S. embassy in Tehran in November 1979, how-ever, the United States still had no standing counterterrorist task force. As a result, a rescue team had to be assembled from scratch, and it took six months of preparation before the rescue operation could be launched. Charged with rescuing the hostages was the newly created Delta Force, with the support of U.S. Navy and Air Force airlifts. The tragic end of this attempt is well known. Technical problems and tacti-

The Battle for Hearts and Minds

cal failures caused the operation's abortion, and it ended in disaster in April 1980. Nevertheless, after this failed rescue operation, U.S. SOF received more funding and better equipment and training. Consequently, SOF became an important foreign policy tool for U.S. policymakers.[4]

SOF specialize in clandestinely rescuing hostages. SOF's military tasks focus on infiltrations into enemy territory to carry out sabotage as well as search-and-destroy and rescue missions and forward air control. Western militaries have extremely limited true SOF capabilities, probably no more than 3,000–5,000 troops for all of NATO.

In addition, Western governments have specialized forces that carry out overt actions. The United States has approximately 45,000 such troops; its NATO allies have 20,000–30,000. The U.S. Army Rangers battalions, which specialize in seizing airfields, are among the better known of these units; another is the 82nd Airborne Division, the world's largest parachute force. These forces seize key targets and prepare the ground for the general-purpose forces that follow.

Even though NATO countries have more than three million individuals in their collective armed services, only a very small portion of them are SOF or specialized armed forces—too few to engage in sustained combat operations. Clearly, it is too late to increase this capability for the campaign in Afghanistan and other countries hosting terrorists. Even if a decision were made to create more of these units, only a small number of young people would be willing or able to join these forces; according to some estimates, less than 10 percent make it through the grueling selection process.

The status of the West's human intelligence (HUMINT) capabilities is similar. For data collection, the intelligence communities of the United States and its NATO allies focus primarily on satellite imagery, signals intelligence, and electronic intelligence. Satellite imagery guides both SOF and HUMINT to targets. Although satellite imagery obtains important strategic information, SOF and HUMINT are the best way to obtain tactical information on the ground, especially because terrorist groups make only limited use of cellular telephones and satellite communications. Since the U.S. cruise missile attacks on his training camps in August 1998, Osama bin Laden no longer uses his satellite telephone, which had made him easy to detect. Instead, he issues "mission orders," instructing his lieutenants orally, in writing, or on videotape that television stations broadcast widely. Consequently, the United States and its allies have no choice but to infiltrate his network.

Tapping into this network is an enormous task, however, because the al Qaeda organization has bases and cells in 50–60 countries, including the United States and most European nations, where so-called sleeper agents live. The individuals who carried out the attacks on the World Trade Center and the Pentagon had been ordinary residents in the United States and other Western countries. Therefore, agents from Islamic states' intelligence communities must infiltrate networks and cells both inside and outside the Islamic world, while Western governments must at the same time recruit agents in the Islamic communities in their own countries. Consequently, effective use of HUMINT requires intensive cooperation among intelligence services worldwide.

Without sufficient HUMINT capabilities, as well as SOF and specialized forces that can effectively address unexpected threats and unconventional warfare—the only option open to the West's opponents—the United States and its allies will find the campaign on terrorism almost impossible. In its most basic form, asymmetrical warfare utilizes one side's comparative advantage against its enemy's relative weakness. Successful asymmetrical warfare exploits vulnerabilities—which are easy to determine—by using weapons and tactics in ways that are unplanned or unexpected. The weakness of Western societies is perceived as their desire to reduce collateral damage by emphasizing technological solutions, the need to maintain coalitions, and the need to adhere to the international rule of law. Moreover, Western industrialized societies are economically and socially vulnerable. Thus, dealing with these new threats requires groups of well-trained, well-equipped, and highly motivated individuals who can infiltrate and destroy terrorist networks.

At the tactical level, the opponent conducting asymmetrical warfare tries to change the course of action in order to prevent the achievement of political objectives. These tactics—including guerrilla warfare, hit-and-run attacks, sabotage, terrorism, and the capture of soldiers who are then shown on television—will confront allied ground forces in Afghanistan and other places that harbor terrorist training camps and headquarters.

At the strategic level, the opponent using asymmetrical tactics exploits the fears of the civilian population, thereby undermining the government, compromising its alliances, and affecting its economy. The September 11 attacks were only partly successful on this score. The fear of further attacks has led to uncertainty about the future among the populations of most Western nations and as a result their economies have fallen into recession. On the other hand, the attackers very likely miscalculated not only the resolve of the leadership and population of the United States but also most of the world's willingness to form and maintain coalitions to fight terrorism.

Direct military action against insurgents and terrorists requires both SOF and HUMINT gathering. Both assets are scarce, however, and not available in the quantities necessary to fight and win sustained wars. Moreover, deploying SOF is extremely risky, and effective engagement requires skills and techniques that come very close to war crimes. Therefore, the United States and its allies need to develop a new defense-planning concept.

Operation Enduring Freedom

Operation Enduring Freedom revealed the difficulties of fighting unconventional wars against irregular forces. The war in Afghanistan was largely fought by proxy with U.S. SOF, specialized forces, and air power mainly functioning as *force multipliers*. Most battles were Afghan-led and U.S.-supported. Success hinged largely on the Afghan United Front (AUF), which had endured since 1996 as a semi-regular fighting force. By September 2001 its commander Ahmadshah Massoud had built up

12,000 troops with artillery and tanks. U.S. reconnaissance, SOF with ground laser target designators, and air power enabled the AUF to win decisive victories.

Fighting by proxy, however, does not always work. The battle of Takur Ghar in southern Afghanistan on March 3–4, 2002, when U.S.-led forces tried to overrun one of the cave complexes used by the Taliban and Al Qaeda, revealed shortcomings in U.S. military coordination and communication, reminiscent of the Mogadishu battle in Somalia nine years before. Intelligence sources grossly underestimated the enemy's strength and staying power, initially identifying some 150 to 200 fighters, and then drastically revising those numbers to 600 to 700 after several days of battle. Within hours of the operation's commencement, the Charlie Company of the 10th Mountain Division faced intense resistance; eleven soldiers from the 101st Airborne Division came under fire; allied Afghan forces were also attacked and unable to achieve their objectives. Eight U.S. soldiers were killed, most of them in an ambush as they deployed from a helicopter. More than 40 U.S. soldiers were wounded. To regain the battlefield advantage the United States quickly carried out a series of air strikes with fighter jets, attack helicopters, and gunships. After a week of heavy fighting the momentum had shifted back in favor of the United States and its allies.

More than a year after the start of Operation Enduring Freedom large parts of the Afghan countryside still lay outside the central government's control. During the first few weeks of 2003, fighting between coalition forces and remnants of Taliban and Al Qaeda forces increased. Al Qaeda appeared to be enlisting and training new recruits, Taliban leader Mullah Omar and Al Qaeda leader Osama bin Laden had still not been arrested or killed, and warlord Gulbuddin Hekmatyar was reported to have formed an alliance with the remaining Taliban and Al Qaeda forces. Fighters from these three groups banded together in the eastern and southern Afghan provinces, attacking coalition forces and denying them control over large parts of the country.

Despite their overwhelming combat power, high-tech coalition forces are not able to deal decisively with a loose, low-tech network of fighters and terrorists—an enduring problem that is not rapidly solvable. A fundamental shift from platform centric warfare to network centric warfare (NCW) holds the solution.[5] NCW, which is based on the idea that information sharing is the key to success, allows the networking of a geographically dispersed force. Information technology will be used to achieve decisive military advantage by networking individual units, providing them unprecedented operational awareness, and enabling them to react better than traditionally possible under fluid conditions. Thus, NCW gives the force an asymmetric information advantage. NCW requires highly advanced Command, Control, Communications, Computers, Intelligence, and Strategic Reconnaissance (C4ISR). Satellites and manned and unmanned reconnaissance planes will transfer data to "shooters," such as aircraft or individual soldiers. The result should be unprecedented battlefield awareness that might even lift the fog of war. A future military network will consist of battle space entities or nodes, such as shooters and platforms, and the links between them. Decisionmaking inputs, as well as the decisions themselves, create the information in the network. All this is subsequently passed across the network, from one node to another. Linking these nodes will greatly increase effectiveness, as the battles space entities will perform a more all-round role, information-sharing will increase, and decisionmaking will become more accurate.

NCW may retire traditional command and control processes. Thus, former U.S. Air Force colonel John Boyd's famous 'observation, orientation, decision, action' (OODA) loop will be replaced by much more integrated and parallel command and control cycles, based on superior battle space awareness and knowledge. These will require a different mindset since, unlike traditional command-structures, hierarchy is diminished and combined arms operations are less emphasized. Junior commanders will take decisions, potentially with strategic implications.

Although much remains uncertain, concepts such as NCW are clearly likely to dominate future wars. They would restore the offensive as the dominant form of war, with speed and movement as key elements. Speed will allow forces to shift quickly around the battlefield to check, block, and strike almost contiguously. The objective of such concepts is not to kill as much of the opposing forces as possible, but to paralyze and to wear him down and to eventually crush his will. The increased ability to know the battlefield as well as to comprehend the enemy will fundamentally change the dynamics of fire and maneuver.

Operation Enduring Freedom provided a glimpse of this future. One lesson from the war in Afghanistan was that the military has already learned to exploit networked information to conduct real-time and coordinated precision operations against a dispersed enemy. In Afghanistan, the time lag between sensor and shooter was sharply reduced. Information technology linked sensors to military capabilities, from the most advanced such as B-2 bombers, to aging systems such as forty-year old B-52 bombers, and even to soldiers on horsebacks. Junior commanders called in air strikes.

When 400 Taliban rebelled at a fort near Mazar-e-Sharif in December 2001, a sergeant pinpointed positions and radioed for air support from F/A-18s carrying 2,000 pound bombs. Responsive action occurred within just 15 minutes. Almost 90 percent of the targets were preplanned, but manned and unmanned systems, such as Global Hawk and Predator unmanned aerial vehicles (UAVs), RC-135, U-2, E-8C, E-2A, and P-3 reconnaissance planes, satellites, SOF, and HUMINT identified them. About 60 percent of the ordnance dropped was precision guided. During Operation Desert Storm in 1991 some 7 to 8 percent of all ordnance was precision guided, while about 40 percent was during Operation Allied Force in 1999. The Joint Direct Attack Munition (JDAM), a conventional "dumb" bomb with a $21,000 GPS device that steers it to any target, day or night and under all weather conditions with pinpoint accuracy, was key to the operation's success.

The Limited Value of Contemporary Western Concepts

For historical and cultural reasons, the armed forces of Western countries have been disinclined to prepare for military action that was considered uncivilized. As a consequence, policymakers, the military, and the public are psychologically ill-prepared for this war. They have become used to concepts such as limited collateral damage, proportionality of response, and the absence of body bags. The current situation, however, calls for a willingness to abandon these ideas, at least partially, a sacrifice that may be difficult for some individuals and nations to make.

During his visit to Pakistan on October 5, British prime minister Tony Blair called for "proportionate strikes ... [that should] not be directed against the Afghan people." These concepts have little value when carrying out military operations against insurgents and terrorists for a number of reasons.

- *Collateral damage.* Because asymmetrical fighters do not usually wear uniforms, combatants are indistinguishable from civilians. These fighters depend on the local civilian population for logistics and shelter in rural areas, and in urban areas the population is used as a shield. Moreover, because the Afghan population is loyal to tribes and clans, differentiating between combatants and noncombatants is almost impossible. Thus, the concept of limited collateral damage is almost useless in unconventional warfare, in which civilian casualties cannot be avoided.

- *Proportionality of response.* Proportionality refers to the response to an attack being in relation—and proportional—to the interests at stake. The events of September 11 threatened not only America's national security but also its leadership and credibility. For a superpower this is a very powerful incentive to use its full might and to take all measures necessary. In theory this could require the use of nuclear weapons if other means are insufficient, such as to destroy hardened underground bunkers of caves. However, keeping fragile coalitions together requires *less* than a proportional response. Therefore, using nuclear weapons is a non-option, despite the debate on nuclear bunker busters triggered by the Nuclear Posture Review.[6]

- *Absence of body bags.* Because vital interests of the United States and its allies are at stake, the concept of an absence of body bags carries little value either. Both Blair and President George W. Bush have the popular political support to withstand the inevitable heavy human losses. General Joseph Ralston, NATO's supreme allied commander, warned, "We cannot be in the mindset of a zero-casualty operation."[7] Whether most European allies are also willing to pay this high price is doubtful. Initially, the Belgian and Dutch governments saw invoking Article 5 of the NATO treaty as a symbolic measure and a demonstration of transatlantic solidarity. Other governments agreed so that they would be consulted on U.S. decisions and have some influence on U.S. decisionmaking. Except for the United Kingdom, few European NATO allies acknowledged that the decision to invoke Article 5 implies sending their own troops to Southwest Asia.

Thus, combating insurgents and terrorists requires mental firmness, a quality evident in the United States and the United Kingdom today but uncertain in other allies. The traditional concepts of proportionality and limited collateral damage, however, do not have much value under the present circumstances.

Coercion and Coercive Diplomacy

Another obstacle to using military means effectively to combat the new threats that terrorism poses is the limited insight that academics, and therefore policymakers, offer into the theories of coercion and coercive diplomacy, as well as governments' lack of experience using them to achieve the desired outcome. Coercion is defined as the deliberate and purposeful use of economic and military power to influence the choices of one's adversaries; coercive diplomacy focuses on the latent use of the instruments of power to influence those choices. The studies on which these theories are based, however, do not have much relevance for policymakers today. The terrorist attacks on the United States demonstrate the need for policymakers and the military to reevaluate the concepts that underlie their approaches to balancing political ends and military means.

the campaign to win the support of the populace of the opponent. In other words, the United States and its allies must also wage a battle for the hearts and minds of the people, in this case, in the Islamic world. This effort—using several approaches, including humanitarian aid and propaganda—must be made along with diplomatic measures and military operations. The humanitarian aid that accompanies the bombs being dropped in Afghanistan in the current fight demonstrates that the United States recognizes the importance of this campaign.

Israel serves as an example of the difficulties that a nation confronts in a war against terrorists and of the way the battle to win the hearts and minds of the population can accompany military measures. Terror persists in Israel, despite the fact that the country has military assets that are important for waging this type of war, including defense forces and intelligence services that are among the best in the world, policymakers and a public who are willing to take risks and to accept casualties, and widespread public support for the military even if mistakes are made. Yet the country cannot prevent or deter terrorist acts or attacks with rockets from southern Lebanon. Israel's experience shows that armed forces—trained, structured, and equipped for conventional war—are incapable of dealing with insurgents. Israel had no choice but to develop new tactics, employ different weapons systems, and use small task forces to carry out small-scale operations; but even this shift in modus operandi has not guaranteed success.

Bin Laden, who is accused of being the force behind the September 11 attacks, fights a battle similar to the Intifada but on a global scale. His objective seems to be to unite the Islamic world under a political-religious figure, or caliph, by removing pro-Western regimes, the state of Israel, and the U.S. presence from the Islamic world.

Israel's experience also shows that, at best, governments can only manage the problem of terrorism. Its solution requires offensive military action, heavy security measures to prevent radical elements from carrying out their attacks, and the building of coalitions with moderate political figures.

Israel's experience with gaining the support of the civilian population is important. For example, when the security zone in southern Lebanon still existed, Israel carried out a counterinsurgency campaign within it while providing aid to the Lebanese population therein, including projects to rebuild infrastructure and programs to provide health care. On the other side of the coin, radical movements such as Hamas use nongovernmental organizations extensively for these purposes.

Bin Laden is popular because of his "good works" in the Islamic world, especially in Pakistan and Afghanistan. Indeed, in most Islamic countries, radical groups of fundamentalists have developed a social and cultural infrastructure to build an Islamic civil society and fill a vacuum that their countries' governments have neglected. For example, during the 1990s in Egypt, Jordan, the West Bank and Gaza, Afghanistan, and Pakistan, radical movements provided health care, education, and welfare for those nations' poor. After the 1992 earthquake in Cairo, these organizations were on the streets within hours, whereas the Egyptian government's relief efforts lagged behind. In fact, Qur'an study centers have become the single most important source for recruiting new members for the radical movements.

These types of campaigns waged by radical Islamic movements have very successfully undermined the legitimacy of governments and gained the support of the local civilian population. Consequently, the diplomatic and military actions of the United States and its allies should go hand in hand with a campaign for the hearts and minds in order to win the support of the Islamic world's population. In addition to food rations, U.S. aircraft have dropped leaflets and small transistor radios to enable the Afghans to receive Washington's message. Nevertheless, even a dual strategy of humanitarian aid and military intervention does not guarantee success. Other factors must be taken into account.

Clashing Civilizations

The major obstacle to success in the campaign against terrorism is not military, political, or diplomatic, but cultural. Because of strong anti-Western sentiments in the Islamic world, a coalition to counter terrorism is fragile by nature but critical to the success of military measures. The geostrategic changes that occurred in the 1990s have contributed to anti-Western feelings in large parts of the world. First, the West "won" the Cold War, with the United States remaining the sole superpower; and in international relations the "hegemon" is always met with distrust. Second, in 1998 the differences between the United States and non-Western nations countries became clearer as a result of a new version of interventionism.

The year 1998 seems to be a turning point in recent history. Events that took place in 1998 and 1999 indicated that the U.S. approach had once and for all shifted to a narrower and more selective foreign and national security policy of unilateralism and preservation of the nation's dominant position in the world. A number of events contributed to this image:

- In response to the bombings of the U.S. embassies in Kenya and Tanzania, the United States intervened unilaterally—and without a UN Security Council mandate—in Sudan and Afghanistan in August 1998. The U.S. goal was to strike a blow against bin Laden's alleged terrorist network.

- In December that same year, Operation Desert Fox took place, in which the United States and the United Kingdom carried out bombing raids against Iraq. The military action was meant as retribution for Saddam Hussein's obstruction of the UN Special Commission's inspections of Iraq's development of weapons of mass destruction. In 1999 and 2000, the bombings continued, albeit with limited intensity.

- In 1998, the U.S. government decided to increase its defense budget (which had undergone a period of decline) by 5.6 percent, a development that some nations viewed with apprehension.[15]

- In March 1999, Operation Allied Force—led by the United States and without a mandate by the UN Security Council—intervened in Kosovo to force Milosevic to end his terror against the Albanian Kosovars and to find a solution to the situation in Kosovo.

- In July 1999, the United States presented its national missile defense initiative, designed to protect the country against limited attacks by rogue states using ballistic missiles. This development demanded a review of the 1972 Anti-Ballistic Missile Treaty. With the U.S. Senate's refusal to ratify the Comprehensive Test Ban Treaty, a general prohibition on conducting nuclear tests was dropped.

Meanwhile, the perceived threat posed by rogue states and terrorists potentially equipped with WMD gained credence. Catastrophic terrorism had emerged as a threat during the Clinton presidency with the 1993 World Trade Center bombing, 1996 Oklahoma City bombing, 1998 bombing of U.S. embassies in Africa, and 2000 attack on the USS Cole in Aden, not to mention numerous foiled attacks, such as a plot to blow up the Lincoln Tunnel and a 1995 plot to blow up 11 U.S. commercial aircraft simultaneously over the Pacific.[16]

As a result of these events, many non-Western countries began to perceive the United States as a superpower that wants to change the status quo and create a "new world order" according to its own views. Because of the fundamental difference between Western and non-Western ideas, Russia, China, and Islamic countries distrust interventions that are based on normative principles, such as democracy and humanitarianism. According to Chinese commentators, for example, interventions by the United States indicate that the West can impose its liberal values on the rest of the world without fear of confrontation with Russia.[17]

Europeans and Muslims alike widely believe that President George W. Bush has embarked on a new unilateralist course since September 11, 2001, aimed at maintaining U.S. hegemonic power. They fear that this emerging unilateralism is based on a narrow realist vision of U.S. interests that requires selective engagement with both Europe and Asia and a domination of world politics with superior armed forces. Multilateral organizations such as NATO and the UN, they believe, are set to play a reduced role, only where they serve U.S. interests and never where they undermine the United States' freedom to act. The public debate that emerged in Europe soon after September 11 about the consequences of a U.S. unilateralist foreign policy for transatlantic rela-

political Islam, is only one aspect of this resurgence, which began in the 1970s when Islamic symbols, beliefs, practices, and institutions won more support throughout the Islamic world. As a product of modernity, the core constituency of Islamic resurgence consists of middle-class students and intellectuals. Even the fundamentalists who carried out the September 11 attacks were well-educated, middle-class men.

Because the resurgence of Islam is fundamentally an anti-Western movement, building coalitions incorporating Islamic nations in the battle against terrorism is not easy. The coalition that was built in the aftermath of the September 11 attacks was primarily based on attitudes against bin Laden, who seeks to establish an undivided *umma* (community of believers) under a political-religious leader—thereby presenting a challenge to most regimes in the Islamic world. Nevertheless, most regimes and large parts of their populations share some of bin Laden's anti-Western sentiments. Consequently, the coalition is fragile and, at best, willing to give only passive support. Thus, many Islamic people will consider a military campaign that is carried out by Western forces as, to use bin Laden's words, "a Zionist Crusade." Unfortunately, a controversial 1996 assertion that conflicts between cultures will dominate future international relations remains germane in the new millennium.[21]

The war on terrorism could improve the West's relations with China and Russia, but, if handled unwisely, it could also lead to a confrontation with the Islamic world. The United States' nightmare scenario is that friendly regimes in the Islamic world will fall and anti-Western regimes willing to play the oil card and support terrorists will emerge. Thus, the immediate consequence of the war on terrorism could be both ineffectiveness and a struggle for energy resources so vital to the Western world.

Limiting Expectations

As the war against terrorism shifts into full gear, the United States and its allies must meet significant practical and conceptual challenges if the campaign is to be successful. A war against terrorists or insurgents can be manageable, at best, if certain approaches are adopted. In principle, the following options, which are not all mutually exclusive, are available to the United States and its allies, depending on the target of the campaign:

- Pursue a military strategy of control in failed states that terrorists use as sanctuaries. Control involves search-and-destroy missions by SOF, supported by specialized forces and airpower. This option requires the United States and its allies to expand the number of SOF and specialized forces significantly.

- Adopt a strategy of coercive diplomacy or coercion against unfriendly regimes to pressure these regimes to end their support of terrorist movements. If they do not comply with these demands, these regimes should be removed from power, which is easier said than done. This strategy requires new thinking about the optimum way to coerce regimes.

- Use HUMINT gathering methods extensively to infiltrate the terrorists' networks in friendly countries and then destroy the terrorist bases from within. This option also requires the United States and its allies to expand their HUMINT capabilities substantially and to embark on even closer cooperation with intelligence services in other countries.

- Wage a campaign to win the hearts and minds of the Islamic people. This option would enable the United States and its allies to gain the support of the populace and thereby drive a wedge between the population and the terrorists or insurgents.

Nevertheless, even if these options are adopted and prove successful at least in the short term, an overriding issue must be addressed in order to achieve long-term success. The primary obstacle to success in the war against terrorism is a cultural one. To some degree, the battle is a clash of civilizations. Political Islam is fundamentally anti-Western, thus the prospect for success is limited. Using military means may exacerbate the potential that this campaign will be cast as a clash of civilizations, ultimately making the problem of terrorism even worse.

Notes

1. U.S. Department of Defense, *Quadrennial Defense Review Report*, September 30, 2001.

2. L. J. Shadwell, *Lockhart's Advance through Tirah* (London: W. Thacker & Co., 1898), pp. 100–105.

3. "Rumsfeld," *International Herald Tribune*, September 19, 2001, p. 6.

4. S. L. Marquis, *Unconventional Warfare: Rebuilding U.S. Special Operations Forces* (Washington, D.C.: Brookings Institution, 1997), p. 2.

5   U.S. Congress, *Network Centric Warfare*. Department of Defense Appropriations Bill 2001, Report of the Committee on Appropriations together with Additional Views, 106th Congress, 2nd Session.

6. Department of Defense, *Nuclear Posture Review*, submitted to Congress on December 31, 2001.

7. "Rumsfeld," p. 6.

8. See Thomas A. Schelling, *Arms and Influence* (New Haven: Yale University Press, 1966); Alexander L. George and W. E. Simons, eds., *The Limits of Coercive Diplomacy* (Boulder, Colo.: Westview Press, 1994); Robert A. Pape, *Bombing to Win: Air Power and Coercion in War* (Ithaca, N.Y.: Cornell University Press, 1996). See also Lawrence Freedman, *Strategic Coercion* (Oxford: Oxford University Press, 1998); Colin S. Gray, *Modern Strategy* (Oxford: Oxford University Press, 1999); Richard N. Haass, *Intervention: The Use of American Military Force in the Post–Cold War World* (Washington, D.C.: Carnegie Endowment for International Peace, 1994); Michael O'Hanlon, *Saving Lives with Force: Military Criteria for Humanitarian Intervention* (Washington, D.C: Brookings Institution, 1997); and B. R. Pirnie and W. E. Simons, *Soldiers for Peace* (Santa Monica, Calif.: RAND, 1996).

9. Schelling, *Arms and Influence*, pp. 2–3.

10. Ibid., pp. 69–91; see also Thomas Schelling, *The Strategy of Conflict* (New York and London: Oxford University Press, 1965).

11. George and Simons, *Limits of Coercive Diplomacy*, p. 7.

12. "U.S. Strategists Begin to Favor Threat to Use Nuclear Weapons," *International Herald Tribune*, October 6–7, 2001, p. 4.

13. Pape, *Bombing to Win*, p. 316.

14. Prime Minister Tony Blair, speech to the Labor Party Conference, London, October 2, 2001.

15. International Institute for Strategic Studies, "U.S. Military Spending," *Strategic Comments* 6, no. 4 (May 2000).

16   S. Simon and D. Benjamin, "America and the New Terrorism," *Survival* 42, no. 1 (Spring 2000): 59–75.

17. J. Teufel Dreyer, *The PLA and the Kosovo Conflict* (Carlisle, Penn.: U.S. Army War College, May 2000), p. 3.

18. F. Fukuyama, *The End of History and the Last Man* (New York: Free Press, 1992).

19. "Berlusconi Vaunts West's Superiority," *International Herald Tribune*, September 27, 2001.

20. M. Ignatieff, *Whose Universal Values? The Crisis in Human Rights* (The Hague: Paemium Erasmianum, 1999).

21. Samuel P. Huntington, *The Clash of Civilizations and the Remaking of World Order* (New York: Simon & Schuster, 1996).

Paul Dibb

The Future of International Coalitions: How Useful? How Manageable?

The most dramatic political result of the September 11 terrorist attacks on the United States has been the construction of a global coalition against terrorism. The diversity of this coalition is unprecedented. It includes the United States' NATO allies, Japan, and Australia. It also involves such unexpected partners as China and Russia, as well as Pakistan and India. Major international organizations, specifically the United Nations and the leaders of the Asia-Pacific Economic Cooperation forum, have condemned the terrorist attacks, as has the Conference of the Islamic Organization.

For the first time in its 52-year history, NATO has invoked Article 5, under which an attack on one alliance member is considered an attack on all members. Also for the first time, the Australian government has invoked Article 4 of the 1951 ANZUS Treaty (a security treaty among Australia, New Zealand, and the United States) in order to meet this common danger. Great Britain, Canada, and Australia committed military forces to the coalition's operations against Osama bin Laden's terrorist network and the Taliban regime. France, Germany, and Italy have indicated that they may contribute military support personnel to a

Paul Dibb is head of the Strategic and Defence Studies Centre in the Research School of Pacific and Asian Studies at the Australian National University. He previously served as deputy secretary of defence and director of the Defence Intelligence Organization in Australia.

Copyright © 2002 by The Center for Strategic and International Studies and the Massachusetts Institute of Technology
The Washington Quarterly • 25:2 pp. 131–144.

peace stabilization force in Afghanistan, as have several Muslim countries. Japan, in a major departure from its past reluctance to send military units overseas, has deployed naval warships in a support role.

This coalition is remarkable not only because of the large number of countries involved from all around the world, but also the apparent recognition that the fight against terrorism will be a prolonged one—one that will involve diplomatic pressure and financial sanctions, as well as military force. Never in world history have so many countries combined together against a common threat in this manner.

The war against terrorism will be unprecedented as it spreads across a wide range of countries, not only in the Middle East. It will require patience and close coordination. Victories will not be readily apparent in the traditional sense of battlefield successes. As President George W. Bush has said, the collective efforts of the coalition will require "the patient accumulation of successes." Even bin Laden's death will not be the end of the matter by any means. In his book about bin Laden, Yossef Bodansky observes, "Ultimately the quintessence of bin Laden's threat is his being a cog, albeit an important one, in a large system that will outlast his own demise. ..." [1]

Can this unprecedented coalition against terrorism hang together under such difficult circumstances? A coalition, by definition, is a temporary combination of parties that retain distinctive principles. Already, views have differed over the bombing campaign in Afghanistan. Opinions vary—not least within the United States itself—about whether the war should extend to Iraq. The installation of a new regime in Kabul to replace the Taliban is a step fraught with danger, as is the wooing of the military regime in Islamic Pakistan. Although the coalition members do share a common fear of terrorism, the fact remains that only the United States has suffered a severe terrorist attack. The risk that the war may widen will put intense pressure on the coalition.

The events that led to the brokering of the coalition must be examined, as well as the performance of the coalition's military, diplomatic, and financial coordination. Finally, what are the risks for the future of

one that recognizes the need for international cooperation. This change in U.S. posture reflects the seriousness of the terrorist threat it faces and the need to put together an international coalition that can be sustained over a considerable period of time. This effort has involved significant policy trade-offs and adjustments to previous U.S. policy stances with countries such as Pakistan and Russia. The global balance of power remains unchanged, however, leaving the United States in a dominant position. As a result, dismissive unilateralism characterizes its attitude to binding treaties, such as the Anti-Ballistic Missile (ABM) Treaty, and its resistance to multilateral commitments, such as the Biological Weapons Convention.

Robert Zoellick, now the U.S. trade representative, argued at the beginning of 2000 that a modern Republican foreign policy emphasizes building and sustaining coalitions.[4] Until September 11, however, the Bush administration showed precious little interest in this aspect of its foreign policy. Instead, it seemed to be heading down the path of unilateralism. Prominent U.S. commentators, such as William Kristol and Robert Kagan, argued the case for U.S. hegemony. Others, such as Deputy Secretary of State Richard Armitage, talked about U.S. preeminence as a force for good. Whether these labels were accurate or not, with the collapse of the Soviet Union the United States had certainly lost its clear sense of national purpose, and the U.S. alliance system risked losing what had been its compelling rationale. Lacking a clear enemy, the United States grew confused about whether expanding its costly global engagement was really necessary after the end of the Cold War.[5] Allies, including NATO, Japan, and Australia, sensed a lack of focus and attention in Washington. Russia was treated as if it was unimportant, and China was regarded with hostility. Both India and Pakistan were punished for their nuclear weapons programs.

With the events of September 11, all this has now changed. Constructing the antiterrorism coalition has involved important U.S. policy concessions to Russia, Pakistan, and India, as well as to China to get it on the coalition's side if not actually within it. The general expectation of U.S. allies that the United States would be the one to come to their assistance has been reversed; instead, the NATO and ANZUS alliances have been invoked in defense of the United States. Although the diplomatic aspects of coalition building have been impressive, the countries willing to contribute combat forces have been the usual U.S. allies: Great Britain, Canada, and Australia. Other countries were apparently willing to contribute military forces but were turned away. Unlike the 1991 Persian Gulf War and even the Kosovo conflict, the military coalition against terrorism has been a "shadow coalition," which is particularly disappointing, given the perception in much of the Middle East that the U.S.-led war on terrorism is a Western crusade against Islam.

As the war enters a new phase involving peacekeeping and stabilization operations in Afghanistan, the participation of non–Anglo-Saxon countries is vital. France, Germany, and Italy seem to have committed to these efforts—against some strong domestic political opposition. Other countries that have indicated a commitment include important Muslim countries such as Indonesia, Turkey, Jordan, and Bangladesh.

Leading the coalition effectively requires clear-eyed judgments about priorities, an appreciation of others' interests, constant consultations among partners, and a willingness to compromise on some points but to remain focused on core objectives.[6] So far, the United States has fared well in this regard: in just four weeks, before it decided to use military power, it assembled an impressive diplomatic coalition. The military coalition has been less impressive: the United States, with some assistance from the United Kingdom, has almost completely dominated it. At the time of writing, Australian and Canadian military operations were still very limited, as were those of Germany and France. Washington has found it difficult to manage the military operations in Afghanistan as a true coalition, as distinct from a dominant U.S. military force with subordinate allies expected to do what is demanded of them. Much of this situation was unsurprising, given the need to quickly punish the Taliban for their harboring of bin Laden. The management of this aspect of the coalition, however, will require much more finesse in the future, particularly if the war against terrorism expands.

The Coalition: Winners and Losers

Some U.S. commentators argue that establishing a broad coalition is "nothing less than an invitation for paralysis."[7] Even the individual members of a coalition of Western governments will insist on having their say before decisions are made. A coalition is never stronger than its weakest link and, so the argument goes, this coalition will consist of many weak links. Walter Laqueur argues that the United States' most effective course of action would have been to retaliate indiscriminately within a day or two after the attacks against any of the governments suspected of aiding international terrorism. He reasons that terrorism is not based on common sense and elementary logic, and neither is effective counterterrorism. This proposal, however, ignores the uniqueness of the strategy of terrorism: it achieves its goal not through its acts but through the response to its acts.

From what we know of bin Laden, the supposition that he actually wanted to provoke indiscriminate strikes by the United States against certain Middle Eastern Muslim countries is fairly made. As argued more than 25 years ago, terrorism is violence used in order to create fear; but it is aimed at creating fear in order that the fear, in turn, will lead somebody else to embark on some quite different program of action that will accomplish whatever it is that the terrorist really desires.[8] Terrorism is an indirect strategy that wins or loses only based on how one responds to it. If one chooses not to respond at all, or else to respond in a way that diverges from the desires of the terrorists, they will fail to achieve their objectives. The important point here is that the choice is yours—and that is the ultimate weakness of terrorism as a strategy.[9] In this context, the U.S. strategy so far seems correct. Despite extreme provocation, it has not lashed out. Its use of force has been both discriminate and proportionate and, contrary to expectations, has resulted in the collapse of the Taliban.

The United States is leading a moral campaign. In World War II, the firm conviction that evil was being fought greatly simplified the Allied effort.[10] The image of a "just war" nourished the Allies' willingness to fight the war to the bitter end. The difference between the war against terrorism and World War II, of course, is that in World War II the Allied powers were all the victims of aggression, simplifying the task of constructing a wartime consensus. Until and unless terrorists attack other Western powers, maintaining the coalition in the longer term will be difficult. The sense of moral outrage, however, has certainly led to the view that this war is just.

Some believe that political solutions must be given priority over military solutions for the global campaign against terrorism to be successful. The only thing that can undercut bin Laden's brand of global terrorism is a sustained political effort to address the issues that have fueled extremism. In this view, priority must be given to finding a sustainable solution to the Israeli-Palestinian conflict and removing the debilitating economic sanctions against Iraq. This line of reasoning holds that "[t]he link that currently exists between historical grievances, contemporary political injustices, social and economic hardship, closed political opportunity structures, and politicized religion must be broken."[11] Military actions, they argue, are only likely to strengthen these links.

The problem is that this approach to the immediate demands of decisionmaking is unrealistic, particularly when the United States has suffered such a devastating terrorist attack on its homeland. The Israeli-Palestinian conflict can only be resolved in the longer term. Asking the United States to desist from military action and concentrate on the long-term and well-nigh impossible task of solving the underlying grievances in the Middle East is not a practical course in the shorter term. It leads to the entirely unacceptable view of moral equivalence between what bin Laden did and the defects that may or may not exist in U.S. Middle East policy.

Arising out of all of this debate has been a useful clarification of the United States' international policy stance. For much of the last decade—since the end of the Cold War—the United States had become more unpredictable because it lost the focus provided by its enemy for the previous 50 years: the USSR. The end of the Cold War removed a clear and simple rationale for devising foreign policy in Washington.

François Heisbourg described this development as the great risk of entropy, of growing inconsistency in the construction of U.S. foreign and security policy.[12] His despair that foreign policy and security studies in the United States were no longer given the same priority as they received during the Cold War has been reversed.

The question now is, Can Washington devise a new organizing principle of the international system for the twenty-first century? This principle, however, cannot only be "you are with us or you are with the terrorists." China's rise to power, the continuing risk of war across the Taiwan Straits as well as on the Korean Peninsula, nuclear competition between India and Pakistan, and instability in Russia and parts of the former Soviet Union are all hazards to world peace. They will need Washington's careful attention while it fights the new war against terrorism and avoids, if possible, a wider war in the Middle East.

Problematically, cobbling together the coalition against terrorism has resulted in some risky trade-offs in other key aspects of U.S. national security policy. National security adviser Condoleezza Rice believes that U.S. foreign policy should be firmly grounded in national interests, "not [in] the interests of an illusory international community."[13] Arguably, the United States now needs such an international community. This realization does not deny Rice's view that the United States must focus on being able to meet powerfully and decisively the emergence of any hostile military power in the Asia-Pacific region, the Middle East, the Persian Gulf, and Europe—areas where not only U.S. interests but also those of its key allies are at stake. The war against terrorism, however, will require some short-term tactical adjustments.

For example, both Pakistan and India are winners in this new situation in a way that before would have been inconceivable. Pakistan and India were nuclear pariah states. Now, Pakistan is crucial to U.S. military operations in Afghanistan and to U.S. efforts to pursue bin Laden. India's support has been important as the world's largest democracy and a key Asian power with a large Muslim population. As a result, the sanctions applied against Pakistan and India because of their nuclear weapons programs have been lifted, and Washington's diplomatic focus on both of these countries has become much more intense. The question becomes, Can the United States use its newfound leverage with India and Pakistan to broker a resolution to their dangerous military confrontation in Kashmir?

Russia too is a winner. Its relations with the United States have improved dramatically. During President Vladimir Putin's visit to the United States in November 2001, Bush announced a unilateral reduction in U.S. strategic nuclear forces from about 6,000 warheads to 2,200 or less. Russia facilitated U.S. access to military bases in Central Asia. In return, the Russians have made plain their regard for the Chechnyans as terrorists and their belief in "a right to expect that double standards will not be applied."[14] A decade after the end of the Cold War, Russia finally feels that the United States is treating it as a friend and important power, if not a global power, once again.

Japan has improved its status as a U.S ally. Its historic decision to deploy naval ships to the Indian Ocean in support of the war against terrorism should not be underestimated. In the 1991 Gulf War, Japan incurred U.S. displeasure because of its reluctance to contribute military forces (minesweepers) until after the war had finished. Its contribution this time has involved considerable domestic debate. The Japanese now seem willing to reinterpret the "peace constitution" that was imposed on them in 1947. In October 2001, the Japanese Diet passed an antiterrorism special law that authorizes, under strict conditions, a military response to assist the U.S.-led war against terrorism. This historic naval deployment has attracted the ire of China and South Korea; the United States must firmly rebuff any such criticism.

The country that has gained most in its status with the United States is the United Kingdom (UK). Once again, the UK has proven that it is the only ally with credible military forces and sufficient diplomatic clout to stand by the United States. In the bombing and missile attacks on Afghanistan, the UK was the only other country to contribute to the U.S. military mission. In bringing together the coalition, Prime Minister Tony Blair has exhibited diplomatic skills that eclipse those of Bush. Blair's help has been crucial in shoring up support not

The Battle for Hearts and Minds

only among Europeans but also with Middle Eastern countries, Pakistan, and Russia. Australia, by comparison, has contributed significant but token military forces. Additionally, Prime Minister John Howard has been unable to exert any influence with either Indonesia or Malaysia—Australia's Muslim neighbors.

Who are the losers? The most obvious is China. Beijing has seen the United States assume notable influence in Pakistan—a country in which China has invested considerable military and economic assistance. It has also seen the United States gain access to military bases in Central Asia—a region that China considers within its natural sphere of influence. Before the events of September 11, China had developed an important relationship with Russia because both countries were concerned about what they viewed as the new Bush administration's hard-line stance toward them. Russia now is seizing the chance to be accepted as a friend of the West, and it seems ready to pay less attention to its relations with China. Although China says that it supports the war against terrorism, it has contributed nothing to the coalition other than general diplomatic support. Arguably, China has gained something by losing its status as the United States' number one enemy: Taiwan also seems to have gone off the boil in Washington. Bush's announcement in December 2001 that the United States will rescind the ABM Treaty, however, is a severe blow to China's security.

The other loser is Israel. Israel's hard-line military actions against the Palestinians are an embarrassment and potential danger to the coalition against terrorism. Washington may have initially urged Israel to keep its head down while the United States mounted sensitive military operations against bin Laden and the Taliban, but some Arab regimes no doubt believe, rightly or wrongly, that the United States has now allowed Israel freer rein because of its own successful strategy against the Taliban. Statements by the United States that it approves Palestinian statehood in principle, however, are a worrisome development for Tel Aviv. If the war against terrorism should widen to include U.S. attacks on Iraq, Israel's position will become even more delicate. The United States simply cannot afford to be seen as pursuing a war against Islam in the Middle East in cahoots with Israel.

As this war develops, Saudi Arabia may find itself in an increasingly untenable position. It is a friend of the United States, a critical supplier of oil to the West, and host to U.S. military bases that have drawn the anger of bin Laden and other Islamic fundamentalists. The majority of the terrorists who hijacked the aircraft involved in the attacks on September 11 came from Saudi Arabia, bin Laden himself was born there, and Riyadh was one of only three governments to have extended diplomatic relations to the Taliban. The autocratic regime in Saudi Arabia is trying to walk a fine line between its orthodox support for Islam and its friendship with the United States.

Indonesia is the largest Muslim and the fourth most populous country in the world. It occupies an archipelago that stands across narrow straits that control half of the world's maritime traffic. President Megawati Sukarnoputri has equivocated in her support for the United States: a week after the attacks of September 11, she was in Washington giving fulsome support, but once the bombing of Afghanistan started, she implicitly criticized the United States. Although she clearly must keep a careful eye on her domestic Islamic credentials, Washington is now disenchanted with her.

What states support bin Laden? The Taliban regime in Afghanistan is now finished. Although the attitudes of most Arab states, including pro-Western ones, "range from lukewarm to ice-cold,"[15] supporters of terrorism such as Iraq, Iran, and Syria are keeping remarkably quiet. As Charles Krauthammer has observed, on the enemy's side are fanatical but weak forces, supported and sheltered by not a single major power. On the U.S. side, for all near-term practical purposes at least, are NATO, Japan, Canada, Australia, Russia, China, India, Pakistan, and scores of other countries.

What if War Expands?

What happens to the coalition if the war expands? There are three main dangers. The first raises the specter of the coalition becoming bogged down in Afghanistan in a Vietnam-style counterinsurgency war. The second involves the war expanding beyond Afghanistan to other

The Battle for Hearts and Minds

supporters of terrorism, such as Iraq. The third possibility involves another major terrorist attack on the United States, only this time using weapons of mass destruction.

The defeat of the Taliban should minimize the risks of another Vietnam. At the beginning of the bombing campaign, skeptics predicted that the only way to defeat the Taliban involved a U.S. ground force of 500,000. Yet, the combination of precision air strikes (which were much more effective than in the Gulf War), ground offensives by the Northern Alliance, and special operations forces has worked well. The withdrawal of Pakistan's support for the Taliban was a fatal blow. The retreat of Taliban remnants into remote mountainous areas in the south of Afghanistan need not demand a debilitating ground force operation by the coalition. Afghanistan will not become another Vietnam.

A more serious prospect for the coalition is a possible U.S. decision to widen the war to include other countries, such as Iraq, Iran, Syria, Sudan, Somalia, and Yemen, that host either bin Laden's Al Qaeda terrorist network or other dangerous terrorist movements. Influential people in the Bush administration, such as Rice and Deputy Secretary of Defense Paul Wolfowitz, are keen to pursue unfinished business from the 1991 Gulf War with Saddam Hussein. A widening of the war to include Iraq would undoubtedly strain the coalition, particularly with European countries such as France and Germany, as well as Russia. Many in the Middle East would probably regard it as confirmation that the United States is fighting a war against Islam. If evidence implicates Saddam's regime, however, the coalition must agree to punish him. Otherwise, this so-called war against terrorism will falter.

A more dangerous situation would arise if Islamic fundamentalists overthrew General Pervez Musharraf's regime in Pakistan. Unlike Iraq or Iran, Pakistan has developed operational nuclear ballistic missiles. It could easily target U.S. military bases in the Middle East or threaten to widen the conflict to include India—also in possession of nuclear weapons and ballistic missiles—which would raise the war on terrorism to an entirely different level of conflict. Under such conditions, how much of the coalition would remain and what price would U.S. partners demand to stay in it?

The third possibility involves the use by Al Qaeda or some other terrorist group of a nuclear weapon against the United States. The outrage in the United States would show no bounds; the urge to retaliate in kind against some target associated with the terrorists would be strong. This response would break a tacitly agreed norm of international behavior since the end of World War II not to use nuclear weapons. Holding the coalition together in such an apocalyptic situation would be nigh impossible.

These scenarios are speculative. Perhaps the more serious immediate task is to keep the coalition together in the face of increasing accusations that it is waging a war against Islam. To counter this sentiment, the international stabilization force in Afghanistan must include personnel from Muslim countries such as Turkey, Jordan, Bangladesh, and Indonesia—and exclude U.S. troops. As the *Economist* observed, "[T]he West can live in peace with Islam. What is unclear is whether Islam can live in peace with the West."[16] Muslims in many parts of the world flatly say it cannot. When they consider the comparative failure, in material terms, of their once mighty civilization, they feel a deep sense of humiliation.[17]

This issue is complex and must be handled with the utmost sensitivity if the world is not to slide into a confrontation between Islam and the West. We should not commit the error of typing all Islamic countries with the same homogeneous attitudes, as we did, incorrectly, with "world communism." Samuel Huntington asserts that the collapse of communism removed a common enemy of the West as well as Islam and left each the perceived major threat to the other.[18] He predicts "a civilizational war" between Islam and the West. This prophecy must not become self-fullfilling.

Concluding Observations

Predicting how the war against terrorism will unfold is obviously very difficult. So far at least, the United States has handled the situation well. Who would have predicted such an impressive array of countries supporting the United States, including every major power? Additionally—contrary to much media speculation—the United States has acquitted itself exceptionally well in bringing about the defeat of the Taliban in Afghanistan. The death of bin Laden, however, will not be the end of the matter. The war against terrorism will demand infinite patience and satisfaction with incremental successes that are not measured in terms of historical battlefield victories. Maintaining pressure in the financial, legal, and diplomatic war against terrorism over a prolonged period of time will be far from easy.

There is a risk that the coalition will fray at the edges, particularly if the war expands. That danger should be no excuse for a U.S. retreat or a reversion to isolationist sentiment. Ten years after the end of the Cold War, the United States has a new organizing principle to help define its interests. The United States must not define those interests in narrow terms. If anything, the events of September 11 have increased the global commitment to democracy as well as open economic systems and have decisively limited the unilateral and aggressive use of force and violence.[19] The United States can expect its major allies to stand by it in this context, but it must involve them in the coalition's decisionmaking more than it has done so far.

Crises other than terrorism will naturally arise, engaging U.S. national interests. Whenever they arise, the United States must not revert to its previous unilateral, U.S.-first instincts and recognize that, as powerful as it is, it needs to work with other countries to achieve its aims. At times, this reality will demand some uncomfortable trade-offs and concessions. Washington will need to ensure that its current emphasis on greater domestic security does not undermine its traditional international support for human rights and democracy.

This historic coalition must not be discarded if the going gets tough, as it will. The United States is no longer an invulnerable country.

Notes

1.   Yossef Bodansky, *Bin Laden: The Man Who Declared War on the United States* (Rocklin, Calif.: Prima Publishing, 1999), p. 406.

The Battle for Hearts and Minds

2. I owe the thoughts in this paragraph to Avery Goldstein, "September 11, the Shanghai Summit, and the Shift in U.S.-China Policy," in *E-Notes* (Philadelphia: Foreign Policy Research Institute, November 9, 2001), www.fpri.org/enotes/americawar.20011109.goldstein.sept11china.html (accessed January 8, 2002).

3. Ibid.

4. Robert B. Zoellick, "A Republican Foreign Policy," *Foreign Affairs* 79, no. 1 (January/February 2000): 69.

5. William Pfaff, "The Question of Hegemony," *Foreign Affairs* 80, no. 1 (January/February 2001): 228.

6. Zoellick, "A Republican Foreign Policy," p. 69.

7. Walter Laqueur, "Let the Eagle Strike Free," *Australian*, October 2, 2001, p. 13.

8. David Fromkin, "The Strategy of Terrorism," in James F. Hoge Jr. and Fareed Zakaria, eds., *The American Encounter: The United States and the Making of the Modern World* (New York: Basic Books, 1997), p. 345. This article was first published in *Foreign Affairs* in July 1975 and addresses "how to drain the swamps of misery in which hatred and fanaticism breed."

9. Ibid., p. 348.

10. Richard Overy, *Why the Allies Won* (London: Pimlico, 1995), p. 290.

11. Christian Reus-Smit, "The Return of History," in *The Day the World Changed? Terrorism and World Order* (Canberra: Australian National University, 2001), pp. 5–6.

12. François Heisbourg, "U.S. Hegemony? Perceptions of the United States Abroad," *Survival* 41, no. 4 (winter 1999–2000): 17.

13. Condoleezza Rice, "Promoting the National Interest," *Foreign Affairs* 79, no. 1 (January/February 2000): 62.

14. *Nezavisimaya Gazeta*, October 23, 2001 (quoting Russian first deputy minister of foreign affairs Vyacheslav Trubnikov).

15. *Economist*, November 17–23, 2001, p. 18.

16. "Muslims and the West: The Need to Speak Up," *Economist*, October 13–19, 2001, p. 14.

17. Ibid.

18. Samuel P. Huntington, *The Clash of Civilizations and the Remaking of World Order* (New York: Simon & Schuster, 1996), p. 211.

19. Adam Garfinkle, "September 11: Before and After," in *FPRI Wire* 9, no. 8 (Philadelphia: Foreign Policy Research Institute, November 9, 2001), www.fpri.org/fpriwire/0908.200110.garfinkle.sept11.html (accessed January 8, 2002).

Barry Desker and Kumar Ramakrishna

Forging an Indirect Strategy in Southeast Asia

Even as the campaign by the U.S.-led coalition against the radical Islamist Al Qaeda terrorist network and its Taliban protectors in Afghanistan is winding down, recognizing that a terrorist threat still exists in other parts of the world is vital. Any hubris generated by the swift and successful ouster of the Taliban regime and the elimination of Al Qaeda terrorist training camps and personnel should not obscure the fact that Afghanistan is but one theater in the war against terrorism. An estimated 5,000 Islamist recruits from Saudi Arabia, Egypt, Algeria, and other countries have trained as Al Qaeda operatives in Osama bin Laden's camps in Afghanistan. Many of these individuals returned to their homelands to train new recruits and to found new cells. Additionally, about 50,000 volunteers from 50 countries passed through Al Qaeda camps during the Afghan jihad against Soviet occupation more than 20 years ago; many of them returned to their homelands as well, infused with a dangerously radical "jihad mentality." Thus, even after the end of the current campaign in Afghanistan, the international community must still eradicate not just Al Qaeda but also the much larger radical Islamic network worldwide.

Barry Desker is director of the Institute of Defence and Strategic Studies, Nanyang Technological University, Singapore. He was Singapore's ambassador to Indonesia from 1986 to 1993. Kumar Ramakrishna is an assistant professor at the institute.

Copyright © 2002 by The Center for Strategic and International Studies and the Massachusetts Institute of Technology
The Washington Quarterly • 25:2 pp. 161–176.

As a result, intelligence analysts are now focusing on Asia. Rohan Gunaratna, a former chief investigator for the United Nations Terrorism Prevention Branch now based at the Centre for the Study of Terrorism and Political Violence at St. Andrew's University in Scotland, has argued that the center of gravity of terrorism has shifted from the Middle East to Asia since the 1993 Oslo peace accords between Israel and the Palestinians. Gunaratna observes that Asia is currently experiencing the highest incidence of terrorist attacks in the world.[1] In fact, following the security crackdown by U.S. and European governments in the wake of the September 11 attacks, Western intelligence analysts believe that Al Qaeda operatives have been seeking safer waters in Southeast Asia, a region notorious for its porous borders, large populations of urban and rural poor, and both Muslim and non-Muslim armed extremist groups. The U.S. State Department recently named the Philippines, Indonesia, and Malaysia as "potential Al Qaeda hubs."[2]

What strategy will root out the terrorist network within Southeast Asia? At the strategic level, the war against terrorism must be understood as a political and ideological war for the hearts and minds of the borderless, transnational Muslim state, or *ummah*. Hence, instead of pursuing a predominantly military approach to wiping out Al Qaeda cells worldwide, adopting an indirect strategy in which military power is carefully calibrated, and political, economic, and ideological measures are emphasized, is necessary to project the overarching message that the West is a friend of Islam and wants to help Muslims preserve their core values while they make the painful transition to modernity.

Al Qaeda and the Southeast Asian Radical Islamic Movement

Maritime Southeast Asia—a key theater of conflict during the Cold War—has reemerged with good reason as a region of prime strategic importance to the United States. About 20 percent of the world's one billion Muslims live in the area, and Indonesia hosts the world's largest Muslim population—170 million. The majority of the populations of Indonesia, Malaysia, and Brunei are Muslim, and sizable Muslim mi-

The Battle for Hearts and Minds

norities reside in the Philippines, Singapore, and Thailand. Although most of the region's Muslims practice a tolerant form of Islam, oppose terrorism, and do not hold explicitly anti-American views, the links between regional radical Islamic groups and the Al Qaeda network are evident.

The most extensive exposé of these linkages was contained in a statement by the Singaporean government on January 11, 2002, that revealed that it had detained 13 members of Jemaah Islamiah (JI), a clandestine network with cells in Singapore, Malaysia, and Indonesia. The Singaporean government also released a surveillance videotape, prepared by one of the detainees, and handwritten notes in Arabic that were discovered in the rubble of an Al Qaeda leader's house in Afghanistan in December 2001. Three JI cells had targeted shuttle bus services used by U.S. naval personnel as well as U.S. naval vessels transiting Singapore waters. They also kept watch on the U.S., Israeli, British, and Australian embassies; the Singaporean Ministry of Defense; and U.S. companies in Singapore. The group had existed since 1997, and eight members had undergone training at Al Qaeda camps in Afghanistan.[3]

JI has extensive regional linkages. Its leader is Hambali, alias Riduan Isamuddin, an Indonesian resident in Malaysia who is also being sought by the Malaysian and Indonesian police. While in Malaysia, he met two of the hijackers of the airliner that crashed into the Pentagon on September 11 and also reportedly met a man suspected of involvement in the bombing of the U.S.S. *Cole* in Yemen.[4] The Singaporean government's statement said that, under the direction of a foreign Al Qaeda operative and a trainer and bombmaker with the Moro Islamic Liberation Front (MILF) in the Philippines, JI attempted to purchase 21 tons of ammonium nitrate to make several truck bombs. The activities in Singapore were surprising and indicate the extent of the problem elsewhere in Southeast Asia.[5]

Malaysia has also served as a transit point for arms and personnel throughout the region.[6] Nevertheless, of the three Southeast Asian countries on the U.S. State Department's list of potential Al Qaeda hubs, Malaysia arouses the least concern, perhaps because Kuala Lumpur has managed to maintain both its economic and political stability despite being adversely affected by the 1997–1998 financial crisis. The germane issue for the wider struggle against Al Qaeda, however, is the political contest within Malaysia for the hearts and minds of the majority of the population. Dr. Mahathir Muhammad's ruling United Malay National Organization (UMNO) and the main opposition party, Parti Islam Se Malaysia (PAS), an extremely conservative Muslim party, are waging the country's political war. In many ways, Mahathir may be considered a modern, progressive Muslim leader who seeks to mesh traditional Islamic ideas with the requirements of a modern multiracial, globalized society. PAS, which controls two northern Malaysian states, preaches a fundamentalist form of Islam that has much in common with northern India's Deobandism, which ultimately gave rise to the Taliban.[7] In fact, Datuk Nik Aziz Nik Mat, the spiritual leader of PAS, absorbed Deobandi teachings himself while studying in northern India in the 1940s.

In August 2001, Malaysia detained Datuk Nik's son, Nik Adli, a veteran of the Afghan war against the Soviets. According to Kuala Lumpur, Adli was leading a Muslim extremist group plotting to oust Mahathir's moderate, secular government and to create an Islamic state linking Malaysia to Indonesia and the southern Philippines. Because the Malaysian government has not released evidence to support its allegations, PAS naturally accuses Mahathir of seeking to capitalize on the climate of fear over terrorism for domestic political purposes.[8] Kuala Lumpur, however, does have reason to accuse radical Islamic groups of seeking to destabilize the country clandestinely. In July 2000, a previously unknown group called Al Maunah stole weapons from a Malaysian army camp and killed two security personnel before surrendering. In recent months, Kuala Lumpur has detained at least 40 members of another militant Islamic group, the Kumpulan Mujahideen Movement (KMM), which had been implicated in bank robberies, murders, and kidnapping.[9] Al Qaeda has also reportedly established "military links" with the KMM, which operates in both Malaysia and Indonesia.[10]

Whereas the Malaysian state seems to be facing a greater threat of clandestine subversion rather than armed Islamic revolt, Indonesia, where armed Muslim radicals linked to Al Qaeda are operating in the open, presents a different case. Indonesian Mujahideen Council head Abu Bakar Bashir, alias Abdus Samad, whom the Malaysian authorities have identified as one of the "directing figures" of detained militants in Malaysia, continues to operate openly in Indonesia. Furthermore, on December 12, 2001, Lieutenant General Abdullah Hendropriyono, head of Indonesia's national intelligence service, revealed that Al Qaeda operatives were providing assistance to the Indonesian radical Islamic group Laskar Jihad in its battles with Christians in Poso in central Sulawesi. Jafar Umar Thalib, who apparently fought beside bin Laden against the Soviets in the 1980s, heads Laskar Jihad. Since 1999, this group, which seeks to establish Islamic law in Indonesia, has been leading thousands of Muslims into battles with Christians for control of the islands in central and eastern Indonesia. Although Thalib denies any connection with Al Qaeda, Laskar Jihad has set up secret training camps in Indonesia and claims that thousands of its supporters have received ideological and military training there. Laskar Jihad, based in the central Javanese city of Yogyakarta, even established a media center in Jakarta, which hosts a Web site and produces radical Islamic publications.[11] As Diarmid O'Sullivan of the Brussels-based International Crisis Group's Indonesia Project has pointed out, "Laskar Jihad stands out because of its strong ideological motivation and its military strength."[12] Al Qaeda operatives appear to have trained members of the Indonesian Islamic Liberation Front too.

The Philippines is believed to harbor Al Qaeda's regional center. Bin Laden's brother-in-law, Muhammad Jamal Khalifa, arrived in the country in the early 1990s and served as the original Al Qaeda representative in the Far East. Following Khalifa's arrest in Saudi Arabia after September 11, however, Ahmad Fauzi, alias Abdul al-Hakim, has apparently replaced Khalifa.[13] The Philippines is reportedly a major planning hub for Al Qaeda missions worldwide. Lax immigration controls are the country's basic problem, which expedites infiltration by Al

Qaeda operatives now apparently active in Manila. Moreover, radical Islamic Filipinos returning from training camps in Afghanistan in the early 1990s had little difficulty infiltrating the southern Philippines. What has today become the leading radical Islamic group Abu Sayyaf first emerged in 1995 and has grown rapidly from fewer than 200 members in 1997 to about 1,200 men in 2001. Abu Sayyaf has well-established ties with Al Qaeda and has constructed training camps in the southern Philippines modeled on the Al Qaeda setup in Afghanistan. Another significant militant Islamic group, the Moro Islamic Liberation Front (MILF), has also received funding from Al Qaeda.

The Philippines has also served as a regional hub for financing radical Islamic organizations. Khalifa established local branches of the Saudi-based International Islamic Relief Organization (IIRO), which channeled funds to both the Abu Sayyaf and Al Qaeda cells in the country. IIRO even compensated the widows of Filipino Muslim radicals whom security forces had killed, a practice that helps attract young men to IIRO because of assurances that IIRO would look after their families if they were eliminated. IIRO is not the only charitable organization in the Philippines suspected of financing terrorism. Manila is investigating five other Muslim charities active in the Philippines: the Association of Islamic Development, the World Alliance of Muslim Youth, the Darul Hijra Foundation, United Overseas Bangsa Moro, and Islamic Wisdom Worldwide.

As previously stated, the Philippines serves as the major supply source and transit point for weapons and explosives provided to other radical Islamic groups in the region. India's intelligence services have reported that the Pakistani group Harakat al-Mujahideen, which has close ties to Al Qaeda, funnels arms to Abu Sayyaf on boats owned by the Sri Lankan Liberation Tigers of Tamil Eelam. The Filipino radicals then transfer some of the weapons to Indonesian groups. In August 2001, for instance, Malaysian police intercepted a group of Indonesians who were smuggling weapons from Setangkai Island in the southern Philippines to eastern Indonesia. Thanks to the ransom money from its lucrative kidnapping operations—Libya paid $20 million to secure the release of hostages in 2000—Abu Sayyaf is flush with funds with which to purchase new weapons and equipment, such as state-of-the-art speedboats, advanced communications devices, and even weapons obtained from corrupt Filipino troops. Unsurprisingly, some observers believe that Abu Sayyaf has better equipment than the Filipino military.

The Al Qaeda Hydra

President George W. Bush's administration quickly grasped that it needed not only to execute military action against Al Qaeda and its Taliban associates in Afghanistan but also to begin nonmilitary initiatives aimed at disrupting radical Islamic funding, logistics supply lines, and terrorist networks in several countries. These measures, however, really attack the symptoms, not the causes, of the threat from radical Muslims. Al Qaeda clearly knows that it must first defeat the United States in order to set up Islamic territories free of Western influence. Yet, it recognizes that it lacks the military means to engage U.S. forces directly; therefore, it needs to strike at what it considers its foe's critical vulnerability, or soft underbelly: the American people. The September 11 strikes in the United States resulted.

In contrast, the United States and, more generally, the West believe their center of gravity in the war against radical Islamic terrorism resides not in specific states such as Afghanistan, Iraq, Sudan, or Somalia. Rather, it lies in the hearts and minds of the borderless, transnational Muslim nation. Even if the coalition roots out existing Al Qaeda operatives from their secret lairs across the world, cripples the international infrastructure for terrorist funding, and somehow denies radical Muslims the capabilities to produce and deliver weapons of mass destruction (WMD), it would not necessarily eradicate the threat.

Globalization has expedited what Thomas Friedman calls the "democratization" of finance, technology, and information. Consequently, with sufficient determination, a radical Islamic core that is scattered throughout the world, but has access to communications technology to coordinate activities, can reconstitute disrupted logistics and funding networks over time while clandestinely restoring access to WMD capabilities. The reconstruction of terrorist cells, however, is not the main problem.

At a more basic level, as long as sizable pockets of ideologically exclusionist and politically repressed young Muslims in countries from Nigeria to the Philippines remain an angry radical Islamic movement with "sufficient determination," they will always pose an existential threat to Western and especially U.S. interests. For this reason, characterizing Al Qaeda as a "living organism that generates new cells as old ones die"[14] and a "many-headed hydra"[15] is an accurate representation. Forgetting the still-palpable unease among Muslims in the Middle East and in Southeast Asia when the coalition's air campaign against the Taliban began on October 7, 2001, even though most Muslim governments supported it, is easy in the flush of victory over the Taliban's defeat. In Malaysia, PAS called on Malaysian Muslims to wage a jihad against the United States[16] while Jakarta was hit by waves of anti-American demonstrations.[17] Even after the campaign in Afghanistan concludes, and especially if additional military campaigns are undertaken elsewhere in the Muslim world—accompanied by more civilian deaths, however inadvertent—the potential for significant Muslim unrest in Southeast Asia should not be discounted too readily. Deputy Secretary of Defense Paul Wolfowitz's comment soon after September 11 retains its prescience: victory over the radical Islamic threat in general and in Southeast Asia in particular will ultimately require the West to "drain the swamp" of disgruntled, anti-Western Muslims. The West needs to disembowel the radical Islamic hydra, not interminably snip at its many heads.

Emphasizing Political over Military Measures

Because the strategic center of gravity of the war against radical Islamic terrorists resides in the hearts and minds of the Muslim *ummah*, it behooves the West to persuade Muslims to wean themselves away from the radical Islamic movement. In other words, this war is a political and ideological war—political because the West must convince Muslims that the West is a friend of Islam and ideological because the West must assist moderate, progressive Muslim leaders and intellectuals who want Islam to make a successful transition to modernity. In this way, the West's efforts can enable the Muslim masses to coexist peacefully with other creeds while enjoying personal freedom and prosperity. The essential political and ideological nature of the war against radical Islamic terrorism implies that the West has to counter Al Qaeda by using what the French strategist André Beaufré called an indirect strategy—one that elevates nonmilitary instruments of policy over military options.

Seen in this light, three policy measures are particularly important if the West is to improve its image in the eyes of Muslims everywhere, including Southeast Asia. The first step is the reconstruction and rehabilitation of Afghanistan. Having defeated the Taliban regime, the United States and its coalition allies must work together—and be seen working together—to ensure that a viable and durable post-Taliban administration emerges in Kabul. Moreover, Western governments should encourage foreign investment in Afghanistan to expedite postwar reconstruction. The United States must erase the widely articulated Muslim perception, which came in the wake of the closure of the U.S. embassy in Kabul after the Soviet withdrawal in 1989, that the United States "abandoned" Afghanistan in its time of greatest need.[18] The United States needs an enhanced image throughout the Muslim world to undercut the anti-Western propaganda of the radical Islamists.

The second stage of a Western indirect strategy must include progress to resolve the current impasse over the status of Jerusalem and Palestine. As Surin Pitsuwan, the Muslim former foreign minister of Thailand, argued recently, a strong sense of "primordial" resentment exists among "all Muslims around the world, particularly here in Southeast Asia," rooted in the belief that their sentiments about Jerusalem, which after Mecca and Medina is the third holiest site in Islam, have never been seriously accommodated.[19] According to Pitsuwan, the failure of the international community to seek a just solution to the problem has resulted in "frustration, inadequacy, the sense of being left out, the sense of being done injustice"—sentiments that have been "over-

whelming to the point of desperation."[20] Thus, in Muslim eyes, the issue of Palestine and Jerusalem symbolizes the historical arrogance that
Western civilization has displayed toward Islam since the Crusades of
the eleventh through thirteenth centuries. Consequently, the United
States in particular must strive to be viewed as acting justly on the
question of Palestine.

Third, because of the indirect, political nature of this war as well as
the need to persuade Muslims that the West is a friend of Islam, any
necessary military operations against other state supporters of radical
Islamic terrorism such as Iraq, Sudan, and Somalia must be carefully
calibrated and controlled. One cannot overemphasize the importance
of gearing military operations toward supporting, not undermining, the
more important diplomatic, socioeconomic, and public diplomacy measures aimed at persuading Muslims that the West harbors no ulterior
motive—no desire to subjugate them—as the radical Islamic movement
suggests. In a world dramatically shrunk by globalization and the "CNN
effect," radical Islamic propagandists, aided and abetted by sympathetic
television networks such as the Arabic-language Al Jazeera in Qatar,
can rapidly exploit every errant bomb that kills innocent Muslim women
and children to persuade Muslims that the West, despite its friendly
rhetoric, is indeed at war with the Islamic nation. Serious anti-American protests on the streets of Kuala Lumpur and Jakarta following the
onset of the U.S. air campaign on October 7 suggest that this statement
is not overblown.

Fleshing Out a Southeast Asian Indirect Strategy

Within the region, in what ways can an effective indirect strategy be
waged within Southeast Asia? Actors could implement four measures:

- Strengthen the organic capacity of the governments of the Philippines, Indonesia, and Malaysia to root out radical Islamic networks
  within their territories;

- Encourage regional Southeast Asian cooperation to counter terrorism;

- Help the Southeast Asian governments improve the quality of governance for their populations; and

- Assist local governments in promoting a more moderate form of Islam.

For a number of reasons, the United States must not hijack, and must appear to avoid hijacking, the battle against radical Islamic terrorism from the national governments in Jakarta, Manila, and Kuala Lumpur. First, all three countries are former Western colonies. These governments cannot be perceived as handing over responsibility for internal security to a foreign power, thereby undermining their political legitimacy. Second, and more importantly, all three countries have sizable Muslim populations that would not react kindly to the sudden injection of significant numbers of U.S. troops on their soil. Unsurprisingly, all three governments rejected the U.S. administration's offers of direct combat assistance to fight terrorist groups within their national borders. Thus, helping these governments improve their organic capabilities to fight terrorism rather than doing the job for them would be a wise indirect strategy.

At this writing, the approach that should be taken is, in fact, being taken. As Admiral Dennis Blair, commander in chief of the U.S. Pacific Command, observed in December 2001, U.S. military forces would provide logistical and other support rather than combat terrorist groups directly.[21] In other words, U.S. involvement, although "significant," would be "secondary and nuanced."[22] In fact, the Filipino government accepted $100 million in training assistance, military equipment, and maintenance support for the Armed Forces of the Philippines (AFP). The Indonesian government, which on December 12, 2001, officially admitted that Al Qaeda cells were active in its country, has also accepted offers to share intelligence and to have U.S. Special Forces train its security forces. In passing the fiscal year 2002 foreign operations bill in late December, the U.S. Congress maintained the ban on International Military Education and Training (IMET) programs that it first imposed on Indonesia following the 1991 debacle in East Timor. At the same time, however, Capitol

Hill wisely passed the Defense Department appropriations bill, which allows U.S. defense officials essentially to organize much-needed antiterrorist training for the Indonesian Armed Forces (TNI).[23] Particularly relevant for the relatively cash-strapped Filipino and Indonesian armed forces would be receiving new helicopters, aircraft, and patrol boats, as well as advanced training in counterinsurgency techniques—all required to deal far more effectively with armed radical Islamic groups such as Abu Sayyaf and Laskar Jihad. The recent Indonesian record of counterinsurgency operations, for instance, especially in its ongoing conflict with the Free Aceh Movement in northern Sumatra, has been singularly undistinguished, to say the least.[24]

A second component of an indirect strategy for the United States to use in dealing with Southeast Asia would be to strengthen intraregional cooperation countering the activities of radical Islamic terrorists. In fact, Manila has recently made plans with Kuala Lumpur and Jakarta to form a regional antiterrorist coalition, which would focus on intelligence sharing, maritime border security, and possible joint antiterrorist military operations. Additionally, a working group of the Conference for Security Cooperation in the Asia Pacific (CSCAP), meeting in Jakarta in November 2001, suggested that the governments of the Association of Southeast Asian Nations (ASEAN) member nations might find several options useful, including (1) cooperation in building a database of terrorist organizations to be used by governments inside and outside the region; (2) adoption of common standards or best practices in investigating terrorist groups and incidents; and (3) accumulation of the expertise needed to conduct strategic work in identifying intraregional linkages of terrorist networks and financial links between regional networks and extraregional sources. The United States and other developed countries could contribute to this regional effort by providing technical assistance, training, and funding.

The third component of an indirect strategy for U.S. policy toward Southeast Asia would consist of efforts to improve the quality of governance in the region. Whereas Malaysia has had the relatively good fortune of having inherited a well-functioning state bureaucracy from the

British, the Philippines and post-Suharto Indonesia have not featured a strong central administration. Thus, the primary problem the Indonesian state faces is governance: the state apparatus must be strengthened so that directives from Jakarta are implemented on the ground. For example, some claim that rogue elements of the country's armed forces secretly support Laskar Jihad and have provided manpower and weapons. The U.S. government should emphasize to the TNI that, in return for the resumption of U.S. military aid and training, TNI's leaders must mount a serious effort to rein in maverick elements that operate at the local level. The state's ability to pay proper salaries to its public servants, especially the military, is another aspect of better governance. In the Philippines, underpaid AFP soldiers sell arms to Abu Sayyaf, while others make money by alerting the radical group when the police and army are about to strike—a practice that may help explain Abu Sayyaf's longevity and effectiveness.

The ability to generate wealth is critical not only to compensate public servants but also ultimately to meet the basic needs of the country's populace. The current economic downturn has hurt Malaysia's growth, but Indonesia and the Philippines are in even worse financial straits. This situation affects the ability of these two governments to meet their citizens' basic needs. For example, Indonesia's coordinating minister for the economy, Dorodjatun Kuntjoro-Jakti, despite the respectable growth in the country's economy (3.2–3.5 percent in 2001), warned that transitioning from an authoritarian, centralized political system to a democratic, decentralized one would be very difficult while preparing domestic firms to face the challenges of regional economic cooperation when the ASEAN Free Trade Area goes into effect in 2003. The socioeconomic dislocations resulting from a decrepit Indonesian economy mean that a very large pool of economically downtrodden young Muslims are easy prey for groups such as Laskar Jihad, which, like its Middle Eastern counterparts Hamas and Hizballah, advocate armed struggle and, quite importantly, promote social welfare. Thus, the West has a strong incentive to boost trade with and aid to Southeast Asian governments in an effort to strengthen their capacities to help Southeast

Asia's populations enjoy decent living standards, thereby diminishing the appeal of radical Islamism.

Finally and most critically, given that the current conflict has exposed the contest within the Islamic world for the soul of Islam, the West must assist Southeast Asian Muslim communities to promulgate a moderate brand of Islam. In a sense, the ideological battlefield is already aptly configured because of historical reasons. Islam came to Southeast Asia by way of traders who engaged in commerce first and preached their faith afterward. Hence, Islam in Southeast Asia was compelled to "accommodate and reconcile with the existing traditions and values" that the "high cultures of Hinduism and Buddhism" propounded. The net result was the gradual emergence of a Southeast Asian Islam, which was "basically tolerant, peaceful, and smiling," in the words of a leading Indonesian Islamic scholar.[25] Although the 1979 Iranian revolution, as in other parts of the world, nudged Southeast Asian Islam toward a more fundamentalist interpretation, this trend did not necessarily mean that believers became less tolerant. Muslims became more culturally conservative rather than politically militant. More frequent sightings of Islamic dress in society did not, ipso facto, signal the "Talibanization" of Islam in Southeast Asia.

Nevertheless, radical Islamic intellectuals must be undercut. Wahhabism, an extremely fundamentalist and exclusionary form of Islam that originated in eighteenth-century Saudi Arabia has, thanks to Saudi petrodollars, been carrying more than its weight ideologically in religious schools and mosques from Pakistan to Malaysia since the 1960s. The Taliban was "the final and most formidable product of this long-term strategy," and, even though Western analysts have traditionally shied away from using the term Wahhabism, "the fact that Wahhabi-inspired ideas have been promoted in Pakistan, Afghanistan, and Central Asia in the last thirty years through a variety of semi-official and official actors is undeniable."[26] Moreover, since the mid-1970s, Saudi funding from official and private sources has gone to more radical Islamic groups influenced by Wahhabi teachings. Therefore, demurring from including "Wahhabism in one's analysis handicaps understanding."[27]

As one Malaysian intellectual advocates, it is thus imperative that "moderate Muslims … reclaim center stage."[28] At the moment, another well-known Malaysian scholar complains, a "moral and ideological crisis" has beset "the collective Muslim mind."[29] Hence, Pitsuwan laments that the spirit of inquiry which led Arab Muslim intellectuals of the past to attain great heights of achievement in science, philosophy, and the arts has long been absent from the faith. He argues that, today, the general principle in Southeast Asian religious schools appears to be "memorization, stop thinking, stop rationalizing."[30]

Moderate Muslim voices must begin to reclaim ideological ground that has been lost. Muslims in Southeast Asia should be exposed, through all available technical means, to the ideas of contemporary moderate scholars, such as Indonesia's Nurcholish Majid and Iran's Abdul Saroush. Both these scholars are "trying to extract the prophetic truths from the Koran to show the inherent compatibility of modern-day concerns with the sacred texts."[31] Educational agencies and moderate Muslim religious authorities in Southeast Asia should also be urged to design modern Islamic curriculums for use in religious schools; these efforts should receive adequate funding and assistance. Apart from education in science and technical subjects, the young must be exposed to well-articulated moderate alternatives to Wahhabi-inspired exclusionary worldviews. Ulil Abshar Abdallah, an official of the moderate Nadlatul Ulama, Indonesia's largest Muslim organization, conceded that, rather than "mulling over religious paradoxes and disputes about the lives of long-dead saints," moderate intellectuals must match the radical Muslims in "presenting a simple yet comprehensive ideology that can be grasped by common people."[32]

Finally, U.S. public diplomacy measures must saturate Southeast Asian airwaves with images and stories of amity between Western and Muslim societies. Pictures of joyful Afghans pointedly celebrating the demise of the Taliban in the company of Western forces, and photos of U.S. and European Muslims living comfortably with the accoutrements of postindustrial society and, importantly, in daily rapport with their non-Muslim colleagues, can send and repeatedly emphasize the clear message that the West is a friend of Islam and is willing to assist Muslims' successful transition to modernity without sacrificing their core beliefs. To promote this concept effectively, the United States must rebuild the decrepit machinery that conducts its public diplomacy. An essential step is to enhance congressional funding for the Voice of America and Worldnet, enabling them to increase vernacular broadcasts on radio frequencies, television, and the Internet substantially. Washington must help to shape opinions in parts of the world where a negative perception of the United States has developed and where CNN is not the media of choice.

Most critically, however, the West must genuinely address three key issues: (1) reconstruction of post-Taliban Afghanistan, (2) a viable and secure Palestinian homeland, and (3) appropriate conduct of future military campaigns against Muslim states that support Al Qaeda. Only then can the Muslim world regard the West as sincere in proclaiming itself a friend of Islam. Without deeds that send this message, no amount of rhetoric to that effect will be credible to the Muslim *ummah*. As the late great British counterinsurgent Sir Robert Thompson put it, one cannot make bricks without straw.

'Rolling Back' Radical Islamic Terrorism

Almost 50 years ago, during the Malayan government's counterinsurgency campaign against the Malayan Communist Party, the legendary British high commissioner General Sir Gerald Templer declared a "White area" that was generally free of Communist terrorist activity in the settlement of Malacca. The harsh restrictions on movement and other freedoms that the emergency regulations imposed were removed in the White area, and its residents could live normally again. Because people in neighboring states coveted such freedoms, they intensified cooperation with the government, and soon the terrorist infrastructure in their areas collapsed. Templer and his successors patiently "projected success" outward from Malacca until eventually the whole of Malaya was cleared of the Communist threat and declared "White."

The current war against Al Qaeda and the radical Islamic movement that the network embodies is, of course, not an exact fac-
simile of the campaign against Communist terrorism in 1950s Malaya.
Nevertheless, a similar principle of projecting success outward from
Southeast Asia can apply to the war against terrorism. At one level,
this approach involves the important legal and operational task of
mounting a "rollback" of Al Qaeda's funding, personnel, and weapons pipelines leading from Southeast Asia to the Middle East and
elsewhere. In this indirect political and ideological war to capture
the hearts and minds of Muslims around the world, however, projecting success outward means something much more critical: it
implies deliberately and extensively promoting Southeast Asian Islam, along with its intrinsic tolerance of other faiths and creeds as
well as its relative success in embracing secular modernity, as a
powerful, ideological counterweight to the worldview of the radical Islamic exclusionists.

In this respect, Malaysia's intrareligious harmony and prosperity
should be projected more extensively, as should Indonesia's, which
Wolfowitz, former U.S. ambassador to Indonesia, has said, "stands for
a country that practices religious tolerance and democracy, treats
women properly, and believes Islam is a religion of peace."[33] Therefore, the world's largest Muslim country "ought to be a model to the
rest of the world [of] what Islam can be."[34] Just as the ordinary people
of 1950s Malaya dearly wanted to be free from harsh secular restrictions, so too can the images from newly liberated Kabul and Kandahar
clearly demonstrate that ordinary Muslims, like mainstream Jews and
Christians, want to be similarly liberated from draconian religious restrictions. In particular, Muslims want to know that combining personal piety with peace, freedom, and prosperity is permissible; and
they want to learn how to achieve this balance. To the extent that the
West, by helping to preserve and promote tolerant Southeast Asian
Islam, can help Muslims elsewhere answer these questions, it will
have taken a critical step in the quest to disembowel the radical Islamic hydra.

Notes

1. Michael Richardson, "Southeast Asia Bars Help of U.S. Troops," *International Herald Tribune*, December 14, 2001, www.iht.com/articles/41870.html (accessed January 22, 2002).

2. Ibid.

3. "Yishun Target in Group's Plans," *Straits Times* (Singapore), January 12, 2002, sec. A, p. 1.

4. "Militant Leader Met Terrorists in Selangor," *Star* (Malaysia), reprinted in *Straits Times*, January 12, 2002, sec. A, p. 23.

5. "Yishun Target in Group's Plans," p. 1.

6. The Jemaah Islamiah (JI) purchased four tons of ammonium nitrate in Malaysia for use by the Singapore cell. JI members also made trips to Afghanistan via Malaysia and Pakistan. See "A Tale with Many Beginnings," *Straits Times*, January 12, 2002, sec. H, p. 2.

7. Deobandism, a branch of Sunni Islam, originally emerged in British India as a reform movement aimed at regenerating Muslim society as it struggled to live under British colonialism. In recent decades, however, clerics preaching the exclusionary tenets of Wahhabism have heavily impregnated and radicalized Deobandism as practiced in Pakistan.

8. Barry Wain, "Is Malaysia Using the War on Terror as a Political Tool?" *Asian Wall Street Journal*, December 12, 2001, p. 1.

9. "50 Malaysians with Al-Qaeda Links," *Straits Times*, January 12, 2002, sec. A, p. 23.

10. Rohan Gunaratna, "Al-Qaeda: The Asian Connection," *Straits Times Interactive*, January 4, 2002, www.straitstimes.asia1.com.sg/usattack/story/0,1870,94610-1010095200,00.html (accessed January 22, 2002).

11. "Alumni of Camps Run by Bin Laden Are Causing Alarm," *Asian Wall Street Journal*, December 14, 2001, p. 11.

12. Diarmid O'Sullivan, "Indonesia: Radicals Have Homegrown Causes," *International Herald Tribune*, December 26, 2001, www.iht.com/articles/42897.html (accessed January 22, 2002).

13. Gunaratna, "Al-Qaeda: The Asian Connection."

14. Robert A. Levine, "A Pair of Sober Questions about the Slog after Early Victories," *International Herald Tribune*, December 7, 2001, www.iht.com/articles/41118.html (accessed January 22, 2002).

15. Duncan Campbell, "Futile Campaign against the Head of a Hydra," *Guardian Unlimited*, November 21, 2001, www.guardian.co.uk/Print/0,3858,4303748,00.html (accessed January 22, 2002).

The Battle for Hearts and Minds

16. Michael Richardson, "Mahathir Boosted by Terrorism Stance," *CNN.com*, October 31, 2001, www.cnn.com/2001/WORLD/asiapcf/southeast/10/31/malaysia.mahathir/index.html (accessed January 22, 2002).

17. Atika Shubert, "Indonesia Braces for Friday Protests," *CNN.com*, October 11, 2001, www.cnn.com/2001/WORLD/asiapcf/southeast/10/11/ret.indon.protests/index.html (accessed January 22, 2002).

18. M. Ishaq Nadiri, "Rebuilding a Ravaged Land," *New York Times*, November 26, 2001, sec. A, p. 17, late edition.

19. Surin Pitsuwan, "Strategic Challenges Facing Islam in Southeast Asia" (lecture delivered at the Institute of Defence and Strategic Studies and the Centre for Contemporary Islamic Studies, Singapore, November 5, 2001) (hereinafter "Pitsuwan lecture").

20. Ibid.

21. Michael Richardson, "Seeking Allies in Terror War, U.S. Woos Southeast Asia," *International Herald Tribune*, November 29, 2001, www.iht.com/articles/40338.html (accessed January 22, 2002).

22. Dana Dillon and Paolo Pasicolan, "Fighting Terror in Southeast Asia," *Asian Wall Street Journal*, January 16, 2002, p. 6.

23. Michael Richardson, "U.S. to Aid Jakarta Army," *International Herald Tribune*, December 27, 2001, www.iht.com/articles/43089.html (accessed January 22, 2002).

24. See Rizal Sukma, "The Acehnese Rebellion: Secessionist Movement in Post-Suharto Indonesia," in *Non-Traditional Security Issues in Southeast Asia*, Andrew T. H. Tan and J. D. Kenneth Boutin, eds. (Singapore: Institute of Defence and Strategic Studies, 2001), pp. 377–409.

25. Azyumardi Azra, "The Megawati Presidency: Challenge of Political Islam" (paper presented at the "Joint Public Forum on Indonesia: The First 100 Days of President Megawati," organized by the Institute of Southeast Asian Studies and the Centre for Strategic and International Studies, Singapore, November 1, 2001).

26. Shireen T. Hunter, "Religion, Politics, and Security in Central Asia," *SAIS Review* 21, no. 2 (summer–fall 2001): 72–81.

27. Ibid.

28. Karim Raslan, "Now a Historic Chance to Welcome Muslims into the System," *International Herald Tribune*, November 27, 2001, www.iht.com/articles/40072.html (accessed January 22, 2002).

29. Farish A. Noor, personal communication with author, October 21, 2001.

30. Pitsuwan lecture.

31. Raslan, "Now a Historic Chance to Welcome Muslims into the System," www.iht.com/articles/40072.html.

32. Peter Ford, "Listening for Islam's Silent Majority," *Christian Science Monitor*, November 5, 2001, www.csmonitor.com/2001/1105/p1s2-wogi.html (accessed January 22, 2002).

33. Richardson, "Seeking Allies in Terror War, U.S. Woos Southeast Asia," www.iht.com/articles/40338.html.

34. Ibid.

The Battle for Hearts and Minds

Thérèse Delpech

The Imbalance of Terror

In the eyes of history, the 10 years from December 25, 1991, until September 11, 2001, may become known as the interwar years. Just as the 20 years from 1919 to 1939 have no organizing principle to define them, so too the last 10 years may be independently unrecognizable to the future. From the day the Soviet flag was lowered from the Kremlin until the day the twin towers collapsed, the shape of the world to come was impossible to imagine. Granted, new trends distinct from the Cold War were emerging. A limited, regional war in the Persian Gulf had gathered together one of the major coalitions in the history of warfare. Three major actors—the United States, Russia, and China—worked with a curious mix of cooperation and confrontation. Intrastate wars were blooming in the Balkans, Indonesia, Central Asia, and Africa, but ethnic rivalries were hardly the only feature of these conflicts, even in the chaos of Africa. Globalization was an economic, rather than strategic, concept and its very meaning remained elusive. The information revolution was changing the nature of conflict, but exactly how was difficult to assess. Simply stated, no clear picture was emerging from these different elements.

Thérèse Delpech is currently director of strategic affairs at the Atomic Energy Commission, France. She is also senior research associate at the Center for International Studies (CERI), Paris, and member of the International Institute for Strategic Studies (IISS) Council.

Copyright © 2001 by The Center for Strategic and International Studies and the Massachusetts Institute of Technology
The Washington Quarterly • 25:1 pp. 31–40.

One thing, however, was already clear: by the end of the last century, hopes concerning a "new world order" had vanished. The strategic literature was full of "new threats." Rapid change was indeed feared by many, particularly with the appearance of two additional declared nuclear powers in 1998, with the intractable problems posed by Iraq and North Korea, and with the modernization of the Chinese military. Possible failures of deterrence were often contemplated, and missile defenses were supposed to protect people and troops at home and abroad. The question at the beginning of September 2001 was whether such defenses would increase international security or *in*security.

The vocabulary used to describe the international situation did not reflect the striking difference between expectations at the beginning and at the end of the 1990s. For want of something better, observers retained the term "post–Cold War" as the least imperfect way to name the 10 years that followed the Soviet Union's breakup. Now, something different, something unrecognizable, something irreconcilable with concepts inherited from past experiences of either war or terrorism has come into being. This new phenomenon, however, does have a name: asymmetric warfare. Significant thought had already been given to asymmetric threats before September 11, but it had been nothing but a way of thinking. Such an extraordinary attack, in real time and real space, gave asymmetry a horrific shape.

The Terrorist Agenda

Those who planned the attacks seem to have operated from a list detailing the striking differences between the United States and themselves and to have played on those differences as much as they could. Their strategy can be described as follows:

• *Have no center and strike at the heart of the superpower.*

Although the United States may have become increasingly non-Clausewitzian in its approach to warfare, the terrorists adhered to the old recipe of warfare's most famous theoretician: inflict the most powerful blow at the center of gravity of your enemy. The World Trade Center, as a symbol of U.S. economic might and U.S.-led globalization, was precisely that point. The decapitation of U.S. political and military power with strikes on the Pentagon and possibly the White House or the Capitol was supposed to finish off the task. President George W. Bush correctly described the terrorist attack as an act of war. This trauma has been far worse than during the 1950s when Sputnik revealed the vulnerability of U.S. territory. Although that threat was much more serious, putting the entire United States within a fraction of an hour's journey of Soviet nuclear missiles, it remained unreal because it was theoretical. Today's threat is no longer "potential": lower Manhattan lies in ruins. The terrorists correctly calculated the psychological effect.

- *The United States wants life at any cost? Kill as many civilians as possible.*
  In his first *fatwa*, or religious declaration, Osama bin Laden in 1996 urged Muslims to kill U.S. military men abroad. In 1998, he expanded this "religious duty" to all U.S. citizens, civilian and military. Shortly after the second *fatwa*, hundreds died in the Kenyan and Tanzanian embassy bombings, most of them Africans. The latest escalation on September 11 is impressive. The terrorists so shocked the U.S. psyche that Bush received unprecedented popular support (91 percent of the U.S. population) even after he said that no victory would be possible without casualties, most probably heavy ones. As the conflict unfolds, more frightening scenarios surface, involving unconventional means. This enemy has no moral limits.

- *Reveal U.S. vulnerability to rustic means of war.*
  To defeat the high-tech superpower, knives, fuel, and planes would suffice. The hijackers conducted a live demonstration for would-be terrorists. The message is clear: do not fear the United States' power; the United States is a giant with feet of clay. Worldwide eavesdropping can easily be defeated and the most effective missile shield provides no protection against this type of attack. Does this notion mean that the terrorists did

not use modern technology? Certainly not. They used the Internet for communication and encryptions. They made electronic money transfers from Dubai to the United States and back until just before the attacks. Moreover, networking, an essential component of postmodern society, was key to the terrorists' strategy. Yet, in the minds of terrorists, highly developed technology cannot defeat those committed to the cause, and willing to die for it, no matter how simple their methods.

- *Fight the kind of war the United States hates: an elusive enemy who uses guerrilla tactics.*

From the terrorists' standpoint, the only possible responses to the September 11 attacks would be either that of 1998, which proved totally ineffective (perhaps because of Pakistani betrayal); a Soviet-style invasion, which would lead to a second disaster for another major power; or guerrilla-style warfare, where the United States is not at its best. Lessons from experiences in Vietnam and more recently in Somalia were not lost on the terrorists. Afghanistan presents a particularly difficult and inhospitable terrain. Even the Soviet "Speznats" were unable to defeat the mujahideen. Granted, the United States has also learned lessons—not just from 1998, but also from Soviet errors—and has new technologies that allow it to destroy key military infrastructures immediately and trace fighters even in difficult terrains. Still, what exactly does the U.S. technological advantage provide in a fight against a tribal army in its mountainous homeland?

- *The United States makes military plans years ahead, so surprise them continuously.*

Surprise has always been the nightmare of the military, but the U.S. military may particularly hate it. If no consistent strategy is recognizable, if no anticipation can be expected, preparation is almost impossible. With strikes both at home and abroad, domestic support may prove more fragile over a long period, particularly if unconventional means are used against unprotected civilians. Adapting to surprise might become an important element of future planning.

telligence services (reportedly from those of Pakistan and Iraq). Evidence exists that certain terrorists have had contacts with undercover services on several continents (in Europe, the Middle East, South Asia, and Southeast Asia) and that some provided the terrorists with the Social Security numbers of deceased people. The latter is typical of state agents' work. Moreover, the terrorists' ability to defeat U.S. eavesdropping, monitoring, and counterintelligence over an extended period of time also suggests that undercover specialists may have assisted the perpetrators. Thus the attack most probably involved a mixture of state and nonstate action. Incontrovertible evidence of any state complicity might never surface, however, further complicating the mission to eradicate international terrorism. This lesson for the future is a dire one: states may learn that they can use nonstate actors to inflict major blows on an adversary without having to be held accountable for their actions.

- *The strategic challenge of failed states.*

The fact that large expanses of territories in so-called failed states escape government control need no longer be considered a regrettable feature of the postmodern world, but rather a strategic challenge that should be addressed urgently. Anarchic countries are both a breeding ground and a haven for terrorists. Apart from Central Asia, Africa comes to mind as a dramatic illustration of a locale that cannot be left any longer in its too-often chaotic shape. Nation-building and peacemaking, far from being secondary tasks that can be easily dismissed, should become central not only in European but also in U.S. security policy.

- *Possible failures of deterrence.*

Deterrence, in the context of asymmetric warfare, is probably less relevant than in more classical scenarios, because surprise and shock are essential part of asymmetric strategies. Failures of deterrence should particularly be considered in the case of nonstate actors engaged in unrestricted wars, whether they act alone or with the sponsorship of a nation-state, because they have little to lose, particularly when suicide is used as a weapon.

- *Defenses could be equally ineffective.*

This precept is notably true if the main preoccupation in the United States remains long-range ballistic missiles. Long-range ballistic missiles, in fact, appear less threatening than cruise missiles, which have been mentioned only rhetorically so far. About 80,000 cruise missiles are deployed in 70 countries. A dozen countries retain land-attack cruise missiles and antiship cruise missiles; unmanned aerial vehicles are proliferating. All the key cruise-missile technologies are widely available, and the end-products of that technology are all potential delivery systems for chemical and biological agents. Cruise missiles present air defense systems with an enormous challenge, to detect the missile early enough to mount an effective defense. A new emphasis on protection against cruise missiles is needed now.

- *The strength of an absolute ideology against our moderate societies.*

The danger of "religious" wars is greater than that of wars between "civilizations" because religions have a significantly greater power than civilizations. Al Qaeda uses religion not only to be able to recognize God as the sole constituency, but also to use the absolute power of religious faith in countries where literacy does not allow people even to read the Qur'an. Al Qaeda's declared ambition is to annihilate not just religions other than Islam (the destruction of the ancient Bamiyan's Buddhist statues in February 2001 is an eloquent testimony), but also anyone who does not accept its perverse version of Islam (bin Laden's people have burned Shi`ites alive in Afghanistan). No concession, however great, would be enough to end bin Laden's "mission" because, unlike many previous terrorist organizations, it does not intend to create a state nor does it wish to introduce political reforms. Its objective is metaphysical: a titanic struggle between "good" and "evil" forces, in which any means can be used to achieve the end.

- *A new world is taking shape.*

All conflicts have one quality in common: they all contribute to re-shaping international relations, sometimes in dramatic ways. This conflict, by starting out to destroy al Qaeda and other terrorist organizations with global reach, may end up reshaping the world. Waging the fight with this new world in mind is essential. An increased potential for miscalculation and surprise will probably occur in the future. Predictability should therefore be improved whenever possible during this conflict, especially in areas where strong tensions exist. In Europe's past, differences in strategic approach have resulted in grave errors, but the odds of misinterpretation between countries with different cultures are incomparably greater. The Bush administration has been wise to refute the vague and dangerous concept of "wars of civilizations," but words are not enough. Second, U.S. security will depend increasingly on its ability to keep alliances alive, to build coalitions, and to sustain multilateralism. The world will be policed collectively or not at all.

Containing violence has always been the key to security. In *Leviathan*, Thomas Hobbes argued that people needed the state to insulate them from violent death. In the twentieth century, one of the most violent in history, the state itself was the major vehicle that produced violence through wars and revolutions. During the Cold War, the concept of mutual assured destruction expressed an unprecedented magnitude of violence between the two superpowers, contained at great risk with nuclear weapons. The world now faces a different, highly dispersed form of radical violence that results most identifiably from the failures of politics throughout the planet. If the ability to contain violence, particularly in its most extreme forms, is a common objective, then those failures should now be addressed. Otherwise, terrorism will destroy society, first in the Muslim world, where it is most threatening, and then elsewhere as well.

Addressing past failures will require significant changes. First, political courage is needed: where terrorism is concerned, there should be no room for ambivalence or tolerance. A dramatic reassessment of past policies in a large number of countries will be necessary. Some Muslim leaders have already dared to say that groups that call themselves Islamic "hijacked" their countries in order to further destructive political goals; the veil of secrecy that covers the activities of such groups should now be removed. On the Western side, the end of support for corrupt and repressive regimes that sponsor terrorism, such as Saudi Arabia, appears essential.

Second, when this campaign is fought, vague confidence in free markets and political liberalism will not meet the challenge of a lasting peace. Nothing less will do than a return to the origins of political values in ethics. A new international order based on justice and arbitration is the only way to avoid clashes liable to unleash the devastating potential of the twenty-first century's violence and war technologies.

Note

1. David Ronfeldt and John Arquilla, eds., *Networks and Netwars: The Future of Terror, Crime, and Militancy* (Santa Monica, Calif.: RAND, 2001).

Part I

State Failure and Nation Building

Robert I. Rotberg

The New Nature of Nation-State Failure

Nation-states fail because they can no longer deliver positive political goods to their people. Their governments lose legitimacy and, in the eyes and hearts of a growing plurality of its citizens, the nation-state itself becomes illegitimate.

Only a handful of the world's 191 nation-states can now be categorized as failed, or collapsed, which is the end stage of failure. Several dozen more, however, are weak and serious candidates for failure. Because failed states are hospitable to and harbor nonstate actors—warlords and terrorists—understanding the dynamics of nation-state failure is central to the war against terrorism. Strengthening weak nation-states in the developing world has consequently assumed new urgency.

Defining State Failure

Failed states are tense, deeply conflicted, dangerous, and bitterly contested by warring factions. In most failed states, government troops battle armed revolts led by one or more rivals. Official authorities in a failed state sometimes face two or more insurgencies, varieties of civil

Robert I. Rotberg is director of the Kennedy School's Program on Intrastate Conflict and president of the World Peace Foundation. He edited *State Failure and State Weakness in a Time of Terror* (Washington, D.C.: Brookings Institution Press, 2003).

unrest, differing degrees of communal discontent, and a plethora of dissent directed at the state and at groups within the state.

The absolute intensity of violence does not define a failed state. Rather, it is the enduring character of that violence (as in Angola, Burundi, and Sudan), the direction of such violence against the existing government or regime, and the vigorous character of the political or geographical demands for shared power or autonomy that rationalize or justify that violence that identifies the failed state. Failure for a nation-state looms when violence cascades into all-out internal war, when standards of living massively deteriorate, when the infrastructure of ordinary life decays, and when the greed of rulers overwhelms their responsibilities to better their people and their surroundings.

The civil wars that characterize failed states usually stem from or have roots in ethnic, religious, linguistic, or other intercommunal enmity. The fear of "the other" that drives so much ethnic conflict may stimulate and fuel hostilities between ruling entities and subordinate and less-favored groups. Avarice also propels antagonism, especially when discoveries of new, frequently contested sources of resource wealth, such as petroleum deposits or diamond fields, encourage that greed.

There is no failed state without disharmonies between communities. Yet, the simple fact that many weak nation-states include haves and have-nots, and that some of the newer states contain a heterogeneous collection of ethnic, religious, and linguistic interests, is more a contributor to than a root cause of nation-state failure. In other words, state failure cannot be ascribed primarily to the inability to build nations from a congeries of ethnic groups. Nor should it be ascribed baldly to the oppression of minorities by a majority, although such brutalities are often a major ingredient of the impulse toward failure.

In contrast to strong states, failed states cannot control their borders. They lose authority over chunks of territory. Often, the expression of official power is limited to a capital city and one or more ethnically specific zones. Indeed, one measure of the extent of a state's failure is how much of the state's geographical expanse a government genuinely controls. How nominal is the central government's sway over rural towns, roads, and waterways? Who really rules up-country, or in particular distant districts?

In most cases, driven by ethnic or other intercommunal hostility or by regime insecurity, failed states prey on their own citizens. As in Mobutu Sese Seko's Zaire or the Taliban's Afghanistan, ruling cadres increasingly oppress, extort, and harass the majority of their own compatriots while favoring a narrowly based elite. As in Zaire, Angola, Siaka Stevens's Sierra Leone, or Hassan al-Turabi's pre-2001 Sudan, patrimonial rule depends on a patronage-based system of extraction from ordinary citizens. The typical weak-state plunges toward failure when this kind of ruler-led oppression provokes a countervailing reaction on the part of resentful groups or newly emerged rebels.

Another indicator of state failure is the growth of criminal violence. As state authority weakens and fails, and as the state becomes criminal in its oppression of its citizens, so general lawlessness becomes more apparent. Gangs and criminal syndicates assume control over the streets of the cities. Arms and drug trafficking become more common. Ordinary police forces become paralyzed. Anarchy becomes more and more the norm. For protection, citizens naturally turn to warlords and other strong figures who express ethnic or clan solidarity, thus projecting strength at a time when all else, including the state itself, is crumbling.

Fewer and Fewer Political Goods

Nation-states exist to deliver political goods—security, education, health services, economic opportunity, environmental surveillance, a legal framework of order and a judicial system to administer it, and fundamental infrastructural requirements such as roads and communications facilities—to their citizens. Failed states honor these obligations in the breach. They increasingly forfeit their function as providers of political goods to warlords and other nonstate actors. In other words, a failed state is no longer able or willing to perform the job of a nation-state in the modern world.

Failed states are unable to provide security—the most central and foremost political good—across the whole of their domains. Citizens depend on states and central governments to secure their persons and free them from fear. Because a failing state is unable to establish an atmosphere of security nationwide and is often barely able to assert any kind of state power beyond a capital city, the failure of the state becomes obvious even before rebel groups and other contenders threaten the residents of central cities and overwhelm demoralized government contingents, as in contemporary Liberia and recent Sierra Leone.

Failed states contain weak or flawed institutions—that is, only the executive institution functions. If legislatures exist at all, they are rubber-stamp machines. Democratic debate is noticeably absent. The judiciary is derivative of the executive rather than being independent, and citizens know that they cannot rely on the court system for significant redress or remedy, especially against the state. The bureaucracy has long ago lost its sense of professional responsibility and exists solely to carry out the orders of the executive and, in petty ways, to oppress citizens. The military is possibly the only institution with any remaining integrity, but the armed forces of failed states are often highly politicized, without the esprit that they once exhibited.

Deteriorating or destroyed infrastructures typify failed states. Metaphorically, the more potholes (or main roads turned to rutted tracks), the more likely a state will exemplify failure. As rulers siphon funds from the state, so fewer capital resources are available for road crews, and maintaining road or rail access to distant provinces becomes less and less of a priority. Even refurbishing basic navigational aids along arterial waterways, as in the Democratic Republic of the Congo (DRC), succumbs to neglect. Where the state still controls the landline telephone system, that form of political and economic good also betrays a lack of renewal, upkeep, investment, and bureaucratic interest. Less a metaphor than a daily reality is the index of failed connections, repeated required dialing, and interminable waits for repair or service. If state monopolies have permitted private entrepreneurs to erect cell telephone towers and offer mobile telephone service, cell telephones may already have rendered the government's landline monopoly obsolete. In a state without a government, such as Somalia, the overlapping system of privately provided cell telephone systems is effective.

In failed states, the effective educational and health systems have either been privatized (with a resulting hodgepodge of shady schools and medical clinics in the cities) or have slowly slumped to increasingly desperate levels of decrepitude. Teachers, physicians, nurses, and orderlies are paid late or not at all, and absenteeism rises. Textbooks and essential medicines become scarce. X-ray machines cannot be repaired. Reports to the relevant ministries go unanswered; and parents, students, and patients—especially rural ones—slowly realize that the state has abandoned them to the forces of nature and to their own devices. Sometimes, where a failed state is effectively split (Sudan), essential services are still provided to the favored half (northern Sudan) but not to the half engulfed by war. Most of the time, however, the weakened nation-state completely fails to perform. Literacy falls, infant mortality rises, the AIDS epidemic overwhelms any health infrastructure that exists, life expectancies plummet, and an already poor and neglected citizenry becomes even poorer and more immiserated.

Failed states provide unparalleled economic opportunity, but only for a privileged few. Those close to the ruler or the ruling oligarchy grow richer while their less-fortunate brethren starve. Immense profits can be made from currency speculation, arbitrage, and knowledge of regulatory advantages. But the privilege of making real money when everything else is deteriorating is confined to clients of the ruling elite or to especially favored external entrepreneurs. The responsibility of a nation-state to maximize the well-being and personal prosperity of all of its citizens is conspicuously absent, if it ever existed.

Corruption flourishes in failed states, often on an unusually destructive scale. Petty or lubricating corruption is widespread. Levels of venal corruption escalate, especially kickbacks on anything that can be put out to bid, including medical supplies, textbooks, bridges; unnecessarily wasteful construction projects solely for the rents they will generate; licenses for existing and nonexisting activities; the appropriating by the ruling class of all kinds of private entrepreneurial endeavors; and generalized extortion. Corrupt ruling elites invest their gains overseas, not at home. A few build numerous palaces or lavish residences with state funds. Military officers always benefit from these corrupt regimes and feed ravenously from the same illicit troughs as their civilian counterparts.

An indicator, but not a cause, of failure is declining real national and per capita levels of gross domestic product (GDP). The statistical foundations of most states in the developing world are shaky, most certainly, but failed states—even, or particularly, failed states with abundant natural resources—show overall worsening GDP figures, slim year-to-year growth rates, and greater disparities of income between the wealthiest and poorest fifths of the population. High official deficits (Zimbabwe's reached 30 percent of GDP in 2001) support lavish security spending and the siphoning of cash by elites. Inflation usually soars because the ruling elite raids the central bank and prints money. From the resulting economic insecurity, often engineered by rulers to maximize their own fortunes and their own political as well as economic power, entrepreneurs favored by the prevailing regime can reap great amounts of money. Smuggling becomes rife. When state failure becomes complete, the local currency falls out of favor, and some or several international currencies take its place. Money changers are everywhere, legal or not, and arbitrage becomes an everyday national pursuit.

Sometimes, especially if climatic disasters intervene, the economic chaos and generalized neglect that is endemic to failed states can lead to regular food scarcities and widespread hunger—even to episodes of starvation and resulting international humanitarian relief efforts. Natural calamities can overwhelm the resources even of nonfailed but weak states in the developing world. But when unscrupulous rulers and ruling elites have consciously sucked state competencies dry, unforeseen natural disasters or man-made wars can drive ignored populations over the edge of endurance into starvation. Once such populations have lost their subsistence plots or sources of income, they lose their homes, forfeit already weak support networks, and are forced into an endless cycle of migration and displacement. Failed states offer no safety nets, and the homeless and destitute become fodder for anyone who can provide food and a cause.

A nation-state also fails when it loses a basic legitimacy—when its nominal borders become irrelevant and when one or more groups seek autonomous control within one or more parts of the national territory or, sometimes, even across its borders. Once the state's capacity deteriorates and what little capacity still remains is devoted largely to the fortunes of a few or to a favored ethnicity or community, then there is every reason to expect less and less loyalty to the state on the part of the excluded and the disenfranchised. When the rulers are seen to be working for themselves and their kin, and not for the state, their legitimacy, and the state's legitimacy, plummets. The state increasingly is perceived as owned by an exclusive class or group, with all others pushed aside.

Citizens naturally become more and more conscious of the kinds of sectional or community loyalties that are their main recourse and their only source of security and economic opportunity. They transfer their allegiances to clan and group leaders, some of whom become warlords. These warlords or other local strongmen derive support from external and local supporters. In the wilder, more marginalized corners of failed states, terror can breed along with the prevailing anarchy that emerges from state breakdown and failure.

A collapsed state is an extreme version of a failed state. It has a total vacuum of authority. A collapsed state is a mere geographical expression, a black hole into which a failed polity has fallen. Dark energy exists, but the forces of entropy have overwhelmed the radiance that hitherto provided some semblance of order and other vital political goods to the inhabitants embraced by language affinities or borders. When a state such as Somalia collapses (or Lebanon and Afghanistan a decade ago and Sierra Leone in the late 1990s), substate actors take over. They control regions and subregions, build their own local security apparatuses, sanction markets or other trading arrangements, and even establish an attenuated form of international relations. By definition, they are illegitimate and unrecognized, but some may assume the trappings of a quasi-state, such as Somaliland in northern Somalia. Yet, within the collapsed state prevail disorder, anomic behavior, and the kinds of anarchic mentality and entrepreneurial pursuits—especially gun and drug running—that are compatible with networks of terror.

Contemporary State Failure

This decade's failed states are Afghanistan, Angola, Burundi, the DRC, Liberia, Sierra Leone, and Sudan. These seven states exemplify the criteria of state failure. Beyond those states is one collapsed state: Somalia. Each of these countries has typified state failure continuously since at least 1990, if not before. Lebanon was once a failed state. So were Bosnia, Tajikistan, and Nigeria. Many other modern states approach the brink of failure, some much more ominously than others. Others drift disastrously downward from weak to failing to failed.

Of particular interest is why and how states slip from endemic weakness (Haiti) toward failure, or not. The list of weak states is long, but only a few of those weak and badly governed states necessarily edge into failure. Why? Even the categorization of a state as failing—Colombia and Indonesia, among others—need not doom it unquestionably to full failure. Another critical question is, what does it take to drive a failing state into collapse? Why did Somalia not stop at failure rather than collapsing?

Not each of the classical failed and collapsed states fully fills all of the cells on the matrix of failure. To be termed a failure, however, a state certainly needs to demonstrate that it has met most of the explicit criteria. "Failure" is meant to describe a specific set of conditions and to exclude states that only meet a few of the criteria. In other words, how truly minimal are the roads, the schools, the hospitals, and the clinics? How far has GDP fallen and infant mortality risen? How far does the ambit of the central government reach? How little legitimacy remains? Most importantly, because civil conflict is decisive for state failure, can the state still provide security to its citizens and to what ex-

400:1. Foreign and domestic investment have largely ceased. Health and educational services are almost nonexistent and shrinking further. Road maintenance and telephone service are obviously suffering. Judicial independence survives, but barely, and not in critical political cases. The state has also been preying on its own citizens for at least two years. Corruption is blatant and very much dominated by the avaricious ruling elite. Zimbabwe is an example of a state that, like Sierra Leone and the DRC at earlier moments in history, has been driven into failure by human agency.

Indonesia, Colombia, Sri Lanka, and Zimbabwe are but four among a large number of nation-states (two dozen by a recent count) that contain serious elements of failure but will probably avoid failure, especially if they receive sufficient outside assistance. They belong to a category of state that is designated weak but that encompasses and spreads into the category of failing—the precursor to true failure. Haiti, Chad, and Kyrgyzstan, from three continents, are representative examples of perpetual weakness. Argentina has recently joined an analogous rank; Russia was once a candidate. Fiji, the Solomon Islands, Tajikistan, Lebanon, Nigeria, Niger, and Burkina Faso remain vulnerable to further deterioration. Even Kenya is a weak state with some potential for definitive failure if ethnic disparities and ambitions provoke civil strife.

The list of states in weakness is longer and hardly static. Some of the potentially stronger states move in and out of weakness and nearer or farther from failure. Others are foreordained weak. Particular decisions by ruling groups would be needed to destabilize members of this second group further and drive them into failure.

The Hand of Man

State failure is man-made, not merely accidental nor—fundamentally— caused geographically, environmentally, or externally. Leadership decisions and leadership failures have destroyed states and continue to weaken the fragile polities that operate on the cusp of failure. Mobutu's kleptocratic rule extracted the marrow of Zaire/DRC and left nothing for his national dependents. Much of the resource wealth of that vast country ended up in Mobutu's or his cronies' pockets. During four decades, hardly any money was devoted to uplifting the Congolese people, improving their welfare, building infrastructures, or even providing more than rudimentary security. Mobutu's government performed only for Mobutu, not for Zaire/DRC.

Likewise, oil-rich Angola continues to fail because of three decades of war, but also because President Eduardo dos Santos and his associates have refused to let the Angolan government deliver more than basic services within the large zone that they control. Stevens (1967–1985) decapitated the Sierra Leonean state in order to strengthen his own power amid growing chaos. Sierra Leone has not yet recovered from Stevens's depredations. Nor has Liberia been resuscitated in the aftermath of the slashing neglect and unabashed greed of Samuel Doe, Prince Johnson, and Charles Taylor. In Somalia, Mohammed Siad Barre arrogated more and more power and privilege to himself and his clan. Finally, nothing was left for the other pretenders to power. The Somali state was gutted, the abilities of the Somali government to provide political goods endlessly compromised, and the descent into failure and then full collapse followed.

President Robert Gabriel Mugabe has personally led Zimbabwe from strength to the precipice of failure. His high-handed and seriously corrupt rule bled the resources of the state into his own pocket, squandered foreign exchange, discouraged domestic and international investment, subverted the courts, and this year drove his country to the very brink of starvation. In Sri Lanka, Solomon and Sirimavo Bandaranaike, one after the other, drove the LTTE into reactive combat by abrogating minority rights and vitiating the social contract on which the country called Ceylon had been created. In Afghanistan, Gulbuddin Hakmatyar and Burrhan ul-Din Rabani tried to prevent Afghans other than their fellow Pushtun and Tajik nationals from sharing the perquisites of governance; their narrowly focused, self-enriching decisions enabled the Taliban to triumph and Afghanistan to become a safe harbor for terrorists.

Preventing State Failure

Strengthening weak states against failure is far easier than reviving them after they have definitively failed or collapsed. As the problem of contemporary Afghanistan shows, reconstruction is very long, very expensive, and hardly a smooth process. Creating security and a security force from scratch, amid bitter memories, is the immediate need. Then comes the re-creation of an administrative structure—primarily re-creating a bureaucracy and finding the funds with which to pay the erstwhile bureaucrats and policemen. A judicial method is required, which means the establishment or reestablishment of a legitimate legal code and system; the training of judges, prosecutors, and defenders (as attempted recently in East Timor); and the opening of courtrooms and offices. Restarting the schools, employing teachers, refurbishing and re-equipping hospitals, building roads, and even gathering statistics—all of these fundamental chores take time, large sums of money (especially in war-shattered Afghanistan), and meticulous oversight in postconflict nations with overstretched human resources. Elections need not be an early priority, but constitutions must be written eventually and elections held in order to encourage participatory democracy.

Strengthening states prone to failure before they fail is prudent policy and contributes significantly to world order and to minimizing combat, casualties, refugees, and displaced persons. Doing so is far less expensive than reconstructing states after failure. Strengthening weak states also has the potential to eliminate the authority and power vacuums within which terror thrives.

From a policy perspective, however, these are obvious nostrums. The mechanisms for amelioration are also more obvious than obscure. In order to encourage responsible leadership and good governance, financial assistance from international lending agencies and bilateral donors must be designed to reinforce positive leadership only. Outside support should be conditional on monetary and fiscal streamlining, renewed attention to good governance, reforms of land tenure systems, and strict adherence to the rule of law. External assistance to create in-country jobs by reducing external tariff barriers (e.g., on textiles) and by supporting vital foreign direct investment is critical. So is support for innovations that can reduce importation and exportation transport expenditures for the weak nations, improve telephone and power systems through privatization, open predominantly closed economies in general, create new incentives for agricultural productivity, and bolster existing security forces through training and equipment.

All these ingredients of a successful strengthening process are necessary. The developed world can apply tough love and assist the developing and more vulnerable world to help itself in many more similarly targeted ways. In addition to the significant amounts of cash (grants are preferred over loans) that must be transferred to help the poorer nations help themselves, however, the critical ingredient is sustained interest and sustained assistance over the very long run. Nothing enduring can be accomplished instantaneously. If the world order wants to dry up the reservoirs of terror, as well as do good more broadly, it must commit itself and its powers to a campaign of decades, not months. The refurbishment and revitalization of Afghanistan will take much more than the $4.7 billion pledged and the many years that Secretary of State Colin L. Powell has warned the U.S. people will be necessary to make Afghanistan a self-sufficient state. Strengthening Indonesia, for example, would take a concerted effort for decades. So would strengthening any of the dangerous and needy candidates in Africa or in Central Asia.

Preventing state failure is imperative, difficult, and costly. Yet, doing so is profoundly in the interest not only of the inhabitants of the most deprived and ill-governed states of the world, but also of world peace.

Satisfying such lofty goals, however—making the world much safer by strengthening weak states against failure—is dependent on the political will of the wealthy big-power arbiters of world security. Perhaps the newly aroused awareness of the dangers of terror will embolden political will in the United States, Europe, and Japan. Otherwise, the common ingredients of zero-sum leadership; ethnic, linguistic, and religious antagonisms and fears; chauvinistic ambition; economic insufficiency; and inherited fragility will continue to propel nation-states from weakness toward failure. In turn, that failure will be costly in terms of humanitarian relief and postconflict reconstruction. Ethnic cleansing episodes will recur, as will famines, and in the thin and hospitable soils of newly failed and collapsed states, terrorist groups will take root.

Ray Takeyh and Nikolas Gvosdev

Do Terrorist Networks Need a Home?

How are international business organizations and global terrorist networks similar? This question is not a riddle but an analogy made by policymakers ranging from Secretary of State Colin Powell to Russian presidential advisor Gleb Pavlovsky. The comparison seems apropos because the multinational corporation and the transnational terrorist network both utilize the existing global economic, transportation, and communications systems to organize and manage far-flung subsidiaries and to move funds, men, and material from one location to another.

The 2001 trial of Madji Hasan Idris, an Egyptian member of the radical Al Wa'd organization, revealed the extent to which terror has operationally adopted the global business model. Al Wa'd would send young Egyptian recruits to camps in Kosovo or Pakistan and then dispatch them to serve in the Philippines, Kashmir, or wherever else they were needed after their training and indoctrination were complete. Cell phones and e-mail kept the network in constant contact, while couriers provided cash advances, airplane tickets, and passports to facilitate operations.

The objectives of terrorist organizations such as Al Qaeda and the symbiotic organized-crime networks that help sustain these groups are also not confined territorially or ideologically to a particular region.

Ray Takeyh is a Soref research fellow at the Washington Institute for Near East Policy and a senior policy advisor at the Institute for Religion and Public Policy. Nikolas Gvosdev is executive editor of *The National Interest* and a senior fellow at the Institute for Global Democracy.

Copyright © 2002 by The Center for Strategic and International Studies and the Massachusetts Institute of Technology
The Washington Quarterly • 25:3 pp. 97–108.

They are instead explicitly global in orientation. In contrast, "traditional" terrorist organizations such as the Irish Republican Army (IRA) or the Kurdish Workers' Party (PKK) have pursued largely limited, irredentist aims. Each terrorist group drew its membership largely from a specific population, even if they sought the sponsorship of a foreign patron for arms and logistical support. Al Qaeda, in contrast, recruits adherents from around the globe and seeks out failed states everywhere to house its own, self-sufficient infrastructure.

Extending the analogy, then, these failed states are the global terrorist network's equivalent of an international business's corporate headquarters, providing concrete locations, or stable "nodes," in which to situate their factories, training facilities, and storehouses. Where the analogy differs is the type of state that each seeks. While the multinational corporation seeks out states that offer political stability and a liberal business climate with low taxes and few regulations, failing or failed states draw terrorists, where the breakdown of authority gives them the ability to conduct their operations without risk of significant interference. Today's terrorist does not need a strong state to provide funding and supplies. Rather, it seeks a weak state that cannot impede a group's freedom of action but has the veneer of state sovereignty that prevents other, stronger states from taking effective countermeasures.

The successful U.S. military campaign in Afghanistan has, in the short run, deprived Al Qaeda of one of its principal centers for bases and training camps. Does it matter? Naturally, Al Qaeda operatives are reportedly seeking to move personnel and equipment to new "hosts"—Somalia, Indonesia, Chechnya, the mountains of Central Asia, Bosnia, Lebanon, or Kosovo. In these places, the writ of state authority is lax or nonexistent, and vibrant civil societies do not exist to deny militants the ability to move and operate in the public mainstream. At the same time, these groups also seek to utilize "brown zones" in Western societies, whether specific neighborhoods or particular types of organizations, where state governments are reluctant to intervene.[1] Do terrorist networks need a failed state or other territorial home where it can base its operations, or can these organizations completely blend into global society?

Why Terrorist Networks Need Failed States

Failed states hold a number of attractions for terrorist organizations. First and foremost, they provide the opportunity to acquire territory on a scale much larger than a collection of scattered safe houses—enough to accommodate entire training complexes, arms depots, and communications facilities. Generally, terrorist groups have no desire to assume complete control of the failed state but simply to acquire de facto control over specified areas where they will then be left alone.

In Bosnia, for example, radical groups took control of a number of districts, such as the village of Bocinja Donja, where they could operate with little scrutiny from the central government and live apart from the rest of society. Control over territory not only permits the construction of institutions, but it also allows groups to develop business interests such as gum mastic plantations in Sudan or small factories in Albania, which help generate income for operations. The failed state also enables terrorist groups and organized crime networks to establish transshipment points. Italian intelligence, for example, is extremely concerned about how Albania has become the hub of the primary, illicit traffic routes that cross the Balkans and involve the dispersal of drugs, weapons, dirty money, and illegal migrants.

For the most part, terrorist groups have gained control over territory in a failed state through a Faustian bargain with authorities, usually by offering its services to the failed state during times of conflict. In Bosnia, Kosovo, Chechnya, Sudan, and Afghanistan, Islamist fighters would arrive to partake in local wars, bringing with them not only manpower but much-needed equipment and finances. Once on the ground, they could exploit the chaos caused by the fighting to set up their operations. The near-collapse of the Albanian government during the 1990s; the chaos unleashed in Colombia, Sierra Leone, and Bosnia because of civil wars; the protection of warlords in a Chechnya that is de facto independent of Russia; and the continuing absence of an effective judicial system in Kosovo have enabled terrorists of all stripes to continue their work without significant interference.

Second, failed states have weak or nonexistent law-enforcement capabilities, permitting terrorist groups to engage in smuggling and drug trafficking in order to raise funds for operations. Turkish intelligence sources report that Osama bin Laden extended logistical support and guerrilla training to the Islamic Movement of Uzbekistan (IMU), whose leaders have maintained close ties with Islamic radicals in Afghanistan. Using the southern Fergana Valley as a transit point, Afghans have transferred weapons and personnel into Central Asia. They also use the valley as a transshipment point for drugs produced in Afghanistan en route for sale in Europe, the proceeds of which Al Qaeda can then use to finance further operations. Russian law enforcement officers maintain that groups in Afghanistan used opium-derived income to arm, train, and support fundamentalist groups including the IMU and the Chechen resistance. Another key narcotics route has been via Turkey into the Balkans, where the drugs can then be marketed in Western Europe. Moreover, the continuing conditions in Bosnia, Albania, and Kosovo have created ripe conditions for human trafficking, arms smuggling, and narcotics distribution—all areas in which bin Laden reputedly has been a "silent investor," utilizing profits to help fund Al Qaeda operations.[2] Colombia has experienced a similar pattern, with both leftist and rightist terrorist groups protecting coca fields and cocaine processing facilities in return for a share of the proceeds. The "brown zones" represented by offshore banking centers further facilitate the interconnection of terrorist groups with the narcotics trade by allowing terrorist groups to deposit funds and ensure their availability to their operatives.

Third, failed states create pools of recruits and supporters for terrorist groups, who can use their resources and organizations to step into the vacuum left by the collapse of official state power and civil society. In Central Asia, radicals have taken advantage of the weak successor states to try to establish new outposts, particularly in the Fergana Valley, where mass unemployment and a shortage of land have afflicted the natives. By playing on the widespread dissatisfaction with the corruption, economic stagnation, and political repression of the Central Asian republics, the Islamists have tapped into new pools of recruits and used the rural and mountainous areas of the region to create safe havens for training terrorists.

Observers view Central Asia as a staging area for militant organizations in Tajikistan, Uzbekistan, Kazakhstan, Kyrgyzstan, China, and Russia. Poor economic conditions in failed states also mean that terrorist groups take advantage of their financial resources to hire recruits and bribe officials. In Colombia, for example, new members of the right-wing "United Self-Defense Forces" receive pay of $180 per month, described as a "healthy sum" in a country with more than 20 percent unemployment. Islamist groups, particularly in the Balkans, found that a useful tool for recruitment was to offer the possibility of high-paying work to unemployed young men in the Persian Gulf states, with the hope of then diverting them into joining mujahideen units.

Finally, failed states retain the outward signs of sovereignty. The presumption against interference in the internal affairs of another state, enshrined in the United Nations (UN) Charter, remains a major impediment to cross-border action designed to eliminate terrorist networks. Despite the high volume of traffic in drugs, weapons, and migrants undertaken by Italian, Albanian, and Russian mafia groups via the port of Durres, for example, no European state has shown much inclination to enter Albania by force and take control of the city. Failed states may be notoriously unable to control their own territory, but they remain loath to allow access to any other state to do the same.

The governments of failed states also can issue legitimate passports and other documents—or provide the templates needed to forge credible copies—that enable terrorists to move around the world and disguise their true identities.[3] Abu Zubaydah, Al Qaeda's chief of staff, had a number of passports and false aliases that have enabled him to move freely, coordinating the activities of sleeper cells; at the time of his capture, he had a number of blank (and possibly forged) Saudi passports.[4] Bin Laden reportedly holds passports issued by Sudan, Bosnia, and Albania.

Moreover, failed states have had—and in some cases continue to possess—official military units that under international law can legiti-

The Battle for Hearts and Minds

mately purchase weaponry. In some cases, such equipment is transferred to terrorist groups; in other cases, the failed state is simply too weak to secure armories, as occurred in Albania. Interpol estimates that, during January–March 1997, terrorists and organized-crime gangs seized hundreds of thousands of assault rifles, machine guns, and rocket launchers from state depots.

Bin Laden's experiences in Sudan following his expulsion from Saudi Arabia in 1991 demonstrated the value of relocating operations to a failed state. Sudan, riven by political instability and civil war, was a classic example of a failed state. Bin Laden established training camps, set up front companies to move assets and generate new revenues, and used the cloak of state sovereignty to shield his operations. Sudan became known as a way station for bin Laden's operatives, a place where terrorists could gather, train, and plan in relative safety and comfort. This pattern repeated itself in Albania and Bosnia, where radical groups, utilizing large donations from Saudi Arabia and the Persian Gulf region, established charitable organizations that doled out humanitarian relief, created schools and orphanages, and even developed a network of banks and credit agencies for the populace. By creating an alternative to a failed state, these groups won supporters both in the ranks of the government and among the general population.[5]

At the same time, terrorist organizations utilized the "brown zones" found in Western societies as secondary bases of operations. Taking advantage of lax asylum laws and immigration procedures, and the low level of scrutiny given to religious and charitable organizations, Al Qaeda has dispatched operatives and sleepers into Western countries, creating a network of safe houses and acquiring vehicles as well as equipment. Moreover, it has intensified its efforts to recruit operatives who are fully integrated members of society—whether second-generation Muslim immigrants or converts—and can move without attracting undue attention. Even after the decisive military strikes launched against Al Qaeda installations in Afghanistan, therefore, the organization and others like it remain a threat.

The Afghanistan Question: Stopgap or Solution?

Washington's global antiterrorism coalition has legitimately focused the initial response to the September 11 attacks on the failed state of Afghanistan and the Al Qaeda network. An effective and judicious use of force by the United States and its allies has been largely successful so far in destroying Al Qaeda's infrastructure on Afghan territory. Islamists themselves have admitted that the loss of the "Islamic Emirate of Afghanistan" represents a major setback to the cause but are confident that Al Qaeda can revive under the proper conditions.[6]

Terrorists are relying on two developments: that long-term occupation and reconstruction in Afghanistan will not follow short-term military action and that the United States has no real stomach for pursuing terrorist enclaves in other, more inaccessible locations. Islamist sources have proclaimed their confidence in the survival of their networks in places such as Kashmir, Kosovo, Chechnya, and Palestine, where they believe that the United States and its allies will choose not to risk significant losses in urban or guerrilla warfare and where no "fifth columns" can undermine the terrorist groups, as occurred in Afghanistan.[7]

The operations in Afghanistan result from a unique and serendipitous convergence of several factors: the existence of anti-Taliban resistance on the ground; the absence of international recognition of the Taliban regime in Afghanistan as a legal government; the general consensus among the world's major powers that decapitation of the Taliban served international order and stability; and, finally, the very real sense of shock in the aftermath of the destruction wrought in Washington, D.C., and New York City. Somalia, which lacks any central government, and the Philippines, where the government asked for U.S. assistance to combat Abu Sayyaf and where a peace plan for granting autonomy to the Muslim southern regions enjoys the support of the state as well as of Muslim moderates, are other areas where concerted military action can be predominantly successful. These areas are the exception, however, rather than the rule.

Solving the problem of global terrorism by conducting military operations in failed states will be difficult to repeat elsewhere. Russian defense minister Sergei Ivanov said, "Any actions, including the use of force, by states and international organizations must be based on the norms and principles of international law and be appropriate for the threats."[8] Few states are eager to extend any sort of carte blanche to the United States to engage in military action anywhere in the world. Moreover, states may have their own security concerns that conflict with the aims of the war on terrorism.

Forces have spotted Al Qaeda operatives in two areas in the south Caucasus: the Pankisi gorge (which links Chechnya and Georgia) and the Kodori gorge (which runs between Georgia and the breakaway republic of Abkhazia). In an ideal world, the simple solution is that Georgia should work closely with Russian security forces, utilizing U.S. equipment and training, to deny Chechen militants the ability to transit Pankisi and to prevent the transfer of weapons and funds into Chechnya from the Georgian side. At the same time, one would argue, the international community should recognize the reality of a separate Abkhazian state, which has effectively existed since 1993, thereby giving Abkhazia the wherewithal to police its borders adequately. Anyone remotely familiar with Caucasian politics, however, knows how unlikely this scenario is. Georgia, for instance, will not undertake any action that either weakens its sovereignty (e.g., grant extraterritorial privileges for Russian security forces to engage in hot pursuit across the border) or undermines its territorial integrity (e.g., recognize the existence of a separate Abkhazia). Last autumn, Georgian paramilitary forces allegedly even sought to engage the services of Chechen fighters, including Al Qaeda operatives, by bringing a group from Pankisi across Georgia into Kodori to utilize them in the struggle against the Abkhazians, with the government turning a blind eye to the whole operation. Indeed, the Georgian government might redirect U.S. aid intended for use against terrorist groups in Pankisi toward retaking Abkhazia by force instead, which could precipitate a larger regional crisis.

Moreover, no one in the region supports the principle of recognizing de facto statelets as de jure independent because the same precedent could then apply to the Armenians of Nagorno-Karabakh against Azerbaijan and even to the Chechens themselves vis-à-vis the Russian Federation. Similar problems in the Balkans regarding Kosovo, the constituent entities of the Bosnian republic, and the Albanian-majority regions of southern Serbia and Macedonia indicate that, for the foreseeable future, areas effectively outside of any state's purview will continue to litter Southeastern Europe and the Caucasus.

The continuing weakness of other states also will prove to be a major liability in the war against terrorism. The arrest of Al Qaeda sympathizers in Yemen risks escalating tribal tensions, which could lead the government to back away from enforcing a true crackdown against proterrorist elements. The arrest of Yemeni and Egyptian fighters in Bosnia last autumn led to vociferous protests in Sarajevo, highlighting the continuing fragility of the coalition government and raising the possibility that, should the Party of Islamic Action return to power, future antiterrorist cooperation could end. In February 2002, riots broke out in Pristina when authorities from the UN Mission in Kosovo took three former Kosovo Liberation Army members into custody for suspected terrorist acts and war crimes. Around the world, therefore, governments will likely play a double game—appeasing Washington by cooperating to some extent, while striking bargains with terrorists to prevent further destabilization.

Pakistan, one of the key members of the antiterrorist alliance, is a weak link. Indeed, President Pervez Musharraf is discovering the difficulties in containing the forces that he himself helped to unleash when he was army chief of staff. The Pakistan of the 1990s was a state mired in ethnic tension, sectarian violence, and an absence of cohesive central rule. The theological centers (the *madrassahs*), political parties, intelligence services, and retired generals had utilized the services of Al Qaeda, with motivations ranging from religious fanaticism to strategic advantage. Pakistan found Al Qaeda useful as a source of guerrilla fighters that Pakistan could send into Kashmir while providing the government in Islamabad with "plausible deniability"; according to the best estimates, up to 40 percent of the Kashmiri guerrillas came from Afghanistan. Reversing course after September 11 is no easy task. Many of the leading extremists and their cadres have avoided the police dragnets unleashed by Musharraf and simply bide their time, often in refuges where Islamabad's writ runs sluggishly. The December 2001 assassination of the brother of Interior Minister Moinuddin Haider, who is overseeing the crackdown on militants; the attack against the Indian parliament that same month; and the kidnapping and murder of journalist Daniel Pearl in January 2002 are reminders that Pakistan has by no means been "rehabilitated."

Finally, military campaigns to deny terrorists access to failed states do not address the role of Middle Eastern states in financing Islamist terror or their interest in using failed states as dumping grounds for their own militants. By subsidizing disillusioned young men to "fight for Islam" in Afghanistan, Yugoslavia, and Chechnya, many leading Middle Eastern politicians and business figures burnished their own Islamic credentials and removed potentially disruptive figures from the domestic arena.

Military operations against or within failed states designed to destroy bases and infrastructure and neutralize terrorist operatives can only be one aspect of the war on terrorism. At times, military force is not appropriate. Carrier-launched fighter-bombers are useless for uncovering Al Qaeda sleeper cells in Hamburg or shutting down Web sites that provide instructions to terrorist recruits. Food airdrops cannot compensate for the bribes that terrorist groups pay underfunded police officers. The willingness to close the loopholes allowing terrorists to function in the "brown zones" of the West has already begun to recede. In most Western countries, especially Germany, "the right to nearly absolute civil and personal privacy amounts to a state theology."[9] Restrictions may tighten, but fundamental change in a whole host of policies ranging from privacy laws to asylum procedures is unlikely. Proponents must seek the long-term victory against international terrorism in the rehabilitation, not the conquest, of the failed state.

A New Type of Nation Building

The United States and its allies cannot conduct the fight against global terrorism in a vacuum. Effective combat is impossible as long as the failed states that terrorist movements use for refuge are left to flounder. If the United States is serious about rooting out terrorism, it cannot stop at the destruction of a few camps or the freezing of bank accounts. Once the military strikes end, state reconstruction must occur.

Nation building has received a bad reputation in U.S. policy circles, notably because of failures in the Balkans and Somalia, among others, and in part due to the quasi-utopian air surrounding nation building in the 1990s, with greater stress given to empowering downtrodden ethnic groups than on constructing viable state institutions. In fact, many of the idealistic democracy-promotion programs of this period may have had a counterproductive effect by encouraging the diffusion and decentralization of power and the weakening of executive branch institutions.

The situation requires realistic nation building, focusing on existing conditions and working to rebuild and reconstruct viable institutions. The Bush administration has recognized that war against terrorism implies a war against political chaos in favor of strengthening legitimate states. Despite all the claims about globalization creating a new world order, states remain the key actors in the international arena.

In Afghanistan, for example, nation building cannot stop with signing papers in Bonn. A token central government is insufficient. Afghanistan requires effective regional administrations based in Kandahar, Herat, Mazar-e Sharif, and Jalalabad, working with, not around, the regional leaders and warlords. The nation- and state-building efforts of Mexican president Plutarco Elias Calles during the 1920s may set a precedent: regional strongmen were incorporated into the army, given positions within the political administration, or bribed with lucrative business opportunities. Until local institutions are strong enough to assume responsibility for law and order, the international community must ensure that the necessary forces are in place.

The first task in rehabilitating failed states is not holding elections but assisting in the swift reconstruction of the basic infrastructure of society—the health care system, the police force, and so forth—followed by longer-term investment. Linked to that process should be generous aid to reconstruct the bases of community life and to ensure that the wellsprings of civil society—religious organizations, schools, and the media—do not fall victim to extremist forces. In explaining the spread of Islamist extremism across Eurasia, Ravil Gainutdin, the chair of the Muslim Religious Board for European Russia, maintains that financial difficulties have rendered moderate groups unable to afford the costs of print and broadcast media. Reconstructing states will be a wasted effort if extremist groups dominate the airwaves and provide the textbooks used in schools.

The second task is effective military and security assistance. The IMU has been so difficult to crush because, among other reasons, the weak militaries of states such as Kyrgyzstan are no match for a well-armed, well-trained, and well-financed insurgency. Police and security forces need training and equipment that will enable them to intercept and destroy terrorist formations and to crack down on the narcotics trade that supplies much of the income radical groups use to purchase arms and supplies and to bribe impoverished government officials.

The scale of smuggling across the Eurasian arc (from Asia to the Balkans) demonstrates how the culture of lawlessness, abetted by failed states, has taken root. Last year, the Russian Federal Security Service alone confiscated some two tons of narcotics en route from Afghanistan to Europe. Effective financial and logistical support to regional efforts, such as the one envisioned by the draft agreement reached in December 2001 between Indonesia, Malaysia, and the Philippines that created a joint rapid-response force to fight terrorism and border crime, can help strangle the international networks that have benefited from porous borders and undefined jurisdiction to smuggle personnel, funds, and equipment from place to place.

Terrorism will be problematic as long as people are disaffected. Strengthening states around the world, however, prevents scattered, localized cells from transforming into a potent network with a global reach. Recent history demonstrates that relatively weak and isolated insurgencies from Kosovo to the South Philippines became much more deadly and effective once they drew upon an international network for a continuous supply of recruits, funds, and equipment coordinated and dispatched from bases located in failed states. The best means for emasculating international terrorist networks are effective regimes policing their borders and exercising supervision over their territory.

The United States faces the new challenge of transnational terrorists who establish sanctuaries in failed states and attract support worldwide. The traditional approach of combating terrorism, namely, using a combination of economic sanctions, military reprisals, and political pressure, may have succeeded in dissuading individual state sponsors of discrete terrorist groups—states with vested economic and political interests, such as Libya—but will likely fail at coping with this new brand of terror. Special military operations are only the first step in rooting out terror. Substantial economic and political investment designed to reconstruct regimes in failed states will be necessary if the United States and its allies hope not simply to disable terror's infrastructure temporarily, but to prevent such forces from seeking out new adherents and bases of operations in other failed states.

Notes

1. See Guillermo O'Donnell, *On the State, Democratization, and Some Conceptual Problems (A Latin American View with Glances at Some Post-Communist Countries)*, working paper #192 (Notre Dame, Ind.: Helen Kellogg Institute for International Studies, 1993).

2. See, for example, the report issued by the Macedonian Information Agency (MIA), September 20, 2001.

3. Of great concern, for example, is the fate of some 100,000 Albanian passports that "disappeared" during the 1997 unrest, some of which Interpol fears have been used to "legalize" terrorists in Europe. *Ta Nea*, September 14, 2001, p. 11. Thailand, for instance, is trying to take steps to combat the "illicit network ... that produced forged passports and documents [that] has made the country attractive to foreign terrorists." *Nation* (Bangkok), March 11, 2002 (editorial).

4. See *Al-Sharg Al-Awsat*, March 8, 2002, p. 3 (interview of Muhammad Al-Shafi'i with a former "Afghan Arab").

5. For a discussion of this process in Albania, see *Hurriyet*, October 25, 2001; *Albania*, October 31, 2001.

6. See *Al-Quds Al-Arabi*, February 27, 2002 (communiqué reportedly issued by Mullah Omar). Concerning the fragility of the Karzai government, the Iranian newspaper *Jomhuri-ye Eslami* editorialized:

   Even if, due to coercion and foreign military pressure, no reaction is seen for a while, the freedom-loving and independent-spirited people of Afghanistan will not remain passive and idle for long. The turmoil is there, and at the right moment and appropriate opportunity they will rise like a burning fire from under the ashes and devour all the foreigners and their domestic lackeys.

   Jomhuri-ye Eslami, February 24, 2002.

7. Mamduh Isma'il, *Al-Quds Al-Arabi*, January 22, 2002 (providing an Islamist perspective regarding the post–September 11 future of the international Islamist movement, including its ability to survive the losses of its Afghan bases).

8. ITAR-TASS, February 3, 2002.

9. Jane Kramer, "Letter from Europe: Private Lives," *New Yorker*, February 11, 2002, p. 36.

Karin von Hippel

Democracy by Force: A Renewed Commitment to Nation Building

Following the botched Somalia operation, the terms "military intervention" and "nation building" were mostly exorcised from the vernacular of policymakers. Yet, behind the scenes and subsequent to that intervention, the U.S. government has continued to engage in similar activity in Haiti, Bosnia, Kosovo, and now East Timor. The onset of the millennium gives us the opportunity to reflect on what we have learned about these operations since the end of the Cold War. Is our response better today? Where are our soft spots, and how can they be redressed? Examination of developments in nation-building after U.S.-sponsored military intervention in the last decade reveals the factors that put the U.S. government on the path to military action in the first place, the changes in peace-support operations, the advances in nation-building efforts and the recommendations for improving future operations.

Democratization and Nation-Building Defined

The promotion or support of democracy by the U.S. government, also known as democratization, has shifted in focus since the Allied occupa-

Karin von Hippel is the civil affairs officer for the United Nations Mission in Kosovo. This article is adapted from her recently published book, *Democracy by Force* (Cambridge University Press, 1999). The original research for this book was funded by the John D. and Catherine T. MacArthur Foundation. The opinions presented here are solely those of the author.

Copyright © 1999 by The Center for Strategic and International Studies and the Massachusetts Institute of Technology
The Washington Quarterly • 23:1 pp. 95–112.

tion of Germany and Japan after World War II. Then it stood for de-militarization (and denazification in Germany), establishment of demo-cratic institutions, and reeducation of the entire country's population. In Vietnam, and later in much of Central America during the Cold War, democratization came to mean challenging communist advances rather than actually implementing democratic reforms. Only since the end of the Cold War has the campaign once again attempted to fulfill its stated purpose, with the ultimate aim the enhancement of interna-tional peace and security. The promotion of democracy is based on the assumption that democracies rarely go to war with each other and that an increase in the number of democratic states would therefore imply, and indeed encourage, a more secure and peaceful world.

Nation building, which really means state building,[1] has over the years signified an effort to construct a government that may or may not be democratic, but preferably is stable. Today, nation building normally implies the attempt to create democratic and secure states. Thus de-mocratization efforts are part of the larger and more comprehensive na-tion-building campaign, but democratization can also occur in places where the state is secure and does not need to be rebuilt, such as with electoral reform in Mexico.

The 1989 U.S. invasion of Panama provides an appropriate starting point for this study because it straddles the Cold War and post-Cold War interventions. It introduced—albeit unsuccessfully—the democ-racy rationale; that is, to counter the reversal of democratic elections as an excuse to intervene, without an apparent threat of communism. U.S. troops also used the post-World War II plans for the reconstruction of Germany and Japan as their guide for Panama. Somalia then served as a test case for a purely humanitarian crisis that did not affect the de-veloped world. Its failure hindered any massive reaction in the next major humanitarian crisis in Africa, in Rwanda.

Events in Somalia did not stop the U.S. government from intervening in Haiti in 1994, because of the latter's proximity to the United States and problems associated with the increased flow of refugees into Florida. Haiti then became the first case when the aim of the military intervention and the nation-building attempt were the same: to establish a democratic state. It was also the first time the United Nations Security Council sanctioned intervention to restore a democratically elected government. The U.S. government considered Somalia when trying to eschew involvement in Bosnia, but was eventually pressured into acting there militarily beginning in 1995, again on humanitarian grounds, although maintaining the credibility of the North Atlantic Treaty Organization (NATO) and U.S. leadership in Europe factored in as well. The use of force in Kosovo in 1999 was facilitated by the spillover effect from Bosnia, which encouraged European Union countries to support military involvement because of the looming threat in their own backyard.[2]

What Provoked the Military Response?

Certain similarities in the pre-intervention phase in these cases merit mention, if only to serve as possible early warning signals for future crises that might lead the U.S. government toward choosing the military option. Attention to these factors could allow the U.S. government to step back and go in an altogether different policy direction or proceed in a systematic and well-coordinated manner.

The period leading up to the intervention was marked by inconsistent policy, public waffling, and empty threats in these cases: by the U.S. government in Panama and Haiti, by the international community in Somalia, by Europe and then the United States in Bosnia, and by the two together in Kosovo. It is perhaps impossible for democratic states to refrain from such behavior because, as Bruce Russett explained, "In the absence of direct attack, institutionalized checks and balances make democracies' decisions to go to war slow and very public."[3] Other common issues that drive democratic states to intervene, however, can be considered—particularly refugee flows, the media spotlight on humanitarian suffering, increased use of sanctions, and continued defiance by rulers.

A large increase in refugee movements, especially into a powerful neighboring country, is one indicator. In Panama and Somalia, this was not a factor, but it was to a significant degree in Haiti and Bosnia. Later, refugees from Albania fleeing into Italy and Greece, from Kosovo to neighboring countries, from East Timor throughout the region, from Liberia and Sierra Leone to Nigeria and other West African states, as well as refugee shifts within Central Africa, also played a significant role in the decisions to intervene in those countries. Most governments cannot easily prevent refugees from arriving, not only because it is difficult and expensive to police borders, but also for human rights reasons.

Media coverage of these crises, with the ensuing public outcry, also forced policymakers to react. Although it fueled the initial military response in Panama, the "CNN Effect" became a major factor after the Persian Gulf War when safe havens for the Kurds were established. By the time of the Somalia intervention, media coverage pushed the U.S. government, because images of starving children were viewed with discomfort by many Americans. It also was partly responsible for the abrupt termination of the UN operation, as those same Americans witnessed their boys being killed in a brutal fashion by the very people they had gone to help. In the case of Somalia, the U.S. government reacted too impulsively to media portrayals; instead it should have utilized them to debate the merits of continued action and how to rectify the mistakes already made, which arguably might have been more effective.

In Haiti, the opposite occurred. Significant coverage of events during the period leading up to the intervention spurred a healthy debate about a possible intervention and gave those organizations that would be involved ample time to plan. The refugee crisis, however, was exaggerated by the U.S. media, even though during the height of the crisis, Cuban refugees were also arriving in large numbers without any corresponding threat to the Cuban government. Notably, during the lead up to the intervention, articles on Haiti were soon listed in the domestic pages of the U.S. press.

In Bosnia, televised Serb atrocities promoted a serious international dialogue, which belatedly helped convince wavering U.S. and European publics of the need for NATO bombing. This coverage also contributed to the establishment of the International Criminal Tribunal for the

Former Yugoslavia. Full-scale reporting of Kosovo refugees encamped in neighbouring countries, along with some coverage of bands of marauding Serbs in early 1999, also eased the way for an even more significant bombing effort.

Sanctions are often applied as a first response to large refugee flows and media pressure. Yet sanctions usually fail to achieve their desired aim of reversing or ending the crisis, as was blatantly evident in Panama, Iraq, Somalia, and Haiti. In the cases of the former Yugoslavia and arguably South Africa, they have been effective. Sanctions, however, also can have the undesirable consequence of promoting nationalist solidarity amongst the targeted population in defiance against the major powers, rather than causing the public to rise against their leader as the policy intends. Even in the rare event that the public does react, leaders normally take the necessary precautions to remain in power. Moreover, the punitive effects of sanctions are almost always avoided by those with money and power, sometimes by import substitution, but mostly by smuggling.

The policy of applying sanctions is thus inherently myopic and frequently leads to the collapse of the domestic economy. For example, the Haitian embargo, which endured for several years without accomplishing its stated purpose of removing the Cedras regime, adversely affected long-term recovery and increased the need for foreign assistance because essential medical and food supplies were drastically reduced, while most jobs in the basic industries were lost. This caused more refugees to attempt the journey to the United States and greater economic instability. More recently, attempts have been made to target sanctions at specific individuals, but overall they have only served to make the post-conflict renewal period more difficult.

Refugee flows, media coverage, and sanctions in these cases forced the international community, with the support of the UN Security Council, to threaten action against the errant rulers. As these threats mounted, it exposed them to charges that warnings were being ignored and not ameliorating the deteriorating situations in Panama, Somalia, Haiti, Bosnia, and Kosovo. Noriega, several Somali warlords, Cedras and company, the Bosnian Serb leadership, and Milosevic continued to defy international pressure because such policy pre-intervention was confused, did not follow a hard-line, and wavered sufficiently to encourage these wayward rulers into thinking they could continue their activity unabated, particularly when they endangered the lives of foreign soldiers.

This noncompliance eventually compelled the U.S. government to choose force in order to demonstrate that the sole remaining superpower would not be pushed around by nasty, tin-pot, small-time, thug dictators and warlords. The Security Council also needed to demonstrate that its resolutions were intended to be observed, not ignored. Thus it approved—sometimes belatedly—the military option in Somalia, Haiti, Bosnia, and Kosovo. In all these situations, the common assumption has been that if these particular "rulers" were removed, democracy would neatly fall in place. This simplistic analysis overlooks the obvious fact that the entire system of these states needs to be rebuilt because it is completely rotten and that rogue rulers survive and prosper precisely because there is no democratic foundation. The removal of one nasty element only guarantees that another one will quickly fill his place. For example, in Somalia, after Siad Barre was removed, warlords such as General Aideed filled the power vacuum. When Aideed was killed in August 1996, he was replaced by one of his sons, Hussein Aideed, who assumed control of his father's faction.

The inability to cope with each of these four factors—refugees, the media, sanctions, and defiance by errant rulers—produced the "Do Something" effect and entrapped the U.S. government into choosing the most extreme option of force. In justifying the decision to intervene in Haiti, Madeleine Albright, then-U.S. ambassador to the UN, explained,

> Together, we, the international community, have tried condemnation, persuasion, isolation, and negotiation. At Governors Island, we helped broker an agreement that the military's leader signed but refused to implement. We have imposed sanctions, suspended them, and strengthened them. We have provided every opportunity for the de facto leaders in Haiti to meet their obligations. But patience is an

exhaustible commodity ... The status quo in Haiti is neither tenable nor acceptable.[4]

The U.S. government added the public rationale of "defending democracy" and "maintaining our reliability" to the list of when the United States can use force—only after the fact—in these cases, in order to safeguard the international norm of nonintervention in the domestic affairs of other states.[5]

These four factors have not been as prominent in other civil crises and consequently can partially account for the absence of a threat to intervene in Algeria, Burundi, or Sudan, for example, where the conflicts may be as horrific, if not worse. Additionally, the decision to intervene is also based on the relative power and size of the country concerned and likelihood of a successful outcome. For example, it is extremely unlikely that the U.S. government would ever threaten China with intervention. Or witness the moral dilemma that European states and the U.S. government find themselves in with respect to the Russian bombardment of Chechnya, without apparent regard to civilians, in late 1999.

Once the decision to intervene had been made, further entrapment ensued as it became clear that a hasty withdrawal would only ensure that the situation on the ground reverted to that which caused the intervention in the first place. The peace-support operation and the nation-building component thus entered into play.

Changes in Peace-Support Operations

One of the most important shifts in operations concerns the role of the U.S. military in political reconstruction. A conspicuous change has been the gradual reduction of U.S. military control over nation-building activities, with Germany and Japan representing the peak. Indeed, both of these operations were directed entirely by the military, with civilian agencies playing a subordinate role.

Panama was the last operation in which the military overtly directed political reconstruction, although there, at least, the U.S. military had extensive experience and relations with Panamanians. Somalia was the last in which the military made important behind-the-scenes decisions, such as preparation of the nation-building resolutions for the Security Council. By Haiti, Bosnia, and Kosovo, the military's role was primarily confined to maintaining security, although it has participated in political reconstruction discussions at the senior level, while U.S. civil affairs, special forces, and psychological operations troops supported political activity.

Whether they like it or not, the U.S. and European militaries will have a role to play in future peace-support operations. European militaries do not view these operations as suspiciously as their U.S. counterpart because of their historical experience in "gray" military operations during the colonial period and, for the British military today, in Northern Ireland as well. The only other alternative would be an increase in the use of private security firms, called mercenaries by some, raising questions of accountability.

Improvements in civil-military relations have been another striking development since Panama, when there was no initial cooperation due to the need to maintain secrecy about the timing—and indeed occurrence—of the invasion. In Somalia, there was a conspicuous lack of cooperation on all sides and turf wars: between UN headquarters in New York and UN operations in Mogadishu, between civilian and military operators in Mogadishu, and even between U.S. and foreign militaries. Additionally, while preparing for the intervention, similar to Panama, there was no joint planning between the military and the heads of relief organizations, even though the military was originally deployed to provide protection for these organizations. In such a climate, it was hardly surprising that it became extremely difficult to carry out the mandate.

In sharp contrast, the Haiti operation experienced the fewest difficulties in implementation, where military, humanitarian, and development agencies were melded in a tight partnership due to the insistence of Lakhdar Brahimi, special representative of the secretary-general (SRSG). The development agenda was integral from the beginning, civilian and military actors trained together before deployment, and a civilian directed the entire operation. This does not guarantee that Haiti will develop a stable democracy, but at least a well-coordinated initial phase has provided the best possible environment for democratic reforms to take root.

In Bosnia, coordination improved after Carl Bildt's period as high representative during the NATO-led Implementation Force (IFOR), during which he was not given any authority over the military, and therefore had no means to enforce the Dayton Accords. Meanwhile, the UN Transitional Authority for Eastern Slavonia, Baranja, and Western Sirmium (UNTAES), in Croatia, which integrated the two, achieved more success in executing its mandate. The former transitional administrator for UNTAES, Jacques Paul Klein, was later appointed deputy to Carlos Westendorp, the subsequent high representative for Bosnia, and then in August 1999 became the SRSG in Bosnia and Herzegovina, indicating a more assertive shift in policy.

For Bernard Kouchner, SRSG of the UN Interim Administration Mission in Kosovo (UNMIK), a compromise appears to have been reached, as demonstrated in Security Council Resolution 1244 in 1999, in which the SRSG is mandated to "control the implementation of the international civil presence, and ... to coordinate closely with the international security presence to ensure that both presences operate towards the same goals and in a mutually supportive manner." Yet when it works, coordination depends too much on the personalities involved rather than on a prior agreement on standard operating procedures. The United States is attempting to incorporate many of these changes into doctrine to ensure greater consistency, the most recent being Presidential Decision Directive 56 in May 1997, which is more thorough but still needs to be adapted to an international agenda.[6]

The protection of aid workers, humanitarian relief supplies, and foreign troops has also become a significant factor interfering with the realization of the mandates in all the operations except Panama. Even there, ironically, one of the justifications for the invasion was the "threat to American lives," yet only one U.S. citizen had been killed prior to the invasion, while 23 U.S. troops were killed during Operation Just

Cause in Panama. By Somalia, U.S. soldiers were no longer allowed to die, at least not on a humanitarian mission (military casualties were more acceptable during the Persian Gulf War). The fear of body bags thus far is mainly a U.S. preoccupation, although in Bosnia, anxiety about Serb reprisals on British, Dutch, and French peacekeepers put a stop to NATO bombing sorties for some time. Later during IFOR and NATO's subsequent operation, Stabilization Force (SFOR), this fear has impeded the active apprehension of indicted war criminals, particularly Karadzic and Mladic, by NATO troops.[7]

If the U.S. government continues to allow its decisions to be dominated by what Thomas Weiss refers to as "a zero-casualty foreign policy,"[8] then Americans will be unable to provide the necessary leadership in these missions, and relations with their allies will also suffer. It is indeed absurd that a U.S. life abroad is valued more highly than at home. Considering that 30 Americans were killed in Somalia, 19 in Grenada, and 23 in Panama, perhaps being a soldier is a safer occupation than a police officer, foreign correspondent, aid worker, or even a taxi driver in most major U.S. cities. This is not to argue that the lives of U.S. soldiers are dispensable, rather that their security will be enhanced by clearer and more robust rules of engagement. If strong signals are consistently sent out to errant leaders that mistreatment of foreign personnel will be met with serious reprisals, aid workers and soldiers will operate in a more secure environment.

Another important lesson learned from Haiti was that the goals set by the international community must be limited and realistic. Again, this is in contrast to Somalia and earlier in the UN operations in Bosnia (UNPROFOR), when the Security Council Resolutions were overly ambitious and too numerous to be implemented and therefore destined to fail. A final and very important lesson that needs to be fully realized is a public, lengthy commitment to the operation, which is critical for allowing confidence-building measures sufficient time to be adopted. U.S. policymakers frequently refer to the Vietnam-induced fear of "mission creep," which occurred during planning for all these operations. Perhaps calls for early withdrawal merely represent a diversion for the

U.S. Congress, since these operations have been regularly extended. In-dicating a recent shift in policy, Dave Scanlon, SFOR Spokesperson, reported that "SFOR is now working toward an 'end state,' not an 'end date.' Deadlines no longer apply to the mission here ...What is left is to ensure a stable and secure environment so that ... a lasting peace [can be] established."[9]

Advances in Nation Building?

If we use the Allied occupation after World War II as a starting point, it appears at first sight that little has been learned—today's democratic Germany and Japan can contrast sharply with these cases and attest to the success and importance of externally sponsored nation-building ef-forts. As Roy Licklider explained, "The resulting governments are im-pressive testimony that it is possible for outsiders to establish relatively benign governments which locals will support for at least half a cen-tury."[10] Yet it is also important to note that Allied success in imple-menting democratic reforms was enhanced by respect for education and high literacy rates, advanced levels of industrialization, and, of course, unconditional surrender.

The United States, Britain, and France as well had a significant stake in preventing the reemergence of Germany and Japan as powerful and aggressive nations. Stable and democratic states were hence viewed as vital to international security. Panama, Somalia, Haiti, Bosnia, and now Kosovo have not been considered as critical by the U.S. government, though the latter two affect European security and thus figure more prominently in European policy.

Success in Germany and Japan, moreover, was achieved by policies that focused on sweeping economic, political, and educational reforms that affected the entire population for several decades. Again, external interest and support for the same in these post-Cold War cases have not been nearly as significant, although it could also be argued that the first of these interventions only took place in 1989, and democratic reforms need a solid and lengthy commitment before they take root. More targeted international aid could obviously make a difference. But interest here is slight, particularly in Congress, where representatives want to spend less money and exert less energy abroad, especially after the initial hype of the military operation subsides and international civil servants are getting on with the mundane tasks required to rebuild the state.

Interestingly, studies have demonstrated that the U.S. public in general supports spending on foreign affairs. In 1995, for example, the average American believed that the U.S. government was spending at least five times more than the amount actually allocated. When told what the real figures were, the majority endorsed maintaining or increasing that amount, not reducing it.[11] Yet influential representatives in the U.S. Congress continue to push for reductions in foreign-assistance funding. And they have been successful in their campaign: in 1999, less than one-half of 1 percent of the total U.S. budget went to foreign economic and humanitarian assistance.[12]

This amount is not remotely comparable to that which enabled Germany and Japan to become stable democracies, to the benefit of the Germans and the Japanese, not to mention for the United States and its allies in terms of security, trade, and political relations. For example, in 1948, the first year of the Marshall Plan (1948-1952), aid distributed to 16 European states amounted to 13 percent of the entire U.S. budget. This total did not even include all costs incurred during the German occupation and any of the occupation costs in Japan.[13] The equivalent for fiscal year 1997 would be $208 billion, in sharp contrast to the actual appropriation of $18.25 billion.[14] Although many Americans might claim foreign assistance is no longer the priority it was after World War II, it is also true that the threat posed by recent conflicts to international peace and security is more serious than may be apparent and could be mitigated if U.S. government gave them greater attention.

The Trilateral Approach: An Old Look at a New Problem

A strategy for rebuilding and democratizing states after intervention must incorporate three fundamental elements. It needs to reestablish security, empower civil society and strengthen democratic institutions, and coordinate international efforts. Each cannot be fully implemented without the others. For example, strengthened democratic institutions will not endure unless the state maintains the legal monopoly on force.

Elements of this approach were indeed applied in these cases, yet they were only applied in varying degrees and not holistically. The trilateral strategy is nothing new; it resembles that adopted successfully by the Allies in Germany and Japan. Can it be applied to a more modern and hence different type of crisis?

REESTABLISHING SECURITY

Prior to implementing democratic reforms, the government needs to recover as much control over security as possible. In many developing states, they are unable to do this. Instead, governments are forced to share protection with a number of nonstate actors, who may be called warlords, the Mafia, rebels, guerrillas, terrorists, or paramilitaries. The restoration and maintenance of governmental control over security is contingent upon military, police, and judicial reforms.

Some states choose to abolish the armed forces entirely and maintain only the police, as in Costa Rica, Haiti, or Panama. An alternative could be to retrain the military to work on domestic concerns such as border patrols to limit terrorism and trafficking in drugs, arms, and/or nuclear materials, or to provide coastal and environmental protection, disaster management, and rebuilding of infrastructure (e.g., an engineer corps). Military reforms should also include a reduction in defense expenditure.

Police reform is also vital and has been a major component of these cases. In most situations, an entirely new force is necessary, one that could ensure public safety and gain the confidence of the local population. The goal is to achieve a comprehensive change in mindset of the local police and of the public, as previously the police in many of these countries had only served to terrify civilians through extortion and torture, instead of providing protection.

Thus far, newly trained forces have inevitably included some members of the old force, due to the lack of experienced personnel and the belief that it would take longer to train an entire corps of new officers than to re-train some of the old. Such a policy has not been without controversy, although the method applied in Haiti appears to have garnered more domestic support, that is, phasing out the old force in increments while simultaneously recruiting and training new troops. The model used in Bosnia also displays the advances in promoting accountability by international police trainers, while in Kosovo, UNMIK has initiated a similarly transparent multiethnic program.[15]

Judicial reforms are also necessary and linked to other security sector reforms. Many excellent training organizations already exist, such as the International Criminal Investigative Training Assistance Program, supported by the U.S. Department of Justice, while watchdog organizations, such as Human Rights Watch, help to ensure that these bodies maintain high standards. Without accountable criminal investigative procedures, trained judges and lawyers, and prisons that adhere to fundamental human rights standards, police reform would be pointless.

The planned international criminal court could also send the appropriate message to adhere to international law, as well as provide the forum to punish those guilty of mistreatment of international personnel. This court would relieve countries emerging from civil war with scarce resources and overwhelming demands to bring perpetrators to justice. If a warlord suspects that he may be called to task for massive human rights abuses, irrespective of the existence of a central authority, he may be less likely to commit such crimes. For example, a number of Somali warlords paid attention to the Pinochet affair after he was arrested in London in October 1998.[16] At the least, the court would prevent the international community from negotiating with particular warlords if they are indicted, allowing members of civil society to resume positions of authority.

Demilitarization is also a priority, albeit extremely difficult to achieve, particularly in heavily armed societies, such as Somalia (or the United States). This would include disarmament, demobilization, and demining as integral components with the aim of reintegrating militia and soldiers into civil society, as indeed occurred in a thorough manner in Germany and Japan. In the latter two, there was also a purge of the nasty elements in both societies who had contributed to the war, which helped to rebuild trust.

There is no political will in the United States to become so extensively involved in demilitarization due to the fear of casualties, yet until control over security is reestablished, state reconstruction cannot be successfully realized. A permanent security-sector reform unit could be established at UN headquarters, perhaps in conjunction with the UN security coordinator, to coordinate all police, military, and judicial reform activities.

EMPOWERING CIVIL SOCIETY AND STRENGTHENING DEMOCRATIC INSTITUTIONS

Linked to the question of security is the need to consider the influence of nonstate actors, especially warlords. Often responsible for civil war and, at extremes, the collapse of government, warlords maintain their power by controlling strategic resources and valuable real estate, such as diamond mines and ports. The intervening power's choice of authority in any negotiations, therefore, can have serious repercussions, as in the UN operation in Somalia when Aideed was empowered at home and abroad by being branded "Enemy Number One" by the U.S. government. At the time, and indeed today, there are a number of warlords operating throughout southern Somalia, with no one warlord controlling the entire territory.

More attention paid to the warlords occurs at the expense of traditional leaders from civil society. Ignoring the faction leaders entirely is arguably ineffective because they control the situation on the ground and will need to relinquish their hold if peace is to be realized. This eventually occurred in Haiti when the junta agreed to leave the country, admittedly while U.S. troops were on their way. In Bosnia, Karadzic, and Mladic's exclusion from Dayton and subsequent ban from political participation because of their indictment by the Tribunal has allowed other leaders to emerge and participate, although the two still wield enormous influence because they have not been fully ostracized nor arrested.

The international community still negotiated with Milosevic, however, at Dayton. This issue resurfaced in the crisis in Kosovo that erupted in summer 1998 and again in early 1999, when Milosevic was finally made an international pariah during the NATO bombing campaign. Had he been excluded from Dayton and called to task for his responsibility in the wars in Yugoslavia, perhaps the subsequent humanitarian crisis that led to the bombing campaign might not have reached such a dire state.

Leaders from civil society should be included in all negotiations. They maintain respect in their communities and, if sufficiently empowered, could be capable of convincing those with weapons to disarm and negotiate. The inclusion of women should also be emphasized as their role is often enhanced during civil conflicts because traditional, male-dominated structures break down.

The final and perhaps most important reason to focus on leaders from civil society is that democracy is not a priority for warlords, who are mainly concerned with sustaining and aggrandizing their holdings. When warlords discuss the composition of a future state, the debate tends to focus on who will fill which post in the next government—particularly the positions of president, prime minister and minister of finance—not what type of government should be established. Further, the normal assumption is that the new state will be unitary because this type of state is easier to dominate. In direct contrast, members of civil society have a vested interest in promoting democratic reforms that include power-sharing mechanisms and decentralization of power, which help to ensure that one person cannot usurp power.

It is also possible that the international community's rigid adherence to the Montevideo Convention of 1933 exacerbates conflict. To gain recognition under international law, a state needs to have (1) a defined territory, (2) a population, (3) an effective government, and (4) the capacity to enter into international relations. Fulfillment of these conditions is necessary for recognition, yet their erosion or disappearance later in time do not mandate that it should thereafter be withdrawn or suspended.

The application of such a principle would decertify a large number of states, mostly in Africa, in some parts of the former Soviet Union, and the former Yugoslavia, where borders are largely insignificant and porous, disputes rampant, and governments systemically corrupt and unable to control much territory outside the capital. In fact, only the fourth stipulation is still met by some collapsing states. While having a population merely signifies that the territory is not *terra nullius*, in many of these states, several borders are straddled by populations which often hold more allegiance to their ethnic group than to the state.

Warlords technically need only grab the capital city and claim a government, which in turn allows them to receive foreign aid and all the other goodies that come with state recognition. If the international community could instead institute a mechanism for suspending recognition until such time as the state demonstrated a commitment to establish a representative government that respected fundamental human rights, perhaps this would reduce the warlords' scramble for control.

The international community, led by the United States and Europe, can help to buttress the power base of members of civil society by fortifying or establishing democratic and transparent administrative institutions. This can be achieved by utilizing the expertise of the many U.S. and European nongovernmental organizations that work to strengthen the rule of law, enhance respect for human rights, support international electoral observers, improve financial management and accountability, promote decentralization, expand civilian control of the military, and improve electoral processes, legislatures, political parties, the media, the economy, and education at all levels of society. Additionally, the development and implementation of democratic constitutional arrangements with power-sharing mechanisms should also be a priority.

When the next crisis erupts that eventually turns into a nation-building operation, it may be time to consider new approaches to governance, which might even include support for a government that stretches beyond the external frontiers of that state. Indeed, if we are to consider temporarily de-certifying certain rogue states, so too should we contemplate relaxing the rigid adherence to the Westphalian state-based system.[17] One approach may be greater decentralization, at least for African crises, since traditional culture and levels of command and authority operated at the local level long before colonial powers interfered in the continent. Power could be devolved to villages and communities, even including those that cut across international borders. This example could also apply to potential crises in other parts of the world, such as in the former Soviet Union.

Consociational principles could also be used to realign loyalties within a larger regional grouping. Consociational arrangements provide options for power sharing between different groups, with jobs and public moneys distributed according to group sizes. They are based on the concept of separate but equal and are feasible options for deeply divided societies during the period when trust needs to be rebuilt. Each group administers its own community needs, such as education, and minorities are given the right to veto legislation. Consociational principles can be used in any type of political system, from a unitary state to a loose confederation.

As in any political arrangement, safeguards must be instituted to protect minorities, but they will also need external support to ensure their implementation, which again means prolonging the international presence. If such programs are not sustained, the only other way to prevent a recurrence of war is to carve the state into smaller, more ethnically pure pieces. This option sanctifies ethnic cleansing but is unfortunately the one most likely to be chosen because the time commitment is shorter. Consociational arrangements, in contrast, do not force populations to move, because they are allowed to associate with others, no matter where they live.

Finally, the composition of the post-conflict state must largely be decided by its inhabitants to ensure an invested ownership in the peace process and encourage its successful implementation. The best will in the world on behalf of the international community cannot replace local endorsement of democratization. Support for capacity building and inclusion of local actors in the decision-making process, as has been occurring in the Kosovo Transitional Council during UNMIK, is an imperative.

INTERNATIONAL COORDINATION

Just as coordination is important during a peace support operation, so too is it vital during reconstruction. Owing to the insecurity inherent in crisis environments and the preponderance of external actors engaged in mediation and assistance efforts, international coordination has been increasingly considered a crucial element in conflict prevention, management, and resolution. This is especially the case when dealing with a collapsed state because there are no official counterparts on the ground with legitimate negotiating status. Although all would agree that coordination is necessary, the effort to develop common objectives and principles on an international level needs to be enhanced. The five international communities that require coordination are nongovernmental organizations, donors/governments, multilateral organizations, militaries, and, significantly, the private sector.

The role of the private sector has largely been overlooked, even though foreign corporations also play an indirect and sometimes direct role in complex emergencies. Multinational corporations can exacerbate conflicts, but they also can help in their resolution. Many mining and oil companies, for example, have a large stake in unstable regions and often wield enormous influence with whatever remnant of a government exists and, even in some cases, with rebel groups. They also offer the employment that is so essential during rehabilitation.

Coordination of international efforts in reconstruction is particularly vital for the following reasons:

- to facilitate the adoption of common policies and responses;

- to prevent overlap of programs;

- to maximize the effective use of available resources; and

- to promote a secure operational environment for aid activities (e.g., a united front against hostage-taking, harassment, or extortion).

Although the UN already gives certain agencies the task of the lead coordinating role and others have been created in situations of state collapse,[18] a more concerted effort should be made to institutionalize and expand the terms of reference of these bodies for all conflicts as soon as they erupt.

The three components discussed in this section—security, democratization, and coordination—already exist at some level in most peace-supporting and nation-building operations, yet they have not been regulated to the degree necessary to ensure wider adherence. Only when the three components form part of an overall strategic package can we hope to achieve greater synergy in future missions. Anthony Lake concluded, "Neither we nor the international community has either the responsibility or the means to do whatever it takes for as long as it takes to rebuild nations."[19] Although this point is valid, he also admits the failure to comprehend the overall dilemma by his remark "whatever it takes." This inability to conceptualize what it takes to rebuild states is associated with the recent increase in seemingly intractable conflicts but also signifies the lack of interest in addressing these crises in a comprehensive manner. Today's strong democracies in Germany and Japan reflect the value of such a commitment. More attention paid to resolving prevailing crises can thus ensure that future operations achieve similar success.

Notes

1. The term "nation" is often confused with "state," particularly in the United States. Although the term "nation building" incorrectly depicts what the U.S. government is attempting to do, as it rarely strives to create a nation inhabited by peoples of the same collective identity, this term has become synonymous with state building. For example, when the U.S. government and the UN attempted to rebuild Somalia, they did not try to reunite all Somalis living in Djibouti, Kenya, and Ethiopia with Somalis in the former Somali Republic, which would have indeed created a Somali nation; rather, they focused on rebuilding the former Somali Republic.

2. The case of East Timor differs from these cases because it has long been considered by the decolonization committee in the UN as a territory that can decide its future (unlike Kosovo, for example), and the violence that led to military intervention was based on the reaction to the UN-sanctioned referendum. It will not be discussed to any extent in this article, even though it is becoming a nation-building operation, because it was only beginning at the time of the preparation of this article.

3. Letter to the editor, *Economist*, April 29, 1995.

4. UN Document S/PV.3413 (New York: United Nations, July 31, 1994): 12.

5. See John M. Shalikashvili, "National Military Strategy, Shape, Respond, Prepare Now: A Military Strategy for a New Era," 1997, which lists guidelines he set out when he was chairman of the Joint Chiefs of Staff. Shalikashvili's strategy built on that of his predecessor; see Colin Powell, "U.S. Forces: Challenges Ahead," *Foreign Affairs* 72, no. 5 (Winter 1992-93): 32-45. See also Richard N. Haass, *Intervention: The Use of American Military Force in the Post-Cold War World* (Washington, D.C.: Carnegie Endowment for International Peace, 1994), 16-17, citing former Secretary of State Warren Christopher's guidelines, from testimony before the Senate Committee on Foreign Relations in April 1993. Finally, see Anthony Lake, assistant to the president for national security affairs, "Defining Missions, Setting Deadlines: Meeting New Security Challenges in the Post-Cold War World," remarks at George Washington University, March 6, 1996. Shalikashvili, Christopher, and Lake have also correspondingly represented the different foreign-policy communities within the U.S. government: defense, state, and intelligence. The three sets of guidelines are purposely rather vague, which gives the U.S. government latitude in deciding whether to become engaged.

6. The Clinton administration's Policy on Managing Complex Contingency Operations, *Presidential Decision Directive 56*, May 1997.

7. The British military conducted a poll in 1997 to see how many deaths of British soldiers the public would tolerate and found the numbers quite high, about 15 per month. Respondents remarked that soldiers joined on a voluntary basis and should therefore be well aware of the risks they might encounter. Indeed, the British, French, and Dutch all lost more soldiers than the Americans did in the four cases discussed here, while the Pakistanis suffered grave losses in Somalia without withdrawing.

8. Thomas G. Weiss, "Collective Spinelessness: UN Actions in the Former Yugoslavia," in Richard H. Ullman, ed., *The World and Yugoslavia's Wars* (New York: The Council on Foreign Relations, 1996), p. 91.

9. From correspondence with Lt. Cmdr. Dave Scanlon, SFOR spokesperson, April 1999.

10. Roy Licklider, "State Building After Invasion: Somalia and Panama," presented at the International Studies Association annual convention, San Diego, Calif., April 1996.

11. See "Americans and Foreign Aid," Program on International Policy Attitudes, a joint program of the Center for the Study of Policy Attitudes and the Center for International and Security Studies at the University of Maryland, January 23, 1995; or Steven Kull, I. M. Destler, and Clay Ramsay, *The Foreign Policy Gap: How Policymakers Misread the Public* (College Park, Md.: Center for International and Security Studies, 1997).

12. The Challenge of Foreign Assistance (September 1999), www.info.usaid.gov, 6.

13. Curt Tarnoff, "The Marshall Plan: Design, Accomplishments, and Relevance to the Present," *Congressional Research Service, Report for Congress*, January 6, 1997.

14. Author's calculation. Budget information provided by U.S. Department of State, www.state.gov.

15. See "Bosnia and Hercegovina: Beyond Restraint," *Human Rights Watch Report*; and *Report of the Secretary-General on the UN Interim Administration Mission in Kosovo*, S/1999/987 (September 16, 1999): para. 30.

16. Author discussions in Kenya and Somalia, 1999.

17. Jeffrey Herbst, "Alternatives to the Current Nation-States in Africa," *International Security* 21, no. 3 (Winter 1996/1997).

18. The Afghanistan Programming Board, the Monitoring and Steering Group in Liberia, and the Somalia Aid Coordination Body, which were all established on an ad hoc basis, are the best examples of such international coordinating mechanisms in situations of state collapse.

19. Anthony Lake, "Defining Missions, Setting Deadlines: Meeting New Security Challenges in the Post-Cold War World."

Bill Owens and Troy A. Eid

Strategic Democracy Building: How U.S. States Can Help

The war on terrorism provides an unprecedented opportunity for the United States and its supporters to influence—and ultimately to help reform—countries that harbor terrorists or seek to develop or obtain weapons of mass destruction (WMD) and to influence them in ways that more closely align with vital U.S. national interests. Republicans and Democrats alike need to get beyond the current debate over nation building—a term so politically loaded that it is now virtually useless except as a partisan wedge—and move forward together to promote a carefully targeted and sustained policy of strategic democratization.

The United States cannot unilaterally impose democracy on other countries, nor can it dictate the types of governmental institutions that other people choose to adopt—if they are able to choose at all. Political reform must come from within. Encouraging such fundamental reforms in other nations will certainly not come quickly or easily. In some cases, positive change may not happen at all, at least not in this lifetime. Strategic democracy building aims to reinforce the development of demo-

Bill Owens is governor of Colorado and vice chair of the Republican Governors Association. He has led delegations to Europe, Latin America, and Asia, including 10 trips to Russia. Troy A. Eid serves on the governor's cabinet as the secretary of personnel and administration for Colorado. The authors thank Mason Whitney, Sean Duffy, Allison H. Eid, Kim R. Holmes, John C. Hulsman, Livingston Keithley, Heinrich Kreft, Shelley McPherson, James C. O'Brien, Mara L. Warren, Craig Kennedy and the staff of the German Marshall Fund of the United States, and the U.S.-Spain Council for their assistance with this article.

The Washington Quarterly • 25:4 pp. 153–168.

The Battle for Hearts and Minds

cratic institutions in strategically important nations—helping their own reformers to help themselves and their people—and seeks to cultivate new U.S. allies and coalition partners.

Although the context after September 11 may be new, such a strategic approach has already proven successful through programs such as the State Partnership Program (SPP). This program, which now spans three U.S. presidential administrations, began a decade ago under President George H. W. Bush as a joint experiment by the Departments of State and Defense to accelerate the integration of former Eastern bloc nations into NATO. The SPP has since evolved beyond NATO and now includes 34 nations in Central and Eastern Europe, the former Soviet Central Asia, Latin America, and Southeast Asia. The SPP pairs the senior military and political leaders of these nations with senior officers in the U.S. National Guard, state governors, and other high-ranking political officials from 34 states, 2 U.S. territories, and the District of Columbia. Thanks to the SPP, most state governments are helping Washington add to the list of potential allies and coalition partners with which the U.S. government can collaborate politically and militarily in the future. The result is a bipartisan success story that can serve both as a foundation and as a model for other strategic democracy-building initiatives.

The State Partnership Program

The SPP's quiet achievements during the past decade have gone largely unnoticed by many foreign policy specialists in Washington. Perhaps the leading study of the states' involvement in U.S. foreign policy devotes just one sentence to the SPP.[1] The changing nature of the program may explain this oversight at least partially. What was initially conceived primarily as a way to help reform the armed forces of former Eastern bloc nations—and incidentally as a way to strengthen the effectiveness of state National Guard organizations through professional contacts and exchanges—steadily expanded to a more comprehensive set of military and political relationships between states and their partner nations.

As the early 1990s unfolded in Central and Eastern Europe, the collapse of the Soviet Union prompted NATO to contemplate eastward enlargement into several former Warsaw Pact members that were already well on the road to becoming peaceful and stable democracies. Yet, the escalating violence in the Balkans, especially in Bosnia-Herzegovina, throughout the decade also demonstrated that the democratic transformation of Eastern Europe was by no means automatic or preordained. The drive toward NATO enlargement, and more generally the attempt to accelerate the democratization of Central and Eastern Europe, prompted the United States to consider practical democracy-building measures, prior to extending offers of NATO membership, to encourage grassroots political and military reform throughout the former Eastern bloc.

In mid-1992, the Bush administration and NATO officials specifically began exploring ways to support the development of a civilian-controlled military in the Baltic nations of Estonia, Latvia, and Lithuania to coincide with the scheduled withdrawal of Russian troops from the area. These discussions inevitably touched on NATO's anticipated enlargement eastward, thereby broadening the context of the discussion into political as well as military issues.

In December of that year, Bush's National Security Council—joined by the U.S. secretaries of state and defense and the Joint Chiefs of Staff—formally endorsed a plan that relied heavily on the U.S. National Guard to assist military and civilian authorities in Estonia, Latvia, and Lithuania in their steps toward military and political reform. This plan featured a series of military-to-military exchanges and visits as well as joint military-civilian "traveling contact team" missions by NATO experts. Significantly, the plan specified that the National Guard's mission would be both military and political, in keeping with the possibility that the Baltic nations might eventually become candidates for NATO membership.

In the months that followed, these military and civilian teams met extensively with their Baltic counterparts to provide training, resources, and other support in a wide variety of areas, such as enforcing basic human rights guarantees, creating a military legal code based on the rights of soldiers, establishing a professional noncommissioned officer corps and a chaplain corps, and developing other governmental institutions designed to ensure the military's political neutrality and loyalty to a lawful constitution. Over time, the missions of these traveling contact teams incorporated increasingly specialized expertise in areas such as information technology systems, logistics support, legislative and public affairs, personnel management, and organizational development.

The National Guard proved to be an inspired fit for this kind of assignment because it is a dual federal-state reserve military force, reporting either to the president (for national defense missions) and to the state or territorial governors (in cases of civil disturbances or responses to natural disasters and emergencies), depending on the situation. The National Guard pledged to provide a reliable pool of professional citizen-soldiers who could lend their skills and a relatively modest portion of their unit's resources to the effort. At the same time, these men and women could serve as models for the basic behaviors that NATO was expecting its new alliance members from the Baltic nations to emulate.

The National Guard's involvement offered at least two other advantages. The first was to facilitate the political participation of governors, who by law appoint the adjutant generals who command the state National Guard units, as well as other state officials. This process could help develop a broader bipartisan constituency for the program instead of relying solely on the U.S. Congress. A second benefit was cost. The federal government was already footing nearly the entire bill for state National Guard operations. It could now leverage those resources to assist the Baltic nations without the need for substantial new congressional appropriations and with few, if any, direct costs to the participating states.

The Defense Department's European Command (EUCOM) and the National Guard Bureau (NGB) established the SPP in March 1993 by pairing the top military and civilian leaders in Estonia, Latvia, and Lithuania with state National Guard units in Maryland, Michigan, and Pennsylvania, respectively. In selecting these particular states as the first SPP participants, the NGB noted the strong ethnic and cultural ties between their own immigrant populations and those of the partner countries. Although not required, many subsequent partnerships have continued this practice of teaming individual states with nations that, through past immigration patterns, have a historical affinity with their SPP partners in the United States.

From an early emphasis on military-to-military exchanges and similar contacts in the Baltic states, the SPP steadily expanded to include other former Eastern bloc nations, as prioritized by the Pentagon and the State Department. At the same time, by 1995 the SPP's scope had grown to include what military officials called "multifaceted engagement activities … in the social, economic and military spheres."[2] These programs now include both military and civilian exchanges; traveling contact and "familiarization" visits; and training and other forms of assistance focused on emergency management, disaster relief operations, civil and criminal justice, judicial processes, and law enforcement. Under the rubric of democratization, officials from EUCOM and the NGB and SPP state participants also engage in a range of programs and activities aimed at preparing partner nations to satisfy NATO's membership eligibility criteria, including:

- commitment to peace and security measures consistent with North Atlantic Treaty obligations;

- adherence to democratic governance, including transparent governmental decisionmaking and legal processes, and the rule of law;

- respect for territorial integrity and state sovereignty;

- protection of fundamental human rights and rights of ethnic minorities; and

- evidence of economic development, including the transition to a market-based economy and the privatization of selected state-owned industries.[3]

Besides sponsoring official SPP-initiated activities aimed at helping partner countries to meet the criteria for NATO membership, the NGB encourages the ongoing development of informal relationships designed to reinforce these goals. Col. Max Brewer, a senior NGB adviser to the program, views a corresponding benefit of SPP military-to-military contacts as "the relationships between governmental and nongovernmental civilian organizations within the partners. Through the SPP, many countries have established successful governmental, business, educational, and medical relationships with counterpart agencies from the partner state."[4]

From its inception, EUCOM has quietly but firmly touted that U.S. strategic national interests are served through SPP by enhancing NATO's military capabilities and by reinforcing peace and democracy in the region. In a recent report, for instance, the commander in chief of U.S. forces in Europe, Gen. Joseph Ralston, describes the SPP as "a significant section of the United States European Command's overall theater engagement strategy."[5] After recalling the SPP's help in bringing Hungary, Poland, and the Czech Republic into NATO in 1999, Ralston predicts the program "will continue to be an integral part of our strategy to foster stability and democracy in Eastern Europe. ... We also look forward to assisting our other partner countries to achieve free-market economies and civilian-controlled military establishments responsive to the needs of their citizens."[6]

More recently, the SPP has expanded beyond Europe and its NATO roots. Since the second half of Bill Clinton's administration and continuing under President George W. Bush, the SPP is no longer limited to preparing prospective NATO candidates for membership in that alliance. Instead, the SPP has grown to include state partnerships in three other U.S. military command areas: Central Command (CENTCOM) in Central Asia, Southern Command (SOUTHCOM) in Latin America, and Pacific Command (PACOM) in Southeastern Asia and the Pacific Rim. Yet, despite the geographical enlargement of the program (see table 1) each of these partnerships—now covering a total of 36 nations—is still modeled on the program's original goals of enhancing the military capabilities and democratic institutions in partner countries. In the latter case, the SPP has adapted its baseline criteria for achieving

Table I.
State Partnership Program Participants (as of July 2002)

Country	U.S. State Partner	U.S. Military Command
Albania	New Jersey	EUCOM
Azerbaijan	Oklahoma	EUCOM
Belarus	Utah	EUCOM
Belize	Louisiana	SOUTHCOM
Bolivia	Mississippi	SOUTHCOM
Bulgaria	Tennessee	EUCOM
Croatia	Minnesota	EUCOM
Czech Republic	Texas, Nebraska	EUCOM
Ecuador	Kentucky	SOUTHCOM
El Salvador	New Hampshire	SOUTHCOM
Estonia	Maryland	EUCOM
Guatemala	Arkansas	SOUTHCOM
Georgia	Georgia	EUCOM
Honduras	Puerto Rico	SOUTHCOM
Hungary	Ohio	EUCOM
Jamaica	District of Columbia	SOUTHCOM
Kazakhstan	Arizona	CENTCOM
Kyrgyzstan	Montana	CENTCOM
Latvia	Michigan	EUCOM
Lithuania	Pennsylvania	EUCOM
Macedonia (FYR)	Vermont	EUCOM
Moldova	North Carolina	EUCOM
Panama	Missouri	SOUTHCOM
Paraguay	Massachusetts	SOUTHCOM
Peru	West Virginia	SOUTHCOM
Philippines	Hawaii, Guam	PACOM
Poland	Illinois	EUCOM
Romania	Alabama	EUCOM
Slovakia	Indiana	EUCOM
Slovenia	Colorado	EUCOM
Turkmenistan	Nevada	CENTCOM
Thailand	Washington	PACOM
Ukraine	California	EUCOM
Uruguay	Connecticut	SOUTHCOM
Uzbekistan	Louisiana	CENTCOM
Venezuela	Florida	SOUTHCOM

Source: U.S. National Guard Bureau, http://www.ngb.dtic.mil/staff/ia/spp_info_paper.shtml (accessed July 12, 2002).

NATO membership to provide a more general set of requirements and milestones to facilitate the emergence of new U.S. allies and coalition supporters.

According to a fact sheet developed by the NGB, the optimum SPP partnership has the following characteristics:

- The host nation demonstrates genuine interest in the partnership.

- U.S. theater security cooperation and host nation objectives are satisfied.

- The force protection risk is low.

- A minimum of additional resources is required to execute exchanges.

- National Guard core engagement competencies are heavily incorporated.

With these criteria in mind, the Defense and State Departments are currently considering a range of other nations for possible inclusion in the SPP, including Bosnia-Herzegovina; former Soviet republics Azerbaijan and Armenia; and African nations Morocco, South Africa, Niger, Mali, and Benin.[7] Depending on how the secretaries of defense and state assess U.S. strategic priorities in the coming years, the military's needs could ultimately outpace the number of state National Guard units that can participate in the program. Notably, however, the SPP was never intended to become a permanent relationship between the participating states and their partners but rather was designed to help nations achieve their own specific national goals, such as gaining entry into NATO. Once these goals are met, SPP state partners are free to undertake new relationships with different nations.

The SPP guidelines also recognize that partnerships work best when both sides have a mutually reinforcing interest in success. By its own terms, the SPP envisions an ongoing collaboration between both sides to achieve a common set of goals, such as successfully completing the process for NATO accession. As the program moves beyond its original role to include nations that are not seeking to join NATO or any other

U.S.-led military alliance, the partners' expectations of realistic milestones and definitions of success are also changing. Because the promise of NATO membership and its resulting benefits will not serve as an incentive in such cases, a given partner's acceptance and participation in the SPP should be linked to some other set of tangible goals, such as receiving specified U.S. financial assistance and recognition.

To help ensure that each relationship does, in fact, end as programmatic milestones and goals are met, SPP architects have articulated a three-stage life cycle for the program. During the initial phase, which focuses almost entirely on military matters, a three-year SPP plan is developed with input from the partner nation, the partner state, and various Defense Department officials. The next stage, the sustainment phase, is a period of intensive military-related activities with expanded U.S. resource support. SPP officials refer to the sustainment phase as "the active growth and flowering of the relationship between the partners to achieve maximum, positive impact" on U.S. governmental objectives.[8] Civilian activity in the program, including institution building and related activities, takes hold as well during this time.

During the final phase, known as the maturation phase, military activity and funding decline, but civilian engagement with the partner nation continues to rise. "In this phase," Colonel Brewer explains, "sources of funding from civilian agencies are primarily used to maintain the SPP partnership. NGB funding continues as funds allow. ... The partner state may become available to initiate a new partnership [at the Defense Department's request] and begin the cycle again."[9] EUCOM officials are currently evaluating the potential of the three nations that joined NATO in 1999, as well as that of several other countries preparing to enter NATO in the near future, to graduate from the program so that their state partners can undertake new assignments.

SPP guidelines therefore call for gradually shifting partnership responsibilities to civilian authorities at the federal and state level once the military phases of each state partnership have been completed. Apart from the NGB, however, it is not clear whether any federal officials—from either the State or Defense Department—are giving the states much guidance or any funding to continue their partnerships once the maturation stage ends. This apparent lack of continuity and transition planning is a current deficiency in the SPP. This weakness was probably less important when the only goal of the SPP was to help gain membership for a given partner country in the NATO alliance, which provided a political framework for continued cooperation with the United States. Now that many SPP partnerships are increasingly linked to the areas of responsibility of a given U.S. military command, however, as opposed to NATO accession, no one knows whether (and, if so, to what extent) the State and Defense Departments will consider directly supporting state civilian participation in a given partnership during or even after the maturation stage.

One aspect of the SPP, however, has not changed from the program's inception. Its supporters—Democrats and Republicans alike—have always carefully distinguished their efforts from nation building, as have the program's backers in the military. When asked recently if the SPP is building nations, a program spokesperson said no. "We do not teach these countries how to have a government."[10]

Colorado's Partnership with Slovenia

Colorado's current partnership with the Republic of Slovenia illustrates the SPP in action. Maj. Gen. Mason C. Whitney of the U.S. Air Force, now the adjutant general of the Colorado National Guard and a leader in the partnership since its inception, recalls that the NGB originally chose to pair Colorado with Slovenia for several reasons, including (1) geographical similarities, especially between Colorado's Rocky Mountains and Slovenia's Alps, and (2) the historical presence of a small but influential Slovene population in southern Colorado.

Bordering Italy, Austria, Hungary, and Croatia and facing the northern Adriatic Sea, Slovenia, with a current population of nearly two million, won its independence from Yugoslavia in July 1991 following a 10-day war. After enacting a democratic constitution and establishing a parliamentary system of government, Slovenia set out to reform and modernize its armed forces and, in 1993, began its official quest for NATO membership. At that same time, the war in Bosnia had focused NATO's attention on Slovenia and other parts of the former Yugoslavia, leading, also in 1993, to the NGB's decision to match Slovenia with Colorado in the SPP. Then-Governor Roy Romer (D) formally recognized the partnership by executive order on March 31, 1994.

As a result of the partnership, the Colorado National Guard supported various traveling contact teams, military-to-military exchanges, and familiarization visits with Slovenia's political leaders and its defense ministry. These activities were aimed at supporting the country's expected NATO bid. Colorado's SPP partnership marked a key milestone in 1995 when the Slovenian government began the annual planning-and-review process for joining NATO under the alliance's Partnership for Peace program. As part of this process, Slovenia negotiated with NATO its level of participation in various peace and humanitarian activities and its policy against WMD proliferation. The Slovenian Armed Forces (SAF) also developed plans for expanded civilian control, force modernization, systems interoperability, and other improvements required by NATO for integration into the alliance.

The Colorado National Guard assisted in these and other efforts by providing instruction and resources in mutually identified areas such as logistics, force organization, aviation and airfield management, air base development, communications, professional development, employer-employee relations, and personnel training programs.[11] By 1997, SAF personnel were successfully serving on the ground in NATO Stabilization Force (SFOR) peacekeeping operations in Bosnia. NATO forces in Bosnia also used Slovenia's main oceanport, Koper, as a logistics center for troop deployment and as a maintenance depot.

The following year, Slovenia adopted and began implementing its national strategy for NATO integration, a necessary precondition for full alliance membership. Among other things, this strategy calls for increased defense spending and continued development of a highly trained and well-equipped standing military force, including specialized rapid-reaction units, a professional reserve force, and gradual reduction in military conscription through a selective draft. The SPP has hastened the quality improvements in military training that this strategy demands. More than 400 Slovenian military officers have trained in the United States since 1993, including two graduates of the United States Air Force Academy in Colorado Springs.[12]

On the political front, Slovenia's strategy for NATO accession challenged its military and civilian leaders to address specific NATO concerns about the country's ongoing process of democratization, such as harmonizing selected legislation with European Union requirements, protecting ethnic minorities, strengthening the enforcement of private property rights, promoting judicial transparency, and eliminating backlogs in the country's civil court cases.[13] To show his support for these and other Slovenian military and political reforms, as well as for the Colorado National Guard's continuing commitment to the SPP, Governor Bill Owens (R) visited Slovenia in 2000. Bush then selected Slovenia's capital city, Ljubljana, for his first meeting with Russian president Vladimir Putin in June 2001. After the September 11 attacks, Slovenian leaders pledged their support in the war on terrorism, sharing intelligence about potential terrorist links in Bosnia-Herzegovina and offering the country's elite mountain training center as a training area for U.S. forces.

Colorado National Guard officials who have been actively involved in the state's partnership with Slovenia emphasize the important incentives provided by NATO's specific accession criteria in both the military and civilian spheres. According to these officials, the constant pressure on Slovenia to meet the required processes and milestones has been extremely helpful, both in setting partnership expectations and in determining the specific types and levels of assistance to be provided. The Colorado National Guard also stresses that, unlike some other SPP countries, Slovenia already had a fledgling democratic government in place when the country began its drive toward NATO membership. Given the perceived likelihood that Slovenia will soon be extended full NATO membership, possibly as early as the fall of 2002, the country may have already entered the maturation phase of the SPP, raising the possibility that the NGB might ask Colorado to consider a new SPP partnership opportunity elsewhere.

Improving the War on Terror

The September 11 attacks against the United States and the ensuing war on terrorism are testing several of the relationships forged through the SPP. Many of the results so far have been encouraging. For example, SPP partnerships in two former Soviet republics, Uzbekistan and Kyrgyzstan, reportedly helped facilitate the deployment of 4,000 U.S. and allied troops to the area to support operations against Al Qaeda and Taliban fighters in Afghanistan.[14] In another part of the former Soviet Union, U.S. Special Forces are training 2,000 Georgian fighters in mountain fighting, urban combat, and other counterterrorism activities, again building on previous SPP training and relationships.[15]

More generally, NATO's aggregate capabilities and its members' contributions are increasing as more nations become integrated into the alliance, thanks at least in part to their participation in the SPP. This outcome has also positively affected the war on terrorism. Current U.S. efforts to help stabilize and democratize the government in post-Taliban Afghanistan are a case in point. When Slovenian and other new or aspiring NATO peacekeepers are assigned to SFOR or the Kosovo Force in the Balkans, they effectively free other NATO members to participate in peacekeeping missions in Afghanistan. SPP partnerships have similarly aided the collection and sharing of intelligence on Al Qaeda and other terrorist organizations and have helped provide forward bases and logistical support to the allied military campaign. In addition, National Guard sources report informally that SPP relationships have enhanced political support for the U.S.-led war effort.

Quantifying the precise contribution with which the SPP may have strengthened these relationships is difficult. Anecdotally, however, the program appears to have made a positive difference in several key parts of the world at a time when the United States should welcome the help. Since September 11, U.S. citizens have been living in a world where classical concepts of military deterrence have become less effective in confronting at least some of the country's enemies. Therefore, U.S. forces may need to intervene rapidly—and sometimes preemptively—in places that lie well beyond the traditional ambit of the United States' Cold War–era alliance architecture, as the Bush administration's forthcoming national security strategy reportedly urges. The experience of the past decade strongly suggests that the United States may not be able or willing to conduct all these missions alone. Instead, the U.S. government will probably need to assemble U.S.-led multinational coalitions—sometimes with little or no warning—to confront such dangers effectively.

A key lesson of September 11 is that the current ability of the United States to enlist reliable and credible coalition partners in some parts of the world is not nearly as strong as the threats the United States could face. John O'Sullivan assesses what he calls the United States' "sorry search for non-European allies" in the war on terrorism. Contrasting the current capabilities of potential U.S. coalition partners in Asia, the Middle East, and Latin America to what he calls "the functioning and successful military alliance of NATO," O'Sullivan concludes, "No other state or collection of states comes close to Europe as an ally that can seriously assist the [United States] in maintaining global order."[16] O'Sullivan draws this conclusion in an essay arguing for the continued importance of the transatlantic relationship. Even in this context, the author carefully notes the contributions of several non-European democracies, such as Canada, Australia, and New Zealand, to the war on terrorism. Japan also comes to mind.

Without question, the United States will continue to need Europe and NATO both because of Europe's comparative military capabilities vis-à-vis other potential U.S. partners and because of shared democratic values and institutions. O'Sullivan's "sorry search" leads to another compelling point, however, for the United States and its traditional allies: they critically need to expand the list of potential allies and coalition partners for the years and decades ahead—ideally to countries that the United States can encourage over time to join the ranks of free and democratic nations. Laying the groundwork for such long-term political and military relationships will demand the kind of diplomatic leadership that Bush and his administration have so skillfully demonstrated since the September 11 attacks. The process will also require democracy-building efforts, such as the SPP, that promote institutional reform in strategically important countries that, if ignored or left to the mercy of terrorists and their supporters, might eventually threaten Western interests.

Working with States to Pursue the National Interest

As the SPP begins its second decade and shifts further away from its roots in NATO enlargement, the time is perhaps appropriate to take stock of the program and its potential to serve as a model for other democracy-building initiatives. Probably the most intriguing lesson for the future is how the program leverages the power of individual states to serve the national interest. This unique federal-state partnership has resulted, among other things, in the emergence of a small but potentially influential state-level constituency, including state governors and legislators as well as National Guard officials, who can directly attest to the benefits of U.S. democracy building abroad. This constituency increasingly extends beyond state government to include leaders in the business and nonprofit sectors who develop international contacts through the SPP and sometimes graduate into more extensive commercial and professional relationships.

By analogy, the emerging state-level constituency in favor of the SPP is not unlike the states' increasingly strong support, in comparison with that of Congress, for expanded trade and investment ties with other nations. Scholars such as Earl Fry have long contended that state-level international contacts are increasingly important because they help moderate excessive partisanship and parochialism, particularly in the formulation of U.S. foreign policy by Congress. These analysts point out that the passage of the North American Free Trade Agreement, which Congress initially opposed, occurred only after a successful lobbying campaign by the nation's governors and state legislators.[17] Viewed in this context, the SPP helps generate grassroots political support at the state level for U.S. democracy building abroad. Companies and entrepreneurs in Colorado and many other states are closely watching the progress of NATO enlargement as a proxy for predicting future market stability and privatization in Central and Eastern Europe. These businesses and like-minded stakeholders and investors are a visible and active lobbying presence in Washington.

From an institutional standpoint, state governors can effectively advocate democratic reform within emerging nations, and they can speak authoritatively to nations' leaders about how the nuts and bolts of freedom and democracy produce positive change. As the states' chief executives, governors—like national leaders—are typically judged on the results of their policies and programs. They are in direct touch with a broad constituency. They must lead large bureaucracies and interact on a daily basis with elected legislators. Because governors can identify with some of the problems and challenges that elected leaders face in emerging democracies, they can bring a credible and practical approach to conversations about institutional reform and procedural improvement.

Perhaps most promising, the manner in which state governments have worked to expand NATO and other potentially valuable relationships through the SPP—under the overall direction of U.S. military and foreign policy leaders—could broaden the political support for strategic democracy-building policies. Closer integration of state governments into such policies—at the same time harnessing the competitive power of federalism to develop more innovative partnerships and to share best practices—might even help mitigate excessive political wrangling over such policies.

Looking forward, the challenge is to extend and perhaps replicate the SPP model in ways that serve both federal and state interests. With respect to the latter consideration, states participate in the SPP because it benefits them to do so, not because they have (or should have) their own foreign policy goals separate and apart from those of the national government. On the contrary, states gain directly from the training that the SPP provides for their own National Guard units as well as indirectly through the access and contacts the program offers. Conversely, SPP participation costs state governments virtually nothing. Washington pays almost the entire bill in the form of direct congressional appropriations to the NGB, including virtually all the costs of each state National Guard unit's participation in the SPP. States do have the flexibility to supplement the civilian side of the program if they choose—with state appropriations, private monies, or a combination of both—but the decision is theirs, not Washington's. This funding arrangement certainly helps explain why the SPP enjoys so much bipartisan support and embraces most states.

Any expansion of the SPP would need to build on its existing success. One approach is for the federal government to direct and fund expanded state involvement in the SPP by civilian leaders in areas of specific interest and importance, particularly when a given partner country is deemed to have reached "maturation." Professional exchanges and traveling contact visits with state officials from all branches of government could help reinforce the democratic transitions under way in each nation. The SPP should also encourage experts from the private and nonprofit sectors to participate, again under the direction of Washington to ensure that these and other efforts directly meet U.S. foreign policy objectives.

Nurturing Allies Together

By tempering the United States' historical sense of invulnerability, the September 11 attacks also destroyed the illusion that, as the last remaining superpower, the United States can go it alone in world affairs. In the years ahead, the U.S. government will need more, not fewer, friends and supporters to meet the challenges posed by international terrorism, WMD, and other threats. Strategic democracy-building policies such as the SPP can help bring more allies and coalition partners into the fold while perhaps moving the United States toward another increasingly vital source of protection: a more free and prosperous world.

As with past challenges, friends are looking to the United States for leadership to realize the potential of sustained U.S. democracy-building policies in the post–September 11 world. Heinrich Kreft, the respected German scholar and diplomat, typified the cautious optimism that many U.S. allies are quietly expressing: "There is reason to believe that this is a time not just of new and formidable dangers, but also the beginning of a new and epoch-making chapter in history."[18] According to Kreft, the opportunity afforded by the war on terrorism is "comparable perhaps with the years 1945 to 1947, when the [United States] led the way in helping previously totalitarian countries—including Germany and Japan, its principal opponents in World War II—find a secure place within the community of free and democratic nations."[19]

Our friends correctly remind us that, in those momentous years immediately following World War II, Democrats and Republicans disagreed forcefully on many things but not on the need for the United States to encourage the institutional development of strategically important nations toward the path of democratic self-governance. In shaping the future of postwar Japan, for example, leaders as politically diverse as the supreme allied military commander, Gen. Douglas MacArthur, and his leading critics in the State Department, such as George F. Kennan of the Policy Planning Staff, agreed on the critical need to support the process of Japanese democratization. This policy, along with other reforms, led to the so-called MacArthur (or Peace) Constitution, establishing Japan's new government based on the principles of universal suffrage, separation of governmental powers, transparency, and the rule of law. To allow democracy to take root, the United States also pledged to protect the Japanese people from both the Soviet military threat and potential domestic unrest. The allies similarly worked together to protect postwar Germany and to support the process leading to the enactment of West Germany's constitution, the Basic Law.

Some may find it tempting to reject the possibility that Republican and Democratic leaders will ever again come together in the way they did at the end of World War II, to forge a national consensus for actively supporting the development of democratic institutions and values abroad. Before giving way to that temptation, however, one should reflect on the bipartisan success that the SPP has enjoyed during the past decade. Through SPP, leaders from both parties are working to-gether at the state level to encourage strategic democratization abroad, while strengthening support on both sides of the aisle for democracy-building policies in Washington.

Notes

1. Earl H. Fry, *The Expanding Role of State and Local Governments in U.S. Foreign Affairs* (New York: Council on Foreign Relations Press, 1998), p. 5.

2. See Joseph W. Ralston, *State Partnership Stockholders Report* (September 2000), p. 5.

3. See, for example, North Atlantic Council, "National Strategy for Integration of the Republic of Slovenia into NATO," March 11, 1998.

4. Col. Max Brewer, "Life Cycle of the National Guard State Partnership Pro-gram in EUCOM" (memo, March 7, 2002, EUCOM National Guard Program, "The Next Generation" conference, March 20–21, 2002) (hereinafter Brewer memo).

5. Ralston, *State Partnership Stockholders Report*, p. 1.

6. Ibid.

7. Gen. Carton W. Fulford Jr. (briefing, "The Next Generation" conference, March 20, 2002).

8. Brewer memo.

9. Ibid.

10. Col. Mark Kalber, "Partnering Around the World: An Emergency Manage-ment Win-Win," *State Partnership Program Electronic Newsletter*, May 2002.

11. Technical Sgt. Deb Smith, "Cure for the Common Cold War: Slovenia Finds Guard Program Good Home Remedy for New Military Objectives," *National Guard Bureau News*, April 5, 2002, http://www.ngb.dtic.mil/news/2002/04/05/slovenia.shtml (accessed July 12, 2002).

12. "Ten Years of Friendship Yields Benefits for U.S. and Slovenia," *Washington Times*, March 29, 2002, p. 2 (advertising supplement).

13. Ministry of Defense, "The Development of the Slovenian Armed Forces," *Slovenska Vojska* (May 2001), pp. 24–31 (special edition). See also Govern-ment Public Relations and Media Office, "Annual National Program for the Implementation of the NATO Membership Action Plan 2000–2001," *Facts about Slovenia* (Ljubljana, 2001).

14. "The Yankees are Coming," *Economist*, January 17, 2002, p. 7.

15. Charles J. Hanley, "Green Berets to Train Georgians," *Denver Post*, May 20, 2002, p. A-12.

16. John O'Sullivan, "With Friends Like ... Whom?" *National Review*, July 1, 2002, p. 33.

17. Fry, *Expanding Role of State and Local Governments*, pp. 108–109.

18. Heinrich Kreft, "From the Cold to the Grey War," http://www.wwics.si.edu (forthcoming). Alternatively, the article can be found in German. Heinrich Kreft, "Vom Kalten zum Grauen Krieg" ("From the Cold to the Grey War"), *Paradigmenwechsel in der Amerikanischen Aussenpolitik, Aus Politik und Zeitgeschichte* B25 (2002): 14–22.

19. Kreft, "From the Cold to the Grey War"; Kreft, "Vom Kalten zum Grauen Krieg" ("From the Cold to the Grey War"), pp. 14–22.

Michael Chege

Sierra Leone: The State That Came Back from the Dead

British foreign secretary Jack Straw commenced a major foreign policy statement in March with a stinging rebuke against global indifference toward dysfunctional states and a warning of the threats posed by nonstate actors operating outside the limits of any formal governmental control.[1] Pointing to the increasing menace posed by failed states imploding from civil conflict, he admonished that, "when we allow governments to fail, warlords, drug barons, or terrorists fill the vacuum. ... Terrorists are strongest where states are weakest." Hence, the urgent need exists to underwrite state reconstruction in Afghanistan and similarly failed states in Africa, Asia, the Balkans, and the Caucasus.

That same week, President George W. Bush addressed the United Nations (UN) International Conference on Financing Development in Monterrey, Mexico, pledging to double U.S. foreign aid by providing an additional $10 billion in the next three years, as he asserts poverty can provide the setting under which countries become havens for terrorism. Bush emphasized that the most assured path out of mass poverty and for states to become less fickle in the developing world was the building of governmental institutions for "liberty, law, and opportunity" on the foundation of open, market-led economies tied firmly to global trade.

Michael Chege is director of the Center for African Studies at the University of Florida in Gainesville.

Copyright © 2002 by The Center for Strategic and International Studies and the Massachusetts Institute of Technology
The Washington Quarterly • 25:3 pp. 147–160.

Yet, the relationship between poverty, internal conflict, the breakdown of governance institutions, and terrorism is by no means straightforward. Some of the most poverty-stricken and weakly governed states in Africa—Niger, Chad, Burkina Faso, Mauritania, Angola, and the Comoros—barely feature in the unfolding drama of international terrorist networks. Wealthier countries in the Middle East—Egypt, the United Arab Emirates, and Saudi Arabia—have been prime recruitment grounds for terrorist masterminds. Because the margin of error in implementing the new policies linking institutional reconstruction in failed states to poverty alleviation and counterterrorism is very small, understanding the precise linkage between state failure and terrorist-free reconstruction with freedom and prosperity has become a vitally urgent task.

Examining in detail case studies of failed states with terror connections that have turned the corner toward peace and the rebuilding of functional governance institutions is one method of gaining this understanding. Although Sierra Leone is not yet definitively out of danger, its experience as a failed state that came back from the dead labels it a suitable candidate. Sierra Leone is a small state of 4.7 million people, with perhaps the lowest standard of living in the world. From 1991 to 2002, networks of warlords and shady external operators, some of them with links leading indirectly to Al Qaeda, underpinned generalized lawlessness in the country and one of the goriest civil wars in recent memory. Policy lessons relevant to the issues that were raised in London and Monterrey this year can be learned from Sierra Leone's unlikely transition from lurid anarchy to tentative institutional reconstruction.

From Mascot for State Failure to Tentative Recovery

Founded in 1789 as a British colony for freed African slaves yearning for a home after the abolition of the slave trade in Britain's far-flung Atlantic empire (hence "Freetown," its capital port city), Sierra Leone achieved independence from Great Britain in 1961. With Fourah Bay College established in Freetown in 1827, colonial Sierra Leone pioneered higher education in British-run West Africa for the first half of the last century. For most of its 180-year colonial phase, the fundamental political cleavage in Sierra Leone was between the freed immigrants and anglicized "Creoles" and the multiethnic, multireligious (Muslim, Christian, and traditionalist) inhabitants of the country's interior. Sierra Leone also had a small business community of Lebanese and Indians. Party political loyalties assume a loose ethnic divide between north (Temne) and south (Mende). Yet, Sierra Leone did not experience the ethnic fratricide that is often blamed for state collapse in Africa before or after independence. Even after mayhem broke out in 1991, Sierra Leone's craven governments and bloody warring factions apparently observed the policy of equal opportunity employment.

At the hands of an externally sponsored rebel group—the Revolutionary United Front (RUF)—disaster struck Sierra Leone in March 1991, knocking off-balance the barely functional government of President Joseph Momoh. The neighboring failed state of Liberia was then in the throes of a grim civil war. Since 1990, the Momoh regime had provided its only airbase to the West African peacekeeping force (ECOMOG) in Liberia that intended to neutralize Liberia's top warlord at the time, Charles Taylor, now president of Liberia. Sponsoring the RUF invasion was Taylor's way of hitting back at Momoh. He enlisted mercenaries from Burkina Faso (Taylor's main ally in the region) and garnered material and ideological guidance from Libya's Mu'ammar Qadhafi—the political godfather to Taylor, the RUF, and sundry revolutionary groups in Africa promoting a confused mix of anti-Western and antiestablishment ideas. Led by the merciless Foday Sanko, a charismatic if cynical ex-corporal in the Sierra Leone military, the RUF was a collection of "unemployed and unemployable youths [with] ... one foot in the informal or underground economy ... [and] prone to criminal behavior, petty theft, drugs, drunkenness, and gross indiscipline."[2]

Rather than utilize guerrilla training, Sanko and his associates chose to exploit criminality, torture, drugs, plunder, and rape in battle. The RUF distinguished itself in war with forced conscription of adolescent boys; sexual enslavement of girls; shocking human mutilations; and wholesale destruction of settlements, schools, and government buildings. After years of neglect and short of funding, equipment, training, and discipline, the Sierra Leonean armed forces soon capitulated to the invading force. Some fought with the RUF part-time in return for booty, thus earning the appellation "sobels"—part soldier, part rebel. From 1992 onward, the international press transmitted to the world the shocking results of sobel and rebel in action against civilians. The RUF forces posed in drag with weird headgear and held the skulls or the hands of their dead victims, becoming the emblem of senseless carnage by hopeless, semieducated teens.

One of the most influential articles on the emerging global security agenda following the end of the Cold War portrayed the horrifying conditions in Sierra Leone's killing fields of 1994 as the prototype of the imminent strategic danger to Western civilization.[3] Disorder in the remotest corners of the earth, Robert Kaplan predicted, would shatter the placid political smugness of the West generated by the triumph of liberal democracy and capitalism over communism after 1989. The article, "The Coming Anarchy," opened with graphic portraits, rendered in the most vivid prose, of the festering decay of rudderless West African societies cut loose from the new global system by chronically dysfunctional governments that could barely maintain law and order outside the national capitals. In Kaplan's assessment, Sierra Leone's chaotic bloodletting was the archetype of the multiplying disorder in remote, lawless parts of the globe. It arose from failed states overwhelmed by "demographic, environmental, and social stress," in which criminal anarchy was the major preoccupation of restive multitudes of violent, drug-taking youths who gravitated in desperation to the fetid slums of desolate Third World capital cities to escape an impoverished countryside. Against that backdrop, he concluded, the apocalypse of "disease, overpopulation, unprovoked crime, scarcity of resources, refugee migrations, the increasing erosion of nation-states and international borders ... and international drug cartels" could already be seen "through a West African prism."[4]

From what we know today, the bloody, medieval-era warfare in Sierra Leone's interior between 1991 and 2002 was probably worse than Kaplan described. As of 1999, of the country's estimated population of 4.7 million people, more than half (2.6 million) were either internally displaced or became refugees in neighboring states. Nobody knows with any certainty the total number of war casualties. A conservative estimate is 70,000, with hundreds of thousands of amputees and maimed people.

By early 2002, however, Sierra Leone was a vastly different place than Kaplan described, thanks largely to a small but highly efficient contingent of British peacekeepers and the 17,500-strong UN Mission in Sierra Leone (UNAMSIL), the largest UN peacekeeping operation in the world in mid-2002. On January 14, 2002, the commander of UNAMSIL, Kenyan General Daniel Opande, declared the Sierra Leone war officially over after the surrender of some 45,000 demobilized rebels of the RUF, Kamajor militias, armed gangs called the "West Side Boys," and renegade sobels of what remained of the Sierra Leonean army. The fighters' weapons had been symbolically destroyed in various parts of the country in the previous six months. Great Britain was already training a new Sierra Leonean army. With international support, the Sierra Leonean government was itself training a new police force and preparing for a general election scheduled for May 14, 2002.

After 11 years of mayhem, order and peace had returned to most of Sierra Leone. Speaking on the situation in the country last January, veteran BBC West Africa correspondent Mark Doyle reported street crossings in Freetown "with smartly dressed soldiers on point duty shepherding schoolchildren across the road" with unusual gentleness. Deep amid the previously rebel-infested eastern districts of Bo and Kenema, Doyle was no longer concerned with his personal security "because the British and Sierra Leonean soldiers had extended the rule of law to a small part of this remote jungle." Refugees were returning home from Guinea and Liberia. Lungi International Airport was undergoing a facelift and receiving foreign passenger flights.

Most African regional security experts are cautiously hopeful about the long-term prospects of sustaining peace and effective national governance in Sierra Leone. Some rebel groups reportedly cached weapons in the bush and seem truculent about Sanko's impending trial on human rights violations. Much also depends on the actions of the region's veteran meddlers—Qadhafi; Taylor; and Burkina Faso's president, Blaise Campaore. Yet, whether the current positive trend proves sustainable in the long run, the chimera of the "coming anarchy" in Sierra Leone has surely suffered a significant reversal. This change must contain precious lessons for the many who are genuinely committed to the search for durable solutions to state collapse, domestic anarchy, and terrorism in Africa and elsewhere.

The Origins of State Failure

Simply stated, regional experts trace the origins of state failure in Sierra Leone to the slow-motion, self-destructive policies pursued by the government of President Siaka "Pa" Stevens (1968–1985). These trends rapidly accelerated under the venal incompetence of his chosen successor, Joseph Momoh, who led the country from 1985 to 1992. A former trade unionist and ex-mayor of Freetown, Stevens inherited a sound if poor economy based on diamond, iron ore, food, coffee, and cocoa production that was expanding at a reasonable annual rate of 4 percent between 1965 and 1973 against an annual population growth rate of 1.9 percent. Average personal incomes were steadily rising. Primary school enrollment doubled between 1961 and 1973, while life expectancy rose from 37 in 1961 to 47 in 1979. Functional, though increasingly corrupt, public institutions underpinned this improvement.

Sierra Leone's misfortune was Stevens's misunderstanding of the essential factors underlying the economic and governance structures he had inherited and yet his insistence on continuing in power for 17 years. Consumed with ambition and the desire to create a one-party state under his personal control, he gradually emasculated the once-vigorous parliament, finally banning opposition parties and dealing harshly with bona fide political opponents, though never as brutally as did some of his contemporaries. In 1971, military conspirators staged the first of many coup attempts against Stevens. Sanko was among those implicated.

The most far-reaching institutional decay, however, arose from gross economic mismanagement. The 1973 global oil crisis coincided with a dip in diamond and iron ore prices, opening a deficit in external payments that should have been addressed by cuts in public spending, devaluation of the currency, and export diversification. Stevens's government did the exact opposite. In the 1980s, the state failed to agree with foreign corporations on deep-level shaft "kimberlite" diamond investment that would have lessened Sierra Leone's dependence on the alluvial mining that also fueled the RUF rebels in the 1990s. To finance the deficit, the government borrowed lavishly from its central bank (in effect, printing money) and from international commercial and official sources, while extending state ownership and control from the mining sector to food distribution. Inflation rose to 50 percent in the 1980s from 2.1 percent between 1965 and 1973. Growth dipped to a 0.7 percent average between 1980 and 1987. The government reneged on many agreements with the International Monetary Fund (IMF) and the World Bank to stabilize the economy and promote growth. Wages and rural incomes increasingly meant little. For the youths educated with hope in the good years and for those in school, unemployment and a dim future were now a reality.

Economists like to measure the opportunities lost by failure to adopt reforms in monetary terms. The incalculable long-term damage inflicted on public institutions and political legitimacy by misguided policies is of greater national consequence. With swiftly declining real wages, Sierra Leone's public servants, including the security forces, turned to graft and pilferage of government supplies. Public equipment went unserviced. While Stevens spent millions of dollars to host an African summit in 1980, infrastructure fell apart in the tropical sun. State economic control worsened the deterioration. Against the backdrop of a highly overvalued domestic currency, trading at an 80 percent discount against the U.S. dollar in the black market, state licensing of private diamond exports created a lucrative payoff system between those well connected to the Stevens government and the cliques of Lebanese and Indian traders who sold the stones overseas, earning hard currency. The government addressed the increasing scarcity of foreign currency by the import licensing of rice (the food staple) and other consumer goods, creating food lines and yet another wide route for kickbacks. By the time Stevens handed the reins in 1985 to Momoh, a former military officer even less skilled in statecraft than Stevens, public institutions were already a hollow ineffective sham compared to what they had been in the 1960s. In the public's eye, the state lacked legitimacy. Corruption and illegality became the source of livelihood, as public educational and health services vanished. The Momoh government sold mineral prospecting rights under the table, with proceeds going to its chosen favorites. Disoriented young people turned to fantasy, reggae protest music, drugs, Rambo films, inchoate antisystem ideas, and recreational violence with real deaths. In the wings, political opportunists in Liberia, Libya, Burkina Faso, Kenya, Russia, Lebanon, and Afghanistan were waiting to exploit these youths for higher and lethal ends, about which the would-be rebels cared little, if they understood them at all.

With no effective army, police, administration, or judicial system, Sierra Leone was a sitting target for local and external predators. In the waning years of the Lebanese civil war, agents from rival factions—not least among them, Hamas and Hizballah—competed in bribery within Freetown for prospecting rights in the alluvial diamond districts in the southeast to finance the war effort in Lebanon. Dangerous and tedious, riverbed mining was fee-based self-employment by otherwise unemployed youths—not, as is sometimes assumed, a business initiative by the RUF rebels, whose inclination for alcohol and hashish made them poor candidates for such a task. According to a detailed UN investigative report on the subject, Lebanese purchasing agents enjoyed the protection of the RUF, the Taylor government, and Burkina Faso. They purchased the rough diamonds in informal markets in local townships for onward transmission, principally through Monrovia, to international markets.[5] They laundered the easy proceeds toward financing weapons for the West African wars and the Middle East and, as has become evident, Afghanistan.

Yet, as John Hirsch, the U.S. ambassador to Sierra Leone between 1995 and 1998, observes, "Neither the United States nor the United Kingdom devoted any intelligence assets to tracking the trail of money, arms, and diamonds in the West African region."[6] Taylor's actions as a kingpin to help link the diamonds of Sierra Leone (and those of the Congo and Angola), sanctions-busting arms trafficking, and international terrorism are now known. Traveling with a Liberian diplomatic passport and an alias, Sanjivan Ruprah, a notorious Kenyan weapons dealer and Taylor confidant (now under arrest in Belgium for arms smuggling), was a business associate of the Russian master racketeer Victor Bout, who ran "the biggest weapons trafficking network in the world, responsible for supplying the Taliban, terrorist groups from Al Qaeda in Afghanistan, Abu Sayaff in the Philippines, as well as rebel forces in Africa."[7] In these transactions, "conflict diamonds" (stones produced in African rebel-held areas) became the currency of choice.

This knowledge in turn sparked an international humanitarian movement to boycott conflict diamonds and thereby deny sustenance to the inhuman RUF rebels. For Sierra Leone, however, the tainted diamonds, international crime, and terrorism had moved into a power vacuum created by state failure—a self-induced affliction by debauched ruling cliques. The links to international terror sprang from institutional decay to a restive youth that became the cannon fodder of ill-intentioned operators with a global reach. Effective policy responses to the illegal diamond trade and to the need to create peace in Sierra Leone had to take stock of that chain of events.

The Policy Response

In *The Prince*, Niccolo Machiavelli argues strongly against hiring mercenary troops in the building of a state. In the long run, he wrote, a prince is better off losing battles with his own army than winning them with hired guns because, even though skilled in warfare, mercenaries "are anxious to advance their own greatness, either by coercing you ... or by coercing others against your wishes."[8] In postindependence Af-

The Battle for Hearts and Minds

rica—and to the overwhelming disapproval of African states—only the Mobutu government in the Congo could use mercenaries to destroy rebellions in the 1960s and emerge unscathed. As the dangers posed by state failure increase, however, discussion among policymakers and academics on the use of "private security companies" to restore law and order in anarchical states in Africa has renewed.[9] In 2002 the Labour government in Great Britain published a discussion paper intended to regulate companies offering military service to weak but legitimate governments abroad. Machiavelli's dilemma had come to life in an African setting.

Sierra Leone's experience between 1995 and 2002 shed some light on the wisdom, or lack thereof, of hired military groups in failed states. In 1995 the Valentine Strasser military government (which had overthrown Momoh in April 1992) invited Executive Outcomes, a private, South African military outfit, to engage the RUF for a multimillion-dollar fee. By mid-1997 the company had routed the rebels and the sobels, to the popular acclaim of villagers, and forced them to the negotiation table in Abidjan, Côte d'Ivoire, with President Ahmad Tejan Kabbah's government, which had been elected in 1996. In Abidjan, the RUF demanded the withdrawal of foreign troops as a condition for the ceasefire, and with the IMF insisting on a cut in Sierra Leone's spending on defense, Kabbah acquiesced. With Executive Outcomes gone, the RUF slid into its old ways, this time allied with the crooked national army. Under the mercurial Mayor Johnny Paul Koromah, they staged a coup in April 1998 ousting Kabbah and perpetrated massacres on civilians, especially in the capital. Another private military group, Great Britain's Sandlines, was needed to restore Kabbah to power in 1998 with the clandestine support of the Labour government and a contingent of Nigerian armed forces. With the capital secured, after a false start in 2000 the UN peacekeeping force disarmed the rebels in the interior and restored order. Hired forces then provided a temporary, rather than a lasting, solution to Sierra Leone's problem.

If the definition of the state as an organization that holds a monopoly in the legitimate use of force in a given territory is true, then establishing an effective army, police force, and security service must be the top priority in a failed state such as Sierra Leone. British forces secured Freetown from an imminent rebel occupation in early 2000. The Blair administration then initiated action toward realizing that priority as soon as UNAMSIL began stabilizing the military situation. Between June 2000 and September 2001, 600 British officers trained 8,500 members of the new Sierra Leone Army; 350 British officers have since remained in advisory roles. In collaboration with the Commonwealth Secretariat and UNAMSIL, Great Britain is funding and training the new police force. After UNAMSIL departs, the country's sustained, long-term stability will depend on the efficiency and professional integrity of the armed forces. Machiavelli may have been right.

Great Britain has contributed some $120 million toward the reconstruction of Sierra Leone's security institutions and justice system. At its peak in 2001, the UN peacekeeping force of 17,500 had a budget of $744 million. Considering the billions of dollars in Western government and multilateral development aid that had gone to waste in Sierra Leone over the years, partly directed toward building civil society and promoting free and fair elections as a reconciliation and peacemaking tool, noting the highly positive impact of a much smaller amount of carefully targeted military aid is important. Decisionmakers should also give priority to establishing professional armed forces. In 1997 and then again in 1999, Sierra Leone's elected president of 1996, Kabbah, fled the national capital under attack from his own unruly army. The public image and legitimacy of a president so dependent on outside security forces is a poor basis of national reconstruction in any state, let alone a failed one. As Rwanda after the 1994 genocide demonstrates, failure to bring to justice the perpetrators of the mayhem and bloodshed that accompanies governmental collapse makes state legitimacy problematic.

The best social function of the law is serving as a deterrent. Contemporary methods of promoting deterrence in postconflict societies include courts, international tribunals, and truth commissions. In 2000 the UN Security Council adopted a resolution establishing a special court, using Sierra Leonean and international judges and prosecutors, to bring those culpable in the worst killings since 1996 to justice. Voluntary contributions by UN members would provide the funding. Despite repeated pleas from human rights organizations outraged by RUF's mutilations and liberal use of child soldiers, however, the court's $56 million budget was still short by $43 million. The United States has pledged $15 million to the court over three years, the largest single contribution of any government. The full funding of this tribunal should be an urgent priority of all UN members who wish to deter violence in failed states.

Piecing together and rebuilding the panoply of government institutions and infrastructure across the land will obviously require more time. In September 2001, the IMF set the process in motion by approving a $164 million Poverty Reduction and Growth Facility and disbursing some $12 million in March. External donors including the IMF must pay heed, however, to the mistakes they made in engaging the Stevens and Momoh regimes as "development partners" even as the calamity was brewing. Foreign "technical assistance" advisers to the Sierra Leonean government were taking a third of all aid in fees, totaling millions of dollars in the 1980s with precious little to show now for their efforts. Official development assistance to Sierra Leone increased from $18 million in 1975 to $100 million in 1989, effectively rewarding the making of a disaster as the government habitually reneged on implementing any significant reforms. At Monterrey, the leading institutions in the aid industry—the World Bank, the IMF, the UN Development Program, and the regional development banks—claimed to have learned their lesson: aid works best when the borrowing governments abjure corruption and faithfully implement institutional reforms, which were the very conditions Sierra Leone had dodged on its path to ruin. After years of "development partnership" with the baleful Stevens and Momoh regimes, Sierra Leone's recovery program could well be Monterrey's first test. So far, the official aid agencies have not revealed any new road map toward institution-building in that blighted land.

Lessons Learned

From the experiences of Sierra Leone and other failed African countries, one could suggest that the first clear marker of progress toward
state failure is institutional decay in the security forces first and foremost, followed closely by self-induced economic collapse and a floating,
discontented young population prone to recreational violence in a
vacuum devoid of law and order. Institutional collapse, however, is a
necessary but not sufficient condition for the anarchical conditions
found in Sierra Leone between 1991 and 2001 to flourish. Full-blown
state failure and its correlates of armed rival groups and terror requires
opportunistic intervention by neighboring and distant actors exploiting
the situation for their own ends—Libya, Liberia, and Burkina Faso in
the case of Sierra Leone; Pakistan, Iran, and Al Qaeda in Taliban Afghanistan. Connections to international terrorism arise from this second order of intervention. As Somalia since 1991 demonstrates, as
regrettable as state failure is, it need not breed terrorism without powerful and ill-intentioned external actors.

Tracing the origins of the Sierra Leonean war to demographic pressure and the depletion of natural resources would be a mistake. Between 1965 and 1973, Sierra Leone's population grew 1.9 percent, rising
to 2.5 percent in the following decade. Land pressure and deforestation
was not a major national problem. Neither should commentators at-
tribute the state's collapse to globalization and World Bank/IMF pressure to downsize the state in favor of free markets. Under systematic
corruption in a shrinking economy, public institutional capability had
withered before the mid-1980s, when these organizations began funding their luckless economic liberalization programs in Sierra Leone. In
the late 1990s, Paul Collier and his associates at the World Bank propa-
gated the theory that African civil wars originated from greed by "loot-
seeking rebels" rather than grievance-driven dissent, primarily in poor
countries dependent on one export and exhibiting little economic diversification or market orientation.[10] By this yardstick, Somalia's record-
breaking tenure as a failed state ought to be hugely resource-based; yet

other than camels and goats, that country has no major natural resources worthy of major conflict. In Sierra Leone, the RUF moved into a vacuum of state power, collecting a "tax" for what would have been, under regulated conditions, a poverty-eliminating small-scale program to mine diamonds. Indications warrant careful monitoring of irresponsible, institution-destroying autocracies, such as Zimbabwe, Kenya, Burundi, Cameroon, Nigeria, and Côte d'Ivoire, that generate popular cynicism among long-suffering citizens. Together with democratic Nigeria, all these dictatorships exhibit the early symptoms of state failure—a condition congenial to foreign predators.

Once state failure establishes itself and security forces resort to foraging the land and preying on the population, hiring private security agencies is a stopgap measure at best, as the case of Executive Outcomes and Sandlines in Sierra Leone demonstrates. Reconstruction of the police and the national army has no long-term substitute. Since the fall of communism, Western governments, multilateral development agencies, and private foundations have expended large amounts of aid to promote democratic elections, good governance, civil society, and the rule of law. That list must now include professional military and police institutions under accountable, democratically elected governments. Toward that objective, bringing violators of human rights and the law to justice during the period of reconstruction, as the UN is doing in Sierra Leone, deters future abuse. As the world contemplates the effects of September 11, the pitiful political conditions in Sierra Leone's neighbor, Liberia, offer a good example of the dangers of tyrannical warlordism left unpunished and rewarded with power. Aside from the rehabilitation of the security-maintenance arms of the state, rebuilding the justice system and ensuring that justice (not retribution) is done is one of the safest ways to restore public confidence in governments emerging from failure.

Lenders should fund reconstruction of the wider panoply of public institutions such as public utilities, roads, telecommunications, local authorities, and educational and health services with the lessons of the Stevens and Momoh eras in mind. The pressure from external donors on Sierra Leone to take out loans was so great that an IMF official spent the night outside the uncaring finance minister's home to get his almighty signature.[11] Despite the window-dressing rhetoric of "local ownership," "participation," and "institutional capacity-building," the UN, IMF, and World Bank have changed very little about the way they do business in Africa. For the pledge these institutions made at Monterrey to have any consequence in averting mass poverty and governmental collapse, they must urgently rethink their operations in the manner recommended by the Allan Meltzer report of 2000 to the U.S. Congress on restructuring the Bretton Woods institutions—the leading donors to Sierra Leone and the poorest states in Africa.

The events of last September have made further U.S. government neglect of the security risks posed by collapsed, far-off governments impossible. For humanitarian reasons alone, civic organizations in industrial democracies will continue to seek international action on the social disasters that follow in the wake of unraveling governments and nasty little civil wars, even in what were once considered remote, nonstrategic parts of the Third World. Averting governmental failure and addressing its consequences once it occurs is likely to engage the United States and other countries, including those that neighbor anarchical states, for some time to come. There should be room for collaboration between the United States and African states at risk from neighboring failed states.

As with many other political and social problems, prevention is easier than curing. The case of Sierra Leone demonstrates at least that the root cause of the problem lay in the systematic ruin of state institutions by a succession of corrupt and inept dictatorships, indulged by external donors and a network of pirate businessmen. As economic and institutional decay set in, the regimes lost all legitimacy in the eyes of the people they claimed to govern. Then, as public institutions led by the organizations of law and order imploded, the stage was set for anomie as alienated youths hired themselves to rebel leaders and international criminals with a broader agenda.

Africa is a region with many potential candidates for state failure. Policy statements made earlier in the year by Great Britain and the

United States indicate the seriousness with which they consider the problem of failing states. Preventing governments from pursuing self-destructive policies requires first and foremost generating an internal capacity to monitor and contain the damage—which is primarily an African responsibility. Free and fair elections are an ingredient, but a continuing system of accountability, and restitution where necessary, will keep public institutions in good repair. As the reaction to the March 2002 rigged presidential elections in Zimbabwe demonstrate, not all leaders in Africa have proved tolerant of those conditions. As in Sierra Leone, external donors who indulge those leaders may be pushing those states toward a catastrophe that could ultimately hurt the donor nations themselves.

Notes

1. Jack Straw, *Reordering the World: The Long-Term Implications of September 11* (London: Foreign Policy Research Center, 2002).

2. Ibrahim Abdallah, "Bush Paths to Destruction: Origin and Character of the Revolutionary United Front/Sierra Leone," *Journal of Modern African Studies* 36, no. 3 (1998): 207–208.

3. Robert D. Kaplan, "The Coming Anarchy," *Atlantic Monthly*, February 1994.

4. Ibid., p. 3.

5. *Report of the Panel of Experts to the United Nations in Sierra Leone* (New York: United Nations, 2001).

6. John L. Hirsch, "War in Sierra Leone," *Survival* (autumn 2001): 153.

7. Douglas Farah, "Arrest Aids Pursuit of Weapons Network," *Washington Post*, February 26, 2002, p. A1.

8. Niccolo Machiavelli, *The Prince* (New York: Penguin Books, 1981), p. 78.

9. Greg Mills and John Stremlau, eds., *Privatization of Security in Africa* (Johannesburg: South African Institute of International Affairs, 1999).

10. Paul Collier and Anke Hoffler, *Greed and Grievance in Civil War* (Washington, D.C.: World Bank, 2001).

11. William Reno, *Corruption and State Politics in Sierra Leone* (New York: Cambridge University Press, 1995).

Part II

Postconflict Reconstruction

John J. Hamre and Gordon R. Sullivan

Toward Postconflict Reconstruction

One of the principal lessons of the events of September 11 is that failed states matter—not just for humanitarian reasons but for national security as well. If left untended, such states can become sanctuaries for terrorist networks with a global reach, not to mention international organized crime and drug traffickers who also exploit the dysfunctional environment. As such, failed states can pose a direct threat to the national interests of the United States and to the stability of entire regions.

Afghanistan—torn by decades of war, internal strife, and repression—exemplifies the dangers posed by failed states. When the Soviets withdrew from Afghanistan, conventional wisdom in the United States and elsewhere held that Afghanistan did not really affect U.S. interests. Since September 11, however, the threat posed by Al Qaeda and the Taliban was recognized, and the United States has responded forcefully and decisively. Expelling Al Qaeda and removing the Taliban regime that supported it from Afghanistan are only the first steps. Helping create a set of conditions that will deny opportunities for Al Qaeda and

John J. Hamre is president of CSIS. Gordon R. Sullivan is president of the Association of the United States Army (AUSA). Hamre and Sullivan are cochairs of the Post-Conflict Reconstruction Project. A white paper version of this article has been submitted to and reviewed by a bipartisan Commission on Post-Conflict Reconstruction sponsored by CSIS and AUSA.

The Battle for Hearts and Minds

other would-be terrorists to return is the next step. Finally, helping establish political, economic, social, and security structures that will enable the Afghan people to build a better future for themselves will be
key to winning the war of ideas. If the United States and its allies lead,
or provide significant assistance to these efforts, Muslims around the
world will believe Western assurances that the struggle against terrorism is not a war against Islam.

Although Afghanistan provides the first major reconstruction test of
the war on terrorism, it will not be the last. Similar challenges exist
elsewhere, in locations ranging from the Middle East and South Asia to
the Horn of Africa, where terrorist groups have already exploited the
vacuum of state authority and are likely to seek further advantage as
Afghanistan ceases to provide them sanctuary. As much as some in the
United States would like to avoid involvement in nation building,
failed states are a reality that cannot be wished away. Indeed, some of
the possible candidates for failure in coming years are those countries
in which the United States already has a defined national security interest—from Iraq and the Occupied Territories in the Middle East to
North Korea and Cuba. As the situation in Afghanistan has demonstrated, the United States and the international community ignore collapsed or weak states at their peril.

In reality, a broad spectrum of states could be considered failed or
failing. These range from states that no longer have a functioning central government, such as Somalia, and states whose central governments no longer control major parts of their territory, such as Pakistan,
to those whose central governments are no longer able to provide even
the most basic needs for the vast majority of their population, as is the
case in some African countries. Although analysts have identified relatively few completely failed states in recent years, the number of failing
or weak states that face the potential of widespread conflict and state
failure is much greater—approximately 30 cases, or more than 15 percent of the world's countries, by some estimates.[1] These cases affect, or
have the potential to affect, a significant portion of the world's population, economic potential, and regional stability.

Not all failed states are created equal. Not all will be equally important to the United States and the international community. Each stable country must gauge its involvement in failed or failing states according to its own resources and interests. Nor can a "one size fits all" approach be used to address the broad diversity of cases. Although conceptual threads link these situations, the approach to dealing with failed and dangerously weak states must be tailored to each case.

Policy Options for Dealing with Failed States

The United States and other international actors have at least eight major alternatives to consider when facing the problem of a failed state. The first option, which is seldom discussed but often employed, is to do nothing. At first blush, this option may appear to be the easiest course to pursue, in the hope that, if one ignores the problem long enough, the situation will resolve itself without major action on the part of outsiders. Unfortunately, the complex problems of failed states seldom sort themselves out, nor do they remain conveniently localized within one country's borders. More often than not, the problems spread, causing a crisis in an entire region and providing opportunities to international criminals and terrorists who seek to avoid the reach of the law. Afghanistan is only the most recent and most visible case in point. Moreover, often—as in Afghanistan under the Taliban—the way the chaotic situation resolves itself is not to the advantage of the United States and other responsible international actors, but rather to the benefit of the criminal interests that take advantage of the situation.

A second policy option is to try to quarantine a failed state. This alternative is not a no-cost or no-resource proposition, however, as it requires transportation and communication assets to quarantine the state. Monitoring and intercepting potential threats that emanate from the territory are expensive undertakings, as is evident with U.S. surveillance of Somalia today. Naval and intelligence assets can be stretched only so far for so long. Given modern capabilities, quarantining more than specific types of arms or small groups of people may not be possible.

A third option facing policymakers is to acknowledge that a failed state is no longer viable and to "carve it up" or recognize its dissolution into smaller pieces. As with present-day Somalia, however, only some of the smaller pieces are viable. Thus, recognition might reduce the scope of the problem but does not eliminate it. The microstates that might spin off from larger entities often prove to be unsustainable themselves. Even when they are potentially viable, spinning them off sometimes proves to have consequences for regional stability, as in the case of Eritrea. In many cases, as in Kosovo today, should the international community ultimately recognize its independence, such a small, weak state cannot necessarily protect itself in a "tough neighborhood" or mount sufficient legitimate economic activity to remain viable.

A fourth policy option is to seek to integrate or absorb a failed state, or parts of it, into a larger entity, whether this entity is a single state or a body like the European Union. This approach, however, requires a larger, viable political entity that wants to incorporate new units and is able to do so. This option may exist within Europe, but few of the candidates for state failure are located in that part of the world.

A fifth option for dealing with some failed states is to establish some form of international transitional authority. Although this policy has proven fairly successful in recent years in East Timor, Kosovo, and eastern Slavonia, these cases are more likely the exception rather than the rule. These very small territories have truly unique historical situations that made them candidates for major international involvement. Expanding the model to larger states with different histories is highly problematic and surpasses the resources available to underwrite projects of such scale. As many have noted in recent years, for example, the Congo, however much it might need or want direct international administration, is beyond the capacity of transitional administration.

A sixth policy option is to promote some sort of a neighborhood watch system, with countries in the region playing a central role in trying to solve or contain the problem. The Association of Southeast Asian Nations tried to play such a role in Cambodia without much lasting effect. The Economic Community of West African States directly intervened in Liberia and Sierra Leone with mixed results. In both cases, the key to the successes achieved was the combination of re-gional efforts and broader international support.

A seventh option is to back one side in a given conflict and hope both that it emerges as the winner and that it can reorder the affairs of the country. This tack was tried repeatedly throughout the Cold War, often with poor results. Although this option is viable in cases such as the former Yugoslavia and Kosovo, it is a high-risk strategy that should be used only where the interests and prospects for success are high. Ad-ditionally, if outside actors successfully support indigenous actors to win the war, those outside actors often find themselves held responsible by both indigenous actors and the international community to help re-construct the country and solidify the new government. Thus, this ap-proach is not really an option that exempts external actors from additional responsibility for dealing with the situation on the ground, but rather a specific strategy to be used in special circumstances.

The limited utility of these seven alternative policy options demon-strates the need for the United States and the international community to have a strategy and capacity for postconflict reconstruction—the eighth option—if regional stability is to be maintained, economic devel-opment advanced, lives saved, and transnational threats faced. Signifi-cant international interventions to help rebuild countries are certainly not the answer for every failed or failing state; nevertheless, international involvement will be essential in many cases. Other options, even when pursued, will most often succeed when reconstruction capabilities exist and can be used to supplement the measures undertaken.

In essence, the question is not whether the United States and the in-ternational community will have to help reconstruct states, but rather when and how they will do so.

Why 'Postconflict Reconstruction'?

For years, debate in the United States has raged over the concept of na-tion building. Recent military actions in Somalia, Haiti, and elsewhere have renewed the debate; the topic was a major issue in the 2000 presidential campaign; and suggestions to use nation building as a strategy to combat terrorism have reignited the political furor. Although much of the substance of these debates is relevant to a discussion of what to do in failed states and postconflict situations today, reasons for shifting the current debate away from nation building and toward the concept of postconflict reconstruction are several. The latter term is not new—the World Bank has used it since 1995—but it has particular relevance today. The World Bank's definition of postconflict reconstruction focuses on the needs for "the rebuilding of the socioeconomic framework of society" and the "reconstruction of the enabling conditions for a functioning peacetime society [to include] the framework of governance and rule of law."[2] The definition of the term, as used in this article, includes providing and enhancing not only social and economic well-being and governance and the rule of law but also other elements of justice and reconciliation and, very centrally, security.

Postconflict reconstruction capacity, as the term is used in this article, refers to that which is needed to help reconstruct weak or failing states primarily after civil wars. Although many countries also require reconstruction after conventional interstate wars, the challenge is much greater when internal cohesion is questionable. The capacities and approach discussed in this and the following articles, therefore, are addressed principally to the needs following intrastate conflict, even though they might be applied in some cases following interstate conflict.

Using the term postconflict reconstruction to describe current international efforts is preferable to using "nation building" for three main reasons. First, when discussing these issues, as when engaging in operations, it is crucial to recognize the central role of local actors. The citizens of the country in question will build their nation and bring about peace; outsiders can only support their efforts. When discussing international efforts, therefore, the term postconflict reconstruction is perhaps a more accurate representation of the effort: external actors should assist in postconflict reconstruction, not seek to build the nation or state themselves. Outside actors should also be realistic about what they can achieve in the context of a failed state or a devastated postwar environment. The goal, during the short-to-medium run, is to create a minimally capable state, not to build a nation or address all the root causes that imperil peace. Those goals involve a longer-term process that is beyond the scope of what external actors can achieve or lead; actors within the country itself must do so.

A second reason for using the term postconflict reconstruction is its emphasis on overcoming the legacy of conflict. All societies and peoples must build their countries, but only some face the special challenges arising from prolonged, intense, and violent conflict. Many of the rebuilding activities can, and in fact usually do, occur while conflict is still taking place in other parts of the nation. "Postconflict" does not mean that conflict is concluded in all parts of a given country's territory at the same time. The term simply recognizes that most reconstruction tasks cannot be addressed until at least major parts of the country's territory have moved beyond conflict. Therefore, the term postconflict applies to those areas where conflict has indeed subsided, but not necessarily to all parts of a nation's territory.

Finally, "postconflict reconstruction" is preferable to "nation building" because the first term carries less historical baggage. Despite successful efforts in Japan, Germany, and Korea from 1945 to 1960, nation building lost currency during the Vietnam War. Indeed, many of the term's negative connotations are related to that war and to efforts by U.S. armed forces to assemble a "friendly" government as part of the U.S. strategy to win the war. This excessive focus on the military role has carried over to the present day. Presidential candidate George W. Bush, for example, criticized the concept of nation building during the 2000 presidential campaign: "I would be very careful about using our troops as nation builders. I believe the role of the military is to fight and win war and, therefore, prevent war from happening in the first place. ... Morale in today's military is too low. ... I believe we're overextended in too many places."[3] After September 11, the Bush White House has continued to emphasize that the U.S. military is not conducting nation-building efforts in Afghanistan.[4]

In truth, the military is not and should not be the sole or even the principal participant in reconstruction efforts. Although the military may play a crucial role in some cases, a host of civilian actors has a comparative advantage in addressing many of postconflict reconstruction's wide range of needs. Nongovernmental organizations, the private sector, international organizations, multilateral development banks, and civilian agencies of multiple donor governments all have a crucial role to play in addressing governance and participation, justice and reconciliation, and economic and social needs. Some of these groups even have an important role to play on security issues. Given the rapid increase in the number of new international actors; the centrality of indigenous actors owning the building process; and the other demands placed on the limited international supply of disciplined, civilian-controlled armed forces, putting the military at the center of the debate and carrying over polemics that grew out of a bygone era is plain wrong.

What Needs to Be Done: The Four Pillars

In today's world, postconflict reconstruction consists of four distinct yet interrelated categories of tasks, or "pillars":

- **Security** *addresses all aspects of public safety, in particular, creating a safe and secure environment and developing legitimate and effective security institutions.* Security encompasses collective as well as individual security and is the precondition for achieving successful outcomes in the other pillars. In the most pressing sense, providing security involves securing the lives of civilians in the aftermath of immediate and large-scale violence as well as restoring the territorial integrity of the postconflict state.

- **Justice and reconciliation** *addresses the need to deal with past abuses through formal and informal mechanisms for resolving grievances arising from conflict and to create an impartial and accountable legal system for the future, in particular, creating an effective law enforcement apparatus,*

The Battle for Hearts and Minds

an open judicial system, fair laws, and a humane corrections system. These tasks include exacting appropriate penalties for previous acts and building the state's capacity to promulgate and enforce the rule of law. Incorporating the concept of restorative justice, justice and reconciliation efforts include both extraordinary and traditional attempts to reconcile ex-combatants, victims, and perpetrators.

- *Social and economic well-being addresses fundamental social and economic needs, in particular, providing emergency relief, restoring essential services to the population in areas such as health and education, laying the foundation for a viable economy, and initiating an inclusive and sustainable development program.* Often accompanying the establishment of security, well-being entails protecting the population from starvation, disease, and the elements. As the situation stabilizes, attention shifts from humanitarian relief to long-term social and economic development.

- *Governance and participation addresses the need to create legitimate, effective political and administrative institutions and participatory processes, in particular, establishing a representative constitutional structure, strengthening public-sector management and administration, and ensuring the active and open participation of civil society in the formulation of the country's government and its policies.* Governance involves setting rules and procedures for political decisionmaking and for delivering public services in an efficient and transparent manner. Participation encompasses the process for giving the population a voice in government by developing a civil-society structure that generates and exchanges ideas through advocacy groups, civic associations, and the media.

A Strategic Approach to Postconflict Reconstruction

For any postconflict reconstruction effort to succeed, work in these four areas must be carefully integrated. As United Nations secretary general Kofi Annan has noted, "All these tasks—humanitarian, military, political, social, and economic—are interconnected, and the people engaged in them need to work closely together. We cannot expect lasting success in any of them unless we pursue all of them at once as part of a single coherent strategy. If the resources are lacking for any one of them, all the others may turn out to have been pursued in vain."[5]

A coherent strategy is indeed absolutely essential. Although every case is different and must be treated differently, the international community should observe a few general rules if it is to develop a strategy and implement it successfully:

- Primary responsibility and leadership roles must rest with the people of the country in question. At the same time, the local population cannot be left to solve its own problems. The international community can play a critical role in providing assistance.

- A strategic approach based on the constellation of local actors, their interests, and the leadership pool available should focus on how international actors can use their resources to maximize leverage to build a legitimate government, develop key leaders, and progressively marginalize "spoilers."

- Any international presence must address security issues at the very beginning and throughout the course of an intervention. Acceptable security is the sine qua non of postconflict reconstruction. At the same time, security operations must not displace critical initial efforts in justice and reconciliation, social and economic well-being, or governance and participation.

- Unity of effort is crucial. Donors and international actors must establish an appropriate division of labor and plan, coordinate, and execute operations together. Incoherence and competition among outside actors can destroy a local government and society.

- International actors should devolve as much responsibility as possible for strategic direction and implementation to the country teams and unified command mechanisms established among external actors. Trying to keep operational control, of either the military or the civilian side of the intervention, in faraway capitals is a recipe for failure.

- The sequencing and phasing of various parts of an intervention is key. Because every case is different, the international community must develop a comprehensive plan with a logical sequence to support the strategic approach outlined above. In every case-specific strategy, however, the sequence designed must choose areas in which success can be demonstrated early, momentum can be built and sustained, and seeds for success can be sown early in critical areas that may take more time to demonstrate progress.

- The international community's strategy should envision a realistic time horizon and exclude magic bullets or shortcuts. Different actors may be central in different time periods, but the major actors must commit to staying engaged for the duration.

These guidelines are no guarantee for success. Rather, they simply highlight some of the essential lessons that need to be learned and applied in future cases.

The Role of the United States

The United States will often have a critical role to play in international postconflict reconstruction efforts. Obviously, the appropriate U.S. role will vary on a case-by-case basis, depending in large part on the U.S. interests at stake and the role that other international actors choose, or can be induced, to play. When vital interests are at stake, the United States may choose to assume a leadership role, whereas when such interests are absent, the government may choose to make a more limited contribution behind the scenes.

Experience suggests, however, that U.S. leadership can be a critical determinant of an operation's success or failure, given both the unique standing of the United States in the world and the comparatively vast military, political, and economic resources Washington can bring to bear. Bosnia and Kosovo are recent examples of how significant U.S. diplomatic and military involvement turned the tide and created the conditions for success. Perhaps the United States should not take a lead role in every postconflict operation, but the United States often has the capacity to make a difference. Even when it does not, well-targeted U.S. support can make a crucial difference in the success of an intervention, as in East Timor.[6] In yet other cases, such as El Salvador and Guatemala, U.S. engagement as a principal political and financial supporter of a UN-led process can deliver the desired results.

Indeed, when national interests do not support a U.S. leadership role, the United States should not underestimate its ability to catalyze greater burden sharing on the part of the broader international community. When the United States proves its willingness to make a meaningful contribution to an operation, it gives others more confidence in the prospects for success and thus they are often more willing to assume a leadership role and make their own contributions. In short, the United States is frequently in a unique position to motivate others to step up to the plate.

Nevertheless, even when the political will to assist reconstruction exists, most of the current instruments at the government's disposal have been designed to assist the long-term economic and political development of viable states. Providing economic or democracy promotion assistance, for example, requires ministries and recipient institutions that often do not exist in weak or failing states. Likewise, the United States is not prepared to grant trade or other economic benefits unless a local set of institutions can meet a set of standards that almost by definition do not exist in weak or failing states. In this way, we have tied our own hands.

Because the United States cannot afford to address every shortfall in the international community's capabilities to assist in postconflict reconstruction efforts, effective U.S. participation also requires identifying areas where the United States holds a comparative advantage—those capabilities or assets that this country is uniquely or particularly able to bring to the table. U.S. power, for example, gives U.S. negotiators particular leverage in some cases, just as the size of the U.S. market makes enhanced trade opportunities for postconflict countries particularly attractive. Likewise, the global presence and unique logistical and technical capacity of the United States give it a comparative advantage in quick response.

Although the U.S. contribution will vary from operation to operation, decisionmakers will nevertheless have to make judgments about what kind of assistance options they want to be able to make available for future U.S. engagement. This notion of comparative advantage should be central to determining the portfolio of long-term capabilities and mechanisms in which the U.S. government should invest to create those options.

Some in the United States might argue that enhancing U.S. capacity to work in postconflict environments is a recipe for automatically dragging the United States into "other people's messes." In fact, as a superpower with a global presence and global interests the United States does have a stake in remedying failed states. Enhancing our own capacities to deal with them effectively is in our interests. Far from being a recipe to force us to do more in this area, having a clear vision of our comparative advantages and corresponding capacities will give us more, not less, flexibility and leverage to determine what role we should play and what roles other international and indigenous actors should play.

Preparing for the Future

If the United States has learned one thing during the last decade of crises, it is that it cannot wait for the next crisis to begin before it prepares. Even in Afghanistan, where the United States has clear national security interests at stake and high-level governmental commitment, it has used ad hoc mechanisms to address pressing needs. Consequently, the United States has failed to maximize its leverage with both external and internal actors, has lacked coherent responses to certain events, and has been slower, less effective, and less efficient than otherwise necessary.

In order to succeed in the future, the United States must act now. Especially in the post–September 11 environment, the United States cannot wait for the next crisis to try to build its postconflict reconstruction capabilities. Indeed, U.S. leadership will only be credible if the United States gets its own house in order. In some instances, this effort may require new or reformed institutions, while in others it may require new legislative and executive authorities. The U.S. government will need to agree in advance on interagency processes for strategizing and implementing postconflict interventions. It also will need to improve its training capacity so that it fields people prepared for postconflict environments. The United States must also agree on standard operating procedures for coordination in order to maintain operational coherence. Finally, it needs to create funding mechanisms that will allow it to respond in a timely and appropriate manner. It can no longer afford to face every task with nothing but a hammer at its disposal.

The first steps involve identifying the most important issues, the comparative advantages of the United States and other actors, and existing gaps in current capabilities. Because interventions can succeed only if approached holistically, identifying priority gaps in each of the four pillar areas is a good start. The four articles that follow in this issue attempt to do just that. Once the U.S. government has identified key gaps in the areas of security, justice and reconciliation, social and economic well-being, and governance and participation, it will finally be able to prioritize and design a coherent set of U.S. capabilities.

Luckily, the United States will not have to build its postconflict reconstruction capacity from scratch. It already has some key institutions and a wealth of human, organizational, and material resources on which to draw. With a concerted, coherent, bipartisan push, the United States can position itself for the new world that confronts it. The United States should enable itself to catalyze on indigenous and international reconstruction efforts in order to protect U.S. interests. Doing so will also help others to pursue that which U.S. citizens hold most dear—life, liberty, and the pursuit of happiness.

Notes

1. See Robert Rotberg, "The New Nature of Nation-State Failure," *The Washington Quarterly* 25, no. 3 (summer 2001): 85–96 (identifying eight completely failed states). See also National Intelligence Council, "Global Humanitarian Emergencies: Trends and Projections, 2001–2002" (identifying 17 failed countries in 2001 and another 6 countries in immediate danger for failure in 2002).

2. See World Bank, *Post-Conflict Reconstruction: The Role of the World Bank* (Washington, D.C.: World Bank, 1998); Robert Muscat, "The World Bank's Role in Conflict Prevention and Post-Conflict Reconstruction" (prepared for the Task Force on Failed States, World Bank, Washington, D.C., November 27, 1995).

3. George W. Bush, remarks during presidential debate, October 3, 2000.

4. National security adviser Condoleezza Rice stated, "There's nothing wrong with nation building, but not when it's done by the American military." Sebastian Mallaby, "Foundation for a Nation," *Washington Post*, October 29, 2001, p. A17. See also White House press briefing, October 12, 2001; President George W. Bush, CNBC News transcripts, October 11, 2001; Gary T. Dempsey, "Old Folly in a New Disguise: Nation Building to Combat Terrorism," *Policy Analysis* (Washington, D.C.: CATO Institute, March 2002).

5. UN Secretary General Kofi Annan, speech to the UN General Assembly, New York, February 2002.

6. See Robert C. Orr, "Making East Timor Work: The United States as Junior Partner," *National Security Studies Quarterly* 7, no. 3 (summer 2001): 133–140.

Scott Feil

Building Better Foundations: Security in Postconflict Reconstruction

On any given day, tens of thousands of U.S. and international military personnel are engaged in operations that mean the difference between life and death for hundreds of thousands of people. The 1990s saw an expansion of what alternately have been called peace support, peacekeeping, or peace-enforcement operations. Whatever the term, the absence of human security in certain countries and parts of the world emerging from conflict has been a significant and continuing issue that has confronted the United States and the international community. Where U.S. military personnel have been involved in these operations, significant initial progress has been made. People stop killing, and many more stop dying. Although the U.S. military's history is mixed, the record shows that successes outweigh failures, from the significant successes at the end of World War II and the Korean conflict in the 1950s to more modest gains made in Latin America, the Balkans, Haiti, and East Timor. Clearly, the history of Afghanistan and the current situation there illustrate the pressing need to establish the security component of the postconflict equation quickly and permanently. The inability of the international community to create a capable Afghani-

Col. Scott Feil, U.S. Army (Ret.), is executive director of the Association of the United States Army's Program on the Role of American Military Power and codirector of the Post-Conflict Reconstruction Project. A white paper version of this article has been submitted to and reviewed by a bipartisan Commission on Post-Conflict Reconstruction sponsored by CSIS and the Association of the United States Army.

stan in the aftermath of the Soviet withdrawal has had direct and tragic consequences for international and U.S. security.[1]

Postconflict situations, by definition, have at their core a significant security vacuum that is often the proximate cause for external intervention. Indigenous security institutions are either unable to provide security or are operating outside generally accepted norms (i.e., corruption, as in the case of Panama; abuse of power, as in the Balkans; or threats to regional security based on internal instability, as in Africa's Great Lakes region and in Afghanistan). This absence of physical human security differentiates postconflict interventions from interventions conducted solely for humanitarian reasons (e.g., natural disasters), although postconflict situations always have a large humanitarian component.

Undeniably, the four pillars of postconflict reconstruction—security, social and economic well-being, justice and reconciliation, and governance and participation—are all inextricably linked, and a positive outcome in each area depends on successful integration and interaction across them. Yet, security, which encompasses the provision of collective and individual security to the citizenry and to the assistors, is the foundation on which progress in the other issue areas rests. The following definition of security covers the broad nature of those tasks that must be executed and the services that must be delivered, hopefully and eventually, by indigenous actors on behalf of the country itself, but in the interim by outside agencies.

Security as a concept addresses all aspects of public safety, particularly the establishment of a safe and secure environment and the development of legitimate and stable security institutions. Security encompasses the provision of collective and individual security to the citizenry and to the assistors. In the most pressing sense, it concerns securing the lives of citizens from immediate and large-scale violence and restoring the state's ability to maintain territorial integrity.[2] These security tasks may be grouped into the following clusters: control of belligerents; territorial security; protection of the populace; protection of key individuals, infrastructure, and institutions; reform of indigenous security institutions; and regional security.

The role of the external security provider naturally depends on specific circumstances. Indigenous institutions may be able to handle some tasks, so that the international assisting agencies need only support that capacity. In other cases, a country's domestic security apparatus may be unable to perform effectively, forcing outside entities to assume more responsibilities. The goal of the assisting agencies—whether other nations, a coalition, or a mixed government/private partnership—is therefore to execute immediate security tasks that the host nation cannot while reconstructing or strengthening the self-sufficiency of indigenous institutions.

The Security Issue

Just as the absence of conflict is not peace, the imposition of order is not the provision of security. During the last decade, only half of the attempts to stabilize a postconflict situation and prevent a return to large-scale violence have been successful.[3] The potential for a return to violence is so strong that, once international military forces have intervened to improve or stabilize a security situation, they are extremely difficult to extract. Transition to less extraordinary, more traditional forms of long-term developmental assistance, conducted by government agencies such as the U.S. Agency for International Development (USAID), the United Nations Development Program, and the World Bank as well as by civilian engagement by NGOs and private enterprise, often stalls, leading to a two-dimensional problem from both a U.S. and an international standpoint. As conditions improve, international military forces find themselves executing tasks for which their comparative advantage is eroding, yet they are unable to transfer responsibility to either more appropriate international agencies or local actors. They thus end up in open-ended commitments, reducing their strategic flexibility. International soldiers in the Balkans, whose original responsibilities were controlling belligerent groups and countering their actions, are now escorting children to school and conducting drug awareness and prevention training. Although military forces are well suited to coercion, deterrence, and the imposition of order, building a stable security environment in postconflict reconstruction situations has proven costly in terms of both time and money. Much of that difficulty can be traced to an inability to develop, access, organize, and focus U.S. and international capabilities that can contribute to security under these changing conditions.

The basic security question is two-dimensional: who and what must be protected, and from whom?[4] Among the elements to be protected are the general populace (especially the most vulnerable groups, such as women and children); selected key individuals; infrastructure; institutions; humanitarian aid workers; and the intervening security force itself. This focus on protection must couple with a persistent offensive effort to remove the capacity for groups and individuals to engage in illegitimate violence. To control belligerents, any cease-fire must be enforced (either in the context of a larger political agreement or as a confidence-building measure that supports progress to such an agreement). Additionally, comprehensive efforts must be made to disarm, demobilize, and reintegrate combatants either into their hometown communities or into reconstituted or rebuilt military and nonmilitary security forces and organizations (border patrols, customs, territorial reserves, etc.). Territory must be secured through a combination of border/boundary, movement, and point-of-entry controls. Finally, this entire effort must be pursued in the context of regional security initiatives to gain cooperation and prevent unhelpful interference from regional actors. Clearly, this universe of security tasks encompasses much more than a narrowly conceived military role.

Addressing Key U.S. Gaps and Shortfalls

A return to any sense of normalcy depends on the provision of security. Refugees and internally displaced persons will wait until they feel safe to go home; former combatants will wait until they feel safe to lay down their arms and reintegrate into civilian life or a legitimate, restructured military organization; farmers and merchants will wait until they feel that fields, roads, and markets are safe before engaging in food production and business activity; and parents will wait until they feel safe to send their children to school, tend to their families, and seek economic opportunities.

How the intervening force provides this security is of secondary significance, if at all, to the affected population.[5] What is essential is whether this force retains control of the security situation while facilitating a more peaceful and orderly environment and limiting the influence of opponents of the peace process. The question for U.S. policymakers should not be "Do we need robust policemen or constrained military forces?" but rather "How can security be best achieved?"

When a situation is perceived as generally static (accords have been reached) and only slightly more unstable than normal, operations will emphasize efficiency. They will strive to maximize benefits rationally while minimizing risks and costs (including to the security forces themselves) and will consist of a small deployment of minimally armed and constrained forces—so as not to inflame the situation and to present as little affront as possible to the sovereignty of the host nation. In order to meet minimum expected requirements, the intervening forces will need only to "dial up," or add, capabilities to an observer/monitor force. Rwanda in the aftermath of the Arusha Accords in 1993–1994,[6] the Balkans in 1994–1995, and Kosovo in 1998–1999 exemplify this approach.

Alternatively, when the primary criterion is effectiveness and the situation is dynamic and only slightly less violent than during war, intervening forces will use a different approach. Notably in the Balkans in 1995 and 1996, in Sierra Leone in 1999, and in the later stages of operations in Kosovo, ground forces were deployed with the clear capacity to make war and intimidate violent groups. Rules of engagement, not physical capacity, constrained the forces. The security forces thus had the ability both to respond and preempt. Yet, even these extraordinary military efforts, largely successful at the outset, were oriented around belligerent forces and organizations, leaving many of the individual components of the security situation unaddressed, thereby creating long-term security problems. Central actors in the conflict were not held immediately accountable, and members of belligerent organizations reverted to crime as well as corrupt economic and political activities to the detriment of final settlements. Subsequently, rebuilding legitimate indigenous security institutions as part of a minimally capable state did not progress as quickly as possible.

Five key areas offer opportunities to develop, access, organize, and focus capability better to meet pressing security needs:

- unity of effort;

- integrated security forces;

- demobilization, demilitarization, and reintegration (DDR);

- regional security and reconstruction of security institutions; and

- information and intelligence.

UNITY OF SECURITY EFFORT

Dozens of U.S. agencies play a vital role in providing security in postconflict situations. At the national level, the National Security Council (NSC), the Departments of State and Defense, and the Central Intelligence Agency (CIA) are often the lead actors. USAID, the Departments of Justice and the Treasury, and other government agencies are also involved. Although the U.S. ambassador, as a representative of the president, retains overall responsibility for U.S. activity within a given country, the Defense Department has the most robust structure for planning and execution regionally and within a given country. Other agencies in the region may have quite specific responsibilities, rather than broad authorities.

These layers of hierarchy, "stovepipes," and lack of infrastructure create an environment that is not conducive to clear direction and effective and efficient action. Reforms are needed to redress the fragmentation in guidance, planning, and execution of security efforts at the national and regional levels and to provide necessary staffing to the responsible leadership on the ground.

Some headway is being made in this effort. Today, a staff member from Interaction (the umbrella NGO organization) is stationed with Central Command to liaise between military and NGO efforts in Afghanistan. Authorization for this slot will expire, however, in the summer of 2002, and although a single liaison improves information exchange, truly integrated effort requires staff input at the regional command and the operational level for both planning and execution. The U.S. government has integrated staffing between agencies to address specific needs such as those of the counter-drug Joint Interagency Task Forces (JIATFs) established during the 1990s. JIATFs have adapted to integrate staff not only from different domestic agencies, but also staff, equipment, and leadership from the international community. These organizations are based in the United States and are not deployable.

The latest Defense Planning Guidance directs the creation of standing JIATFs within each of the regional combatant commands to assist with planning and the operational control of forces assigned in a crisis or to accomplish a mission in a distant theater of operations. The U.S. Joint Forces Command is crafting the design and operational concepts for these new regional organizations and for a Joint Interagency Coordinating Group (JIACG) located at the regional command headquarters, improving on the model established in the counter-drug JIATF. The new staffs at headquarters and in the field will significantly improve coordination between government agencies and should integrate staff from NGOs that are operating within a region. Establishing an experienced, practiced, and integrated civil-military staff that can conduct assessments, develop operational plans, and provide supervision and centralized guidance to on-the-ground operational organizations will be a major step forward.

Unity of effort also suffers from a lack of consistency in regional responsibilities. The areas of responsibility of different positions within the State and Defense Departments and regional commands do not coincide. For example, while the State and Defense Departments have regional deputy assistant secretaries solely assigned to Africa, the military commander responsible for Africa is also responsible for Europe, parts of Central Asia, and Russia. The military commander (CENTCOM) for the Middle East is also responsible for part of the Horn of Africa. Agencies must therefore plan, operate, and coordinate not only among their own different levels of staff, but also with multiple leaders at each level of other agencies.

To remedy key U.S. gaps and shortfalls, the United States should:

- Provide each regional combatant command's new permanent JIATF with staff to integrate other government agencies, international partners, and the NGO community into its planning and operational functions. The Defense Department should accommodate expanded NGO and interagency staffing at the combatant commander level.

- Integrate USAID's concepts of humanitarian assessment teams and disaster-assistance response teams to include the broader interagency and NGO communities. These assessment and assistance response teams should provide comprehensive assessments of the in-country situation to the NSC, combatant commanders, and the JIACG/JIATF.

- Align the areas of responsibility within the Defense and State Departments, the Joint Staff, and the regional combatant commands.

- Continue to expand military unit training and mission rehearsals and offer participation opportunities to government agencies and NGOs involved in postconflict reconstruction.

INTEGRATED SECURITY FORCES

As conditions change, the overall security situation no longer warrants the large presence of military forces prepared to engage in high-intensity combat with belligerents. This achievement, however, often occurs well before legitimate indigenous security institutions are organized, trained, and equipped to assume security responsibilities. The strains within the intervening military forces as they adapt their roles and force levels to the changing security situation, coupled with the inability of the indigenous security forces to assume increased responsibility, creates a security gap.[7]

To address this gap effectively, organizations that can interact with international agencies and regional state entities must conduct a combination of integrated defensive and offensive measures. The security situation also calls for diverse capabilities—including border patrol; customs support; weapons collection; large-scale (belligerent groups) and targeted (indicted persons) apprehension conducted in coordination with police; and DDR—that do not fall directly within the purview of a military force focused on high-intensity conventional combat.[8]

Conventional wisdom holds that extended peace-support missions degrade a military's combat capability. With combat skills as the core competency of military forces, many have viewed peacekeeping and peace-enforcement operations as "lesser-included cases" ("Soldiers can make peace, but peacekeepers can't fight wars.").[9] This thinking has begun to shift. Some have called for reestablishing not only medium-weight forces that can more rapidly respond while carrying significant combat capability, but also for forces to bridge the capabilities gap between lightly armed and relatively incapable forces that cannot achieve escalation dominance and modernized forces that are tailored for high-intensity combat.[10]

Some countries, instead of trying to emulate the United States in combat capability, have sought to carve out niche functions with a comparative advantage in peacekeeping and peace-enforcement capabilities. The Canadians have gone so far as to shift the central rationale and training focus of their conventional ground forces to preparing for and executing peacekeeping and peace-support operations. Other countries with a tradition of national police organizations that possess paramilitary skills (notably Germany, France, and Italy) offer manpower and training capacity. European countries have had some success with the Baltic Battalion and the Nordic Brigade—multinational forces organized under a broad mission statement that encompasses postconflict peacekeeping and peace enforcement.

A security force with the requisite staffing, organization, and equipment to execute the broad range of integrated security tasks necessary to fill the security gap described above could conduct preemptive measures; support DDR; conduct border surveillance and patrol; engage in crowd control; pursue and engage belligerent groups; and support police apprehensions. Such a force could more effectively accomplish the transition tasks that so often plague postconflict reconstruction efforts, while relieving international military units of many of the operational deployments that allegedly drain combat effectiveness.[11]

To integrate security forces, the United States should mandate the establishment of a bipartisan commission reporting to Congress and supported by the Defense, State, and Justice Departments to examine the feasibility of organizing a U.S. or international integrated security force for use in postconflict reconstruction. The commission should issue recommendations on the structure and integration of this force and the nature of U.S. contributions to its establishment, organization, employment, and sustainment.

DEMOBILIZATION, DISARMAMENT, AND REINTEGRATION (DDR)

Dealing with combatants, whether they are organized in formal national security forces, paramilitary units, or private militias, is one of the most pressing and recurring challenges of any postconflict situation. Failure to respond to this problem adequately and to promote combatants' incorporation into a legitimate security organization, or more frequently a return to civilian life, leads to long-term difficulties across all areas of reconstruction. Although DDR is not a clean three-step process, a viable and seamless strategy must dismantle command and control structures; relocate soldiers to communities; limit the circulation and individual possession of weapons and small arms; and provide employment, educational opportunities, and community reintegration programs. U.S. responsibility and capacity for DDR currently stretches across various government agencies.[12]

To coordinate strategy and promote a more holistic response, the United States should create an office to handle matters concerning DDR. Located within USAID, this unit would possess lead responsibility for developing a coherent strategy for DDR, coordinating it, and managing it financially. The office would include staff from relevant agencies from the State and Defense Departments in order to strengthen planning capacity and the ability to respond to urgent DDR needs.

REGIONAL SECURITY AND RECONSTRUCTION OF SECURITY INSTITUTIONS

The regional context in which reconstruction efforts are undertaken offers both opportunities and obstacles. Although interested regional parties often wield considerable local influence, possess substantial infrastructure, offer proximity, and can act as a source of intelligence and information, they also may be interested in seeing a particular faction represent an important security, cultural, or economic interest that could skew reconstruction efforts. In regions where postconflict reconstruction efforts occur, the mechanisms to channel regional interests into productive and supportive relationships are often limited. The existence of regional security arrangements can help curtail the detrimental influence of those who wish to continue violence or to bend the reconstruction efforts to their own advantage.

Two benefits accrue from enhancing regional security. First, this capacity will provide additional leadership potential when postconflict reconstruction occurs. Put simply, more nations will have the ability to adopt the lead role and intervene to stop or alleviate the conflict at an early stage. Regional interaction gives the United States more confidence in and access to military and government leaders and national facilities. Also, professional security forces that are inculcated with the rule of law and higher standards of conduct reduce the potential for conflict. Beyond bilateral programs, regional organizations can disseminate ethics and skills and build cross-national confidence in tense regions. Successful examples of bilateral and multilateral organizations and training for peacekeeping and peace enforcement include those conducted under NATO's Partnership for Peace initiative, the Multinational Peace Force Southeastern Europe (MPFSEE), and the African Crisis Response Initiative (ACRI).

Peace Corps, which prohibits returning volunteers from working for the agency.

Some current initiatives to remedy these information and intelligence gaps are promising, but they are not yet adequate to the task. Commanders may form humanitarian-assistance survey teams, for example, that can provide initial, up-to-date information on military operations, threat assessments, mapping support, and contact lists, thus sharpening military support for humanitarian assistance. These teams, however, fall short of providing a comprehensive liaison with NGOs. Civil Military Operations Centers (CMOCs) that bring civilian agencies and organizations into military planning, coordination, and execution activities at an appropriate level have been successfully used at the operational and tactical level to exchange information. NGO participation is voluntary, however, and threats to cut military support have at times been used to coerce attendance. Additionally, the CMOC is focused on the operational and tactical requirements of horizontal integration and has no parallel at the strategic or national level.

Technical efforts to manage and disseminate information with the Disaster Assistance Logistics Information System (DALIS) have progressed. This system integrates and tracks logistics requirements and support operations but does not provide "one-stop shopping," a comprehensive picture of the situation on the ground, to NGOs and military and civilian agencies. The United States can improve the sharing of general information without compromising sources or the standings of NGOs.

To increase information and intelligence, the United States should:

- Increase staffing for defense attaché positions and foreign-area officers. Relevant agencies should review their prohibition on employing returned Peace Corps volunteers as analysts and linguists. Using the skills possessed by returning volunteers could protect the status of in-country volunteers and still maintain the impartiality and objective nature of the Peace Corps.

- Give the director of central intelligence the lead in creating a system for sharing information in postconflict reconstruction operations at the national level and between government agencies and the NGO community. The DALIS and other similar systems can serve as models, with the ultimate goal of providing a general information system to selected users on the Internet.

Conclusion

The international community, including the United States, possesses enormous capability to have a positive influence on the security situation in states and regions emerging from conflict. Indigenous populations and agencies remain ultimately responsible for improving and sustaining their situation, and returning the execution of security tasks to the host country must be the paramount objective. In the foreseeable future, calls for U.S. leadership and international participation in postconflict reconstruction will continue. If the United States is to continue to lead the international community and secure its global interests without scattering its military around the globe in long-term deployments in which it does not have comparative advantage, then it must develop and focus military and civilian talent and capabilities to accelerate the transition from external security assistance to sustainable indigenous capacity.

Notes

1. See David Bentley and Robert Oakley, "Peace Operations: A Comparison of Somalia and Haiti," Strategic Forum, INSS, National Defense University, no. 30, May 1995; Steven Metz, "The American Army in the Balkans: Strategic Alternatives and Implications," Strategic Studies Institute, USAWC, January 2001; "Report of the Panel on United Nations Peace Operations," http://www.un.org/peace/reports/peace_operations/docs/part3.htm (accessed April 25, 2002) (hereinafter Brahimi Report).

2. Post-Conflict Reconstruction Project, *Post-Conflict Reconstruction Task Framework* (CSIS and Association of the U.S. Army, May 2002), http://www.pcrproject.org (accessed July 16, 2002).

3. Jean-Paul Azam, Paul Collier, and Anke Hoeffler, "International Policies on Civil Conflict: An Economic Perspective," December 14, 2001, p. 2, http://users.ox.ac.uk/~ball0144/azam_coll_hoe.pdf (accessed July 17, 2002).

The Battle for Hearts and Minds

4. For a discussion of how security concepts have changed with the dynamics of state and nonstate actors, see James Rosenau, "Strategic Links in an Emergent Epoch: From People to Collectivities and Back Again" (conference paper, May 2000); Lloyd Axworthy, "Human Security: Safety for People in a Changing World," April 1999.

5. World Bank, *Voices of the Poor* (1999), p. 186.

6. See Scott Feil, "Preventing Genocide: How the Early Use of Force Might Have Succeeded in Rwanda" (Carnegie Commission on Preventing Deadly Conflict, 1998).

7. William Durch, *Security and Peace Support in Afghanistan: Analysis and Short- to Medium-Term Options* (Washington, D.C.: Henry L. Stimson Center, June 2002).

8. Although the Brahimi report did not recommend a UN force, it did make recommendations on staffing, integrated planning, and rapid deployment. See also Thomas Ricks, "The Price of Power—Ground Zero: Military Must Change for 21st Century," *Wall Street Journal*, November 12, 1999, p. A1; Elaine Sciolino, "Bush Aide Hints Police Are Better Peacekeepers than Military," *New York Times*, November 17, 2000; U.S. General Accounting Office, *European Security: U.S. and European Contributions to Foster Stability and Security in Europe*, GAO-02-174 (Washington, D.C.: U.S. Government Printing Office), November 2001; Ann Scott Tyson, "Wider Mission Stretches Military," *Christian Science Monitor*, May 2, 2002, p. 1.

9. T. R. Fehrenbach, *This Kind of War* (New York: Bantam, 1991). See also Charles E. Heller and William A. Stofft, eds., *America's First Battles: 1776–1965* (Lawrence, Kans.: University of Kansas, 1986).

10. See the Army Transformation Web site, http://www.army.mil/vision/transformationinfo.htm (accessed July 16, 2002). See also Col. Doug MacGregor, *Breaking the Phalanx: A New Design for Landpower in the 21st Century* (Westport, Conn.: Praeger, 1997); Carl Conetta and Charles Knight, *The Logic of Peace Operations: Implications for Force Design*, Project on Defense Alternatives, http://www.comw.org/pda/webun.htm (accessed April 15, 2002).

11. David Jablonsky and James S. McCallum, "Peace Implementation and the Concept of Induced Consent in Peace Operations," *Parameters* (spring 1999): 54–70.

12. See Office of African Affairs, International Security Affairs, Office of the Secretary of Defense, "Policy Options Paper: Improving United States Support to Demobilization, Demilitarization, and Reintegration in Sub-Saharan Africa," May 2002.

13. See Tony Vaux et al., "Humanitarian Action and Private Security Companies: Opening the Debate," *International Alert*.

Michèle Flournoy and Michael Pan

Dealing with Demons: Justice and Reconciliation

After conflict has ceased, societies often lack the mechanisms and institutions for upholding the rule of law and dealing with past abuses— processes that are crucial to rebuilding. Justice and reconciliation, in tandem, must be seen as a central pillar of any assistance for postconflict reconstruction and should receive priority attention early and throughout the life of an operation. Although various efforts to achieve justice and reconciliation can differ greatly in nature, they both establish processes to address grievances, both past and present, in hope of forging a more peaceful future. The past decade of international experience in postconflict assistance suggests that substantial gaps exist in the ability of the United States and the international community to assist in these areas rapidly as well as to develop an integrated strategy to achieve justice and reconciliation. The explosion of lawlessness, corruption, and crime that often accompanies postconflict vacuums can undermine all gains that international assistance makes. Assistance to establish justice must therefore be timely in order to be effective. Indeed, this area has been one of poor performance, if not outright failure, in many interventions.

Michèle Flournoy is a senior advisor at CSIS and codirector of the Post-Conflict Reconstruction Project. Michael Pan is an associate at CSIS and coordinator of the Post-Conflict Reconstruction Project. A white paper version of this article has been submitted to and reviewed by a bipartisan Commission on Post-Conflict Reconstruction sponsored by CSIS and the Association of the United States Army.

Copyright © 2002 by The Center for Strategic and International Studies and the Massachusetts Institute of Technology
The Washington Quarterly • 25:4 pp. 111–123.

Grouping the concepts of justice and reconciliation together may strike some as inconsistent, but the two share a common objective—addressing past abuses and ongoing grievances arising from the conflict. Past atrocities in postconflict societies, such as ethnic cleansing in Bosnia and Kosovo, mass amputations in Sierra Leone, and politically motivated hate crimes in East Timor and Haiti, have demonstrated that the most critical need in the earliest phases of a postconflict operation is often public security, along with the rule of law. Furthermore, postconflict societies often require the introduction of accountability and restorative justice mechanisms to break cycles of impunity and violence. Not only do these procedures prevent the recurrence of conflict, they also provide a valuable forum for individuals and communities to feel a sense of closure and to begin healing old wounds. As Archbishop Desmond Tutu noted, "We could not make the journey from a past marked by conflict, injustice, oppression, and exploitation to a new and democratic dispensation characterised by a culture of respect for human rights without coming face-to-face with our recent history. No one has disputed that. The differences of opinion have been about how we should deal with that past; how we should go about coming to terms with it."[1]

To date, international assistance in the justice arena has focused too narrowly on reestablishing a functioning police force to maintain public safety. This task is indeed critical, but the international community must take a much more comprehensive approach to justice and reconciliation for the intervention to succeed. Specifically, this pillar of postconflict reconstruction should include six key elements: (1) law enforcement instruments that are effective and respectful of human rights; (2) an impartial, open, and accountable judicial system; (3) a fair constitution and body of law; (4) mechanisms for monitoring and upholding human rights; (5) a humane corrections system; and (6) formal and informal reconciliation mechanisms for dealing with past abuses and resolving grievances arising from conflict.

Policymakers and practitioners should make every effort to build on functioning indigenous practices, laws, and institutions that existed before the conflict. *Indeed, the guiding principle for international assistance in the justice and reconciliation arena should always be to seek to empower lo-cal actors and to promote the building of sustainable indigenous capacity while reinforcing respect for human rights and international norms.* In prac-tice, indigenous justice and reconciliation systems must be assessed early in the process to determine what can be salvaged and used and what must be discarded and replaced. Local actors must be given a meaningful role in the design and implementation of programs in order to help ensure sustainability once the period of extraordinary interna-tional intervention ends. Given their poor track record on these issues, the United States and the international community urgently need to reform existing capacities to promote the combined goal of justice and reconciliation better.

Defining Justice and Reconciliation

The justice and reconciliation pillar of postconflict reconstruction in-cludes several distinct but interrelated tasks that may be undertaken during the life of an operation.[2] Four key categories form a useful frame-work for analyzing the U.S. role in supporting credible justice and sus-tainable reconciliation:

- emergency justice measures by international actors to fill the gap un-til indigenous processes and institutions can take over;

- longer-term efforts to rebuild indigenous judicial systems;

- international and national reconciliation mechanisms for addressing grievances and past atrocities; and

- critical predeployment enablers, that is, mechanisms that should be in place prior to external intervention to facilitate a rapid and effec-tive international response.

Emergency justice measures are designed to establish, as quickly as pos-sible, the bare essentials of an interim justice system that can handle the most urgent law and order issues. This effort may involve deploying international police either to monitor and mentor indigenous police forces or, in rare cases such as East Timor, to exercise executive police functions. It may also include the simultaneous deployment of legal experts to help establish an interim legal code, as well as international judges, prosecutors, defense attorneys, and court administrators to help indigenous actors set up interim courts to address immediate issues such as the status and fate of individuals detained by security forces. In this critical period, international institutions should ensure that vital needs in the sphere of justice and reconciliation are properly met. Failure to do so can lead to the loss of gains in areas such as security, governance, and social well-being.

At the same time, the international community should be launching efforts to help develop more permanent indigenous processes and institutions for the administration of justice. Although such assistance usually extends over many years, given the long lead times involved in institution building, the support must be part of the initial response in a postconflict operation. Activities to promote a culture of justice and reconciliation should be transparent and accessible to the broad population in order to support public security and counter any claims of international bias. Typically, international and regional efforts to support the development of a viable rule-of-law infrastructure could include the following steps: development and training of indigenous law enforcement personnel; organization and establishment of an independent judicial system; training for indigenous legal professionals; construction of key judicial infrastructures, including prisons and courts; revision of the constitution and legal codes; and training for indigenous human rights monitors.

A parallel effort to develop and support vital institutions dealing with civil society and nongovernmental activities promoting reconciliation and healing should accompany these measures. The establishment of appropriate liaison mechanisms and ombudspersons for the citizenry should reflect the importance of local feedback and ownership.

Policymakers should also give immediate attention to establishing mechanisms for addressing abuses that occurred during the conflict, such as war crimes or gross violations of human rights. An assessment of the needs of the society in question may indicate that the international community should establish and administer international courts or tribunals to deal with alleged war crimes, to help establish truth commissions to deal with past abuses, and to help create programs to support the rebuilding of communities and the healing and empowerment of individuals. If the international community indeed undertakes such efforts, it should undoubtedly begin as soon as possible but should not expect those efforts to produce instant results. Although judicial institutions are more formal and have a higher profile than civil-society groups and nongovernmental entities involved in extrajudicial dispute resolution, these groups should also receive significant support. Reconciliation initiatives, which are best promoted and implemented by elements within the society, include programs in areas such as public education, mass media, and commemoration, as well as interfaith workshops and cultural exchanges. In this regard, many international organizations are better situated to provide alternative models to meet indigenous needs.

Finally, the United States and the international community should consider the critical enablers that ought to be in place before an actual operation begins; this forethought would facilitate a rapid and effective international response to justice and reconciliation needs. These measures could include compiling rosters of trained personnel available for rapid deployment, advance training in various justice or reconciliation tasks, standard operating procedures and contingency plans in key functional areas, standing capacities for material and private-sector support, and memorandums of understanding and contract vehicles among key international actors.

Addressing Key Capability Gaps and Shortfalls

The United States and the international community have substantial gaps in their capability to provide the justice and reconciliation assistance that may be necessary. Taking a holistic approach to achieving justice and reconciliation in postconflict reconstruction operations can be a Herculean task. Nevertheless, failure to coordinate the delicate and complex relationship between justice and reconciliation carries great risks, as the absence of a viable justice system or adequate reconciliation mechanisms can undermine the security and stability essential to sustainable reconstruction efforts. Because every situation will be different, the international community should have the widest possible range of tools to meet specific needs in an appropriate fashion. Although the United States will not always play a lead role, it should be prepared to provide limited but critical assistance in areas such as training, communications, and logistical support where it has a strong comparative advantage. In many cases, actions taken by the United States will help provide incentives and will demonstrate political support for other international partners that step up to the plate.

U.S. POLICY AND STRATEGY

Perhaps the most fundamental gap in U.S. capacity to assist in the justice and reconciliation arena is the absence of clear policy guidance from the administration on these issues. Previous attempts to organize and implement needed changes within the U.S. government in the area of international assistance for judicial development, including President Bill Clinton's Presidential Decision Directive 71, fell short of their lofty objectives. (The Bush administration has neither adopted nor replaced Clinton's directive, "Strengthening Criminal Justice Systems in Support of Peace Operations." During the Clinton administration's final year, several factors, including the lack of appropriate resources and leadership at the National Security Council (NSC) level, limited the implementation of the directive.)

Currently, no policy basis exists for determining what sort of justice and reconciliation assistance the United States should be prepared to provide, which agencies should have lead responsibility for which tasks, how officials should coordinate interagency programs, and where decisionmakers should make additional investment to improve U.S. capacity in this critical area. Perhaps more troubling, no single office or

individual within the U.S. government is responsible for this set of issues, leading to glaring gaps and improvised responses often dominated
by short-term political goals. This situation is highly problematic at a
time when the proliferation of ad hoc national and international institutions to address long-term justice and reconciliation issues has made
coordination even more critical to preventing the squandering of scarce
financial and political resources.

To fill this critical gap, the administration should:

• Develop and implement a National Security Presidential Directive
  (NSPD) on postconflict reconstruction that addresses U.S. strategy,
  capabilities, and interagency responsibilities and coordination in the
  area of postconflict justice and reconciliation assistance. In addition
  to addressing constabulary force and international civilian police
  (CIVPOL) force issues, this NSPD should define an integrated approach to providing assistance in developing judicial, penal, and legal systems. The directive should also address existing legislative and
  statutory restrictions that impair the efficiency and effectiveness of
  U.S. assistance in this area.

• Establish a Policy Coordination Committee (PCC) for postconflict reconstruction, whose tasks would include developing and coordinating
  strategy for justice and reconciliation activities by the United States.
  Lead responsibility for the PCC should be assigned to a senior director
  at the NSC. This individual would be responsible for leading the interagency process to draft and implement the new NSPD and would be
  empowered to deal directly with Congress. The PCC should also include the offices of U.S. representatives to international institutions
  such as the World Bank and specialized agencies of the United Nations (UN).

RAPIDLY DEPLOYABLE CAPABILITIES

Another critical gap in U.S. and international capacity is the lack of
rapidly deployable capabilities to fill immediate needs for "emergency

justice" temporarily. Within this area, several specific shortfalls are evident. The first is an inadequate mechanism for summoning and deploying appropriately trained international constabulary security forces to safeguard public security until indigenous police forces are able to do so. Although the United States does not have a national constabulary force, a number of other countries, including many of the closest U.S. allies in Europe, have such forces, yet the international community has been unable to gain rapid access to them for postconflict reconstruction operations.

The second shortfall is a shortage of qualified international CIVPOL available for short-notice deployments as monitors and mentors of indigenous police forces or, in rare cases, to exercise executive policing authority. The post–September 11 demands placed on federal, state, and local law enforcement agencies suggest that the United States may not be able to sustain its ability to serve as a major provider of CIVPOL without major institutional reforms. The United States can, however, meaningfully contribute in this area by seeking to improve access to and availability of U.S. expertise in law enforcement.

A third shortfall is the absence of rapidly deployable legal experts who can assist indigenous actors in establishing interim legal codes and interim courts to address pressing judicial issues. Even if the international community manages to deploy adequate numbers of well-trained constabulary and CIVPOL forces rapidly in the future, such forces cannot operate effectively without appropriate laws and courts to hear cases regarding detainment and alleged violations.

A fourth deficiency is the inadequacy of physical matériel, such as generators and transport, required to support judicial initiatives. One of the most critical gaps in material support is the lack of deployable public information assets.

To improve its capability to deploy necessary qualified personnel and equipment rapidly, the U.S. government should:

- Enhance international rapid-response capabilities by launching a diplomatic initiative to increase the availability of national constabulary forces and international CIVPOL as interim guarantors of public security. Specifically, this effort would include endorsement of the European Union's plans to develop a rapid-reaction police force, as well as active U.S. support for the implementation of the UN's Brahimi Report recommendations regarding interim justice capabilities.[3] U.S. agencies could provide training in CIVPOL procedures to countries requesting assistance.

- Design and organize, in cooperation with local and state law enforcement institutions, a civilian reserve police system to support national homeland security needs and postconflict reconstruction. Units from such a volunteer force could be mobilized and deployed on order of the president to serve U.S. national interests in postconflict reconstruction operations. These individuals would have rights and protections similar to military reserve forces.

- Reform the U.S. government's CIVPOL program to take advantage of U.S. comparative advantages. The United States should negotiate agreements with sponsoring international organizations to ensure that U.S. experts in planning, training, organization, and finance are matched with jobs that take advantage of their particular skills and experience. Reforms should include taking steps to assure better quality control and accountability, as well as extending tours of duty to reduce the detrimental effects of high turnover. Furthermore, the White House and Congress should work together to close the jurisdictional loophole to allow for the prosecution of U.S. CIVPOL personnel who commit crimes abroad.

- Promote contracting capacities within the U.S. Agency for International Development (USAID) for rapidly deployable public-information equipment, programs, and experts. Drawing on expertise and experience from nongovernmental organizations (NGOs) such as Internews, USAID should have the ability to help promote justice and reconciliation activities and disseminate legal information through radio, print, and other communication resources.

CAPACITY BUILDING

Similar critical gaps exist in both U.S. and international capacity to assist nations in the long-term tasks of rebuilding or developing judicial processes and institutions. The longest poles missing in this tent are the absence of an agreed, integrated approach to such assistance and the lack of available trained personnel who could be deployed to provide such assistance in a timely manner. The international community also lacks standard operating procedures for assessing justice and reconciliation needs in postconflict societies and mechanisms for gaining access to a wide pool of experts to assist indigenous actors with rewriting legal codes, organizing and operating courts, vetting and training police forces, compensating indigenous judicial officials, strengthening the legal education system, establishing penal systems, and developing a range of nonjudicial reconciliation mechanisms.

Although the United States may not have a comparative advantage in reconstituting judicial systems—especially in countries with civil, as opposed to common, law traditions—it does have significant capacity to provide material support and to assist in the development of bar associations, administrative systems, and units to combat corruption, terrorism and organized crime. For each operation, the United States should conduct an interagency assessment at the outset—one that draws on existing U.S. field personnel, ongoing UN and World Bank programs, and input from local actors—to develop a feasible plan and an integrated approach to building capacity throughout the judicial, police, security, and NGO sectors.

To fill this gap in capacity building, policymakers should:

• Keep the International Criminal Investigation Training Assistance Program (ICITAP) at the Department of Justice while significantly increasing financial support to carry out its mandate. The government should also ensure that the Justice Department's international assistance programs (Overseas Prosecutorial Development and Training [OPDAT] and ICITAP) are better coordinated with other initiatives undertaken by the Department of State, USAID, and the Department of Defense.

- Replace Section 660 of the Foreign Assistance Act of 1961 with new legislation outlining available authorities. Until then, U.S. agency lawyers should take advantage of the often-ignored 1996 "postconflict waiver" in Section 660 to allow U.S. assistance to be used for training indigenous police. Although this step would not automatically assume U.S. involvement in police development, it would allow a more holistic approach to justice institution-building activities in postconflict settings.

- Assign lead responsibility for coordinating private-sector and material support for justice assistance to the State Department's Bureau for Democracy, Human Rights, and Labor (DRL). The bureau's functions in this capacity would include facilitating sister-city bar association partnerships and law school exchange programs, as well as coordinating and disbursing donated or governmental excess property equipment, texts, and furniture. The United States should expand its "space available" programs to include support for courts, offices, and correctional facilities. Working with the Justice Department's Office of Litigation Support, DRL should also design material justice-support packages for procurement on short notice.

- Dedicate a portion of the State Department's human rights budget to discretionary purposes. With appropriate congressional oversight, the State Department would allocate those funds for emerging postconflict reconstruction needs rather than year-old programming. Setting aside $20 million in an already existing DRL account would dramatically improve the surge capacity of justice and reconciliation assistance throughout the entire U.S. government. Funding should be transferred to USAID's Office of Democracy and Governance as necessary to ensure that legal development programs are balanced with civil society–based justice initiatives. Funding should also be used to provide language experts as support for justice and reconciliation efforts in need of translators and interpreters. The government could tap resources at the National Foreign Affairs Training Center, the Foreign Broadcasting Information Center, and the Peace Corps to support these initiatives.

INTERNATIONAL COURTS AND COMMISSIONS

Another set of capability shortfalls lies in the area of U.S. support for both international and national commissions and tribunals. (Current political constraints and U.S. legislative restrictions on the International Criminal Court will limit U.S. engagement to ad hoc international tribunals and commissions.) Despite almost a decade of experience with ad hoc criminal tribunals for the former Yugoslavia and Rwanda, the United States still has difficulty finding appropriate mechanisms to support UN-sponsored initiatives for justice and reconciliation. The vast needs of these initiatives, ranging from evidence collection and legal assistance to adequate funding and qualified personnel, are daunting. Notably, international and local NGOs possess a significant comparative advantage in many of these areas. The issue of disproportionate resources allocated to tribunals compared with those allocated to truth commissions, as well as the disparity in attention and funding for international initiatives and for rebuilding domestic judicial systems, are also worth addressing.

To build support for international tribunals and commissions, the U.S. government should:

- Amend relevant legislation to extend U.S. drawdown authority to support justice and reconciliation institutions based on certification by the president. Current law restricts U.S. assistance to the narrow category of UN-sanctioned ad hoc criminal tribunals. With truth commissions, hybrid tribunals, and specialized UN courts becoming increasingly common in postconflict societies, extending this assistance would have a significant impact at a relatively modest cost.

- Establish a mechanism at the U.S. Institute of Peace or the National Endowment for Democracy to allow tax-deductible, private contributions to UN trust funds to support international tribunals and commissions. Direct contributions to the UN are not tax deductible, unlike contributions to nonprofit organizations and foundations.

- Establish interagency agreements among the State, Justice, and Defense Departments that enable departmental resources, such as the

Armed Forces Institute of Pathology, to provide expert teams in fo-
rensics and evidence collection to help document international
atrocities, such as the past investigations on behalf of the International Criminal Tribunal for Yugoslavia and the International Commission for Missing Persons as well as the portable morgues that were
set up in Kosovo to conduct on-site autopsies.

• Improve the process used to rapidly declassify records on human
rights violations in other countries if requested by international judicial institutions and commissions, assuming release of these records
does not threaten U.S. national security. The Freedom of Information Act, which allows the release of classified documents after 25
years, is inadequate to assist countries investigating past criminal
abuses. Previous attempts, such as the Human Rights Information
Act, have failed to gain the necessary legislative momentum.

CRITICAL ENABLERS

The last set of significant shortfalls lies in the area of critical enablers—
actions that the United States and the international community could
take to improve the speed and quality of their response. Several such
shortfalls are particularly important. Currently, the international community lacks any agreed legal code for use as part of an interim justice
package in postconflict operations. Consequently, every new operation
reinvents this wheel at considerable effort and expense, as well as loss
of valuable time. In addition, no common principles or standard operating procedures are in place to govern the use of CIVPOL, and no standard training or certification procedures have been established. The
UN and other international organizations also lack adequate mechanisms, such as rosters and databases, to gain timely access to trained
and available experts across the range of judicial and reconciliation
functions. These organizations also lack the staff and tools needed for
planning and executing an integrated assistance program in this area.

To develop critical enablers prepared to respond in postconflict settings, the U.S. government should:

- Support Brahimi Report recommendations regarding the development of interim legal codes for ongoing peace operations. Until the report's recommendations are implemented, a nonpartisan institution should convene a commission of international legal experts, including government lawyers and NGO representatives, to develop an international consensus about basic interim laws. The Project on Peacekeeping and the Administration of Justice, undertaken by the U.S. Institute of Peace, is an example of this kind of effort. Furthermore, the government should assist UN efforts to establish common principles, standard operating procedures, and training for CIVPOL, including offering U.S. experts to participate in the effort. When appropriate, the United States should make its training programs available to international CIVPOL candidates.

- Develop and maintain rosters of U.S. judicial specialists, police, penal officers, planners, and human rights monitors who are readily available for rapid deployment to help establish and develop interim justice systems. Responsibility for vetting, background checks, and call-up should be assigned to a stand-alone staff working for the State Department's undersecretary for global affairs, thereby tapping the areas of expertise of the State Department's Bureau of International Narcotics and Law Enforcement Affairs and DRL without creating new administrative burdens for either bureau. A separate roster of mental health and psychological service professionals should be developed to assist the government's interagency teams that are assessing the reconciliation needs of postconflict societies. The government should make these rosters available to the UN Department of Peacekeeping Operations and to the Office of the UN High Commissioner for Human Rights.

- Empower the secretary of state to waive or modify personnel, medical, and other bureaucratic restrictions temporarily on immediately seconding and deploying U.S. government experts to assist critical justice and reconciliation initiatives. The inability of policymakers to meet various federal and state employment requirements often causes unacceptable delays in the internal transfer of federal employees.

- Establish predeployment training to familiarize U.S. experts with international humanitarian law, other applicable international laws, local laws and resources, the requirements of the specific mission, the operating environment to which they are deploying, and existing U.S. government programs and plans already in the area. The National Foreign Affairs Training Center should establish a similar training module and include it in courses for new ambassadors and USAID mission directors.

Conclusion

The damage wrought by mass atrocities and systemic lawlessness usually takes years, if not decades, to repair. The United States does not possess comparative advantages across the entire spectrum of needed assistance, but by enhancing selected U.S. and international capabilities in the key areas of strategy, deployable resources, capacity building, support for international courts and commissions, and critical enablers, it can play a unique and important role in promoting sustainable peace in postconflict environments.

Notes

1. See *Final Report of the South African Truth and Reconciliation Commission*, submitted October 29, 1998.
2. See Project on Post-Conflict Reconstruction, *Post-Conflict Reconstruction Task Framework* (CSIS and Association of the U.S. Army, May 2002), http://www.pcrproject.org (accessed July 10, 2002).
3. See UN Document A/55/305-S/2000/809.

Johanna Mendelson Forman

Achieving Socioeconomic Well-Being in Postconflict Settings

States emerging from conflict are not coincidentally also among the world's poorest. Fifteen of the world's 20 poorest countries have experienced internal conflict in the last 15 years.[1] These wars have spilled refugees over borders, often destabilizing neighboring states. Any visitor to these war-torn societies recognizes that without economic hope peace cannot take hold. Although poverty is not a direct cause of violence or civil war, it is a symptom of the decline of a state's capacity to protect and provide for its citizens.

For postconflict reconstruction generally, success is clearly premised on three conditions: (1) establishing security; (2) restoring good governance, which includes the rule of law; and (3) creating economic opportunity. Recent research on the political economy of developing nations suggests that a good policy environment is essential for economic performance. Good governance is the critical variable in a country's ability to overcome its conflict-ridden past.[2] Despite more than a decade of experience in postconflict reconstruction, the U.S.

Johanna Mendelson Forman is a senior fellow in the Role of American Military Power program at the Association of the United States Army (AUSA) and codirector of the Post-Conflict Reconstruction Project. The author would like to thank Carola McGiffert for her research assistance on this paper. A white paper version of this article has been submitted to and reviewed by a bipartisan Commission on Post-Conflict Reconstruction sponsored by CSIS and AUSA.

Copyright © 2002 by The Center for Strategic and International Studies and the Massachusetts Institute of Technology
The Washington Quarterly • 25:4 pp. 125–138.

government has yet to form a coherent vision for dealing with these tasks. It lacks a deliberate program for linking immediate postconflict needs with medium- and long-term development. Even with the funding available through the U.S. Agency for International Development (USAID), the notion of a smooth transition from one phase of reconstruction to another is still elusive.

Intractable conflict and its economic roots have yet to become a serious subject for congressional deliberation or legislative action. U.S. foreign assistance lacks a focus on conflict prevention. Additionally, none of its tools can handle conflicts driven by resources rather than ideologies. Two major deficiencies that further inhibit U.S. policy to address countries in conflict or with a history of conflict are slow response times in delivering assistance in war-torn countries and any form of flexible credit that would permit local actors to engage in any reconstruction effort. Until recently, socioeconomic tasks were considered part of long-range development assistance programs that could only begin once peace was at hand. We now know that development can take place even when parts of a nation are at war. Research also shows that, at the end of a conflict, a small window of opportunity exists to restore economic hope and social well-being. Without U.S. leadership, it will be lost.

The events of September 11 were central to the U.S. government's rethinking of development assistance. Where once advocating more foreign aid was unpopular, it is now a central feature of President George W. Bush's response to preventing terrorism. As the president has noted, "We must accept a higher, more difficult, more promising call. Developed nations have a duty not only to share our wealth, but also to encourage sources that produce wealth: economic freedom, political liberty, the rule of law, and human rights."[3] This articulation of U.S. development objectives mirrors the work on human security currently underway at the United Nations (UN). It recognizes that poverty alleviation implies not only economic growth, but also personal security as a precondition to any other type of socioeconomic progress.

The Battle for Hearts and Minds

Achieving Social and Economic Well-Being

Of the four pillars of postconflict reconstruction, addressing social and economic well-being is the most varied and therefore the most comprehensive. Ensuring that citizens in war-torn societies can resume a normal existence requires more than just the care and feeding of refugees and the internally displaced. It means providing food security, public health, shelter, educational systems, and a social safety net for all citizens. An economic strategy for assistance must be designed to ensure the reconstruction of physical infrastructure, to generate employment, to open markets, to create legal and regulatory reforms, to lay the foundation for international trade and investment, and to establish transparent banking and financial institutions.

After conflict, certain minimum conditions are necessary to enable a country to progress from decay to development. The following seem essential:

- managing resource-driven conflicts effectively,
- establishing a legal regulatory framework,
- engaging the private sector in reconstruction,
- jump-starting trade,
- establishing basic education services,
- combating HIV/AIDS in postconflict settings, and
- targeting economic conditionality.

Current U.S. Government Capabilities and Gaps

The U.S. government has the capacity to provide humanitarian assistance, recognized as the essential core for saving lives and laying the foundation for social and economic reconstruction. U.S. humanitarian assistance programs, implemented primarily by nonprofit U.S. private voluntary organizations (PVOs) and local nongovernmental organizations (NGOs), are effective for three main reasons. First, they are well organized and funded, allowing them to respond rapidly to both natural and man-made disasters. Second, they have the skills needed both during crises and during the reconstruction process, including emergency management, vulnerability assessments, and development of early-warning systems for disaster preparedness. Third, U.S. government agencies manage short-term relief projects concurrent with efforts to create medium- and long-term economic growth in a rare example of interagency coordination (involving USAID's Office of Foreign Disaster Assistance; the Department of State's Bureau for Population, Refugees and Migration; and the Office of the Secretary of Defense and relevant theater commanders who may be engaged in humanitarian operations). If any issue about humanitarian assistance exists, it relates not to the quality or quantity of U.S. generosity, but to its use as a substitute for diplomatic preventive action and its dissociation from the broader postconflict reconstruction needs that follow a humanitarian crisis.

To achieve economic and social well-being, early assistance in these areas by the U.S. government in coordination with the international community and international financial institutions can help lay a solid foundation for good governance of the economy. Those in leadership positions in affected countries will also need to play an important role in advancing local interests. Bringing stakeholders into the process of economic and social reconstruction will create ownership of both policies and processes. Believing that such a partnership between local and international actors will make it fast or easy to achieve economic development, however, would be foolish. Fragile political environments, the private sector's reluctance to invest in unstable states, the concentration of wealth and resources in the hands of a few powerful figures, the thinness of the financial sector and markets, and weak governance capacity will challenge both external actors and local stakeholders.

EFFECTIVELY MANAGING RESOURCE-DRIVEN CONFLICTS

Research on civil wars in the last decade has pointed to the central role that natural resources play in fueling violence. "War may be a continuation of economics by other means" is a play on Carl von Clausewitz's famous maxim.[4] Civil wars have created great opportunities for profits through underground economies that are often not available during peace. Weakened states, no longer able to manage economic policy and the institutions that govern them, are targets for rent-seeking groups. Criminals engaged in illicit business pay no taxes, and armed groups that can exact cash or resources through extralegal activities act as spoilers to any peaceful conflict resolution. Greed seems to be a key factor in perpetuating civil wars, particularly when providing personal security transforms from a public to a private good. Most citizens lose from war, but a few powerful figures who gain from it can perpetuate fighting. In countries where one natural resource such as oil, timber, or diamonds is a primary export commodity (where export income accounts for more than 25 percent of gross domestic product), the battle to control these resources enhances instability and intensifies conflict.[5]

Despite evidence that reducing the profits of war is one way to restore stability, the U.S. government has yet to develop a coherent strategy that addresses this issue. U.S.-based extractive industries such as mining or oil producers must work with the U.S. government to develop both short- and long-term solutions to this difficult problem. Few if any tools exist to reduce war profits except for the goodwill and responsible action of private corporations. Recently, in Angola the private sector was the one to put Eduardo Dos Santos's government on the spot when an NGO, Global Witness, exposed the discrepancies between the tax revenue collected from oil sales and the revenue reported by the ministry of finance.[6] Transparency in corporate operations and earnings can empower citizens to rally against corrupt, rent-seeking elites. Beyond transparency, a diversified, rather than single-commodity, economy is needed. Development policies that eye economic diversity as a key component of reconstruction may in the long run be the best response to this difficult economic reconstruction hurdle.

To counter the monetary benefits accruing to some from war and remittances, the United States should:

- Encourage the U.S. private sector to develop specific industry-designed codes of conduct on war profits in conflict-ridden countries. As part of this self-regulation, U.S. corporations operating in postconflict environments should promote transparent accountings of their revenues in country so citizens of war-torn states are aware of government revenues from extractive industries.

- Create a public-private trust fund jointly with the World Bank, as part of a natural resources revenue strategy. This trust fund would capture income from international extractive industries operating in postconflict states so that it could be used to meet recurrent costs for essential services and recurrent costs of the government.

ESTABLISHING A LEGAL REGULATORY FRAMEWORK

Creating governing systems that are predictable and impartial, along with establishing economic rules for development, is crucial to any postconflict economic reconstruction. A judicial system must be able to uphold contracts, protect property rights, and ensure that commercial interests have a process that produces reliable and enforceable results. No country can be part of the international economic community without this. Often, the economic aspects of legal reform are treated as secondary to the immediate need to provide justice to victims of war. The two areas, however, are equally important to create the foundation for economic and social rebuilding.

Any legal system must reflect stakeholder laws and traditions, even if the international community plays an initial role in providing technical assistance and resources. Local approaches to justice should integrate existing practices that will provide immediate relief in commercial disputes rather than creating new systems of adjudication that may not be sustainable once assistance ends. USAID has some capacity to support this area, but in the last decade the U.S. government has decreased its assistance in legal regulatory law, delegating this type of assistance to the World Bank, and programming is ad hoc. The Department of Commerce supports some programs to help provide assistance on alternate dispute resolution and for export and trade. Programs in neither agency are geared to dealing with immediate postconflict needs. To solve these problems and implement a legal regulatory framework, the United States should:

• Establish a separate rule-of-law program to help postconflict countries establish basic legal and regulatory systems within USAID's democracy programs. This development should occur as part of its emergency conflict-management activities and part of its larger investment in rule-of-law programming. Such legal regimes must include effective civil codes, not just a criminal justice system.

• Prioritize interagency coordination of legal regulatory activities. The Commerce Department, State Department, USAID, and the World Bank should establish a working group to share information on current activities in postconflict countries. Joint assessment teams should immediately develop one strategic plan for the legal architecture of any reconstruction program to avoid duplication of efforts and wasted resources.

• Increase congressional appropriations to the Treasury Department's Office of Technical Assistance. This change could greatly enhance U.S. capacity to assist countries emerging from conflict to develop the important legal and regulatory architecture for entering the global economic market and for getting their own economies moving. Currently staffed by fewer than 40 people and with a budget of just less than $10 million, the office could provide more technical assistance to postconflict states and further develop banking authorities and financial governance.

ENGAGING THE PRIVATE SECTOR IN RECONSTRUCTION

In any postconflict setting, engaging the local business community is a first step to economic well-being. Those who have survived a conflict, or those who have returned from neighboring states, are often the best hope for restoring local markets and securing local capital for domestic investments. Accordingly, local investment and indigenous business development must receive support, although social spending needs must also be met. The international community may have to support the salaries of the civil service, armed forces, and police, as well as meet pensions and other public-sector obligations. Not only will this action demonstrate the tangible benefits of peace, it will also ensure some stability to those who are essential to restoring economic infrastructure in a postconflict environment.

The international community must also look beyond national economic restoration to consider the importance of local community economic health by investing in microcredit and microlending programs. These initiatives have proven to be important factors in creating immediate access to resources for those affected by conflict. In creating programs for postconflict environments, investment must embrace national incentives to support local business development, while also providing the appropriate type of economic incentives to communities to restore both social and economic capital. All of these efforts lay the foundation for international economic engagement.

Private-sector strategies are not a magic bullet unless U.S. governmental support fortifies them. Instability, coupled with inadequate security, is a major deterrent to international investment. Among the most urgent needs are (1) emergency credit instruments for the private sector; (2) rethinking traditional programs available for normal commercial relations that could be modified for the postconflict period; and (3) specific technical assistance to new governments in need of open markets and support for local investment. Several U.S. government programs to provide emergency credit to exporters exist through the Department of Agriculture. Less emergency credit is available to private investors willing to work in high-risk opportunities because of inadequate programs for the private sector.

Despite certain reluctance by the international private sector to invest in high-risk environments, manipulation of U.S. corporate tax incentives could do much to manage investment risks while also providing medium- to long-range incentives for fostering new markets and international partners. New partnerships between the U.S. government and the private sector would cultivate a better understanding of the needs of countries emerging from conflict.

Wars also create waves of "brain drain." Often the most educated and capable citizens are forced to flee conflict zones, thus robbing states of important human capital and capacity. A return of talent is essential for a country to recover not only its social capital but also its economic growth. Those who leave a country often do not return because restrictive immigration policies of their new homes provide no incentives for them to help their countries after conflict. This is certainly the case under U.S. immigration law. Reversing this loss of talent would go a long way toward creating a capable, economically viable postconflict state.

To increase the private sector's engagement in reconstruction, the United States should:

- Expand support within USAID for emergency microcredit and microlending programs to communities emerging from conflict. The government should coordinate these programs with other efforts of the bilateral donor community as well as those developed by the World Bank. NGOs are often the best, if only, vehicle to provide resource distribution in countries where no banking sector exists.

- Create a specific fund within the Overseas Private Investment Corporation (OPIC) to address emergency high-risk credits to support immediate investments. No one-stop source of credit currently exists for U.S. businesses seeking guarantees to invest in postconflict countries. Both OPIC and the Export-Import Bank (EXIM) have credit criteria too restrictive for postconflict states. This type of a new fund would provide a one-stop credit source for U.S. businesses. It would also waive the requirement that no U.S. jobs be at risk, as the type of jobs created in postconflict states would not be detrimental to U.S. labor interests. The fund could designate countries that are important to U.S. national interests so that investors for places such as Afghanistan could be eligible for access to investment guarantees.

- Give U.S. embassies in postconflict countries additional economic officers whose responsibilities would include supporting investment opportunities and providing intelligence on the potential risks and benefits for the private sector. Contracting specialists for this position would be a fast and convenient way to get business-sector talent to a region quickly. This approach would complement the Commerce Department's U.S. Commercial Service, whose mandate is geared to normal commercial relations.

- Support training through USAID for business students seeking experience in managing postconflict reconstruction. A fellowship program, to include internships in key private-sector enterprises, would support greater understanding about the demands and potential opportunities of high-risk environments.

- Request the Immigration and Naturalization Service to review its immigration rules for U.S. permanent residents who would like to participate in "return of talent" programs to countries undergoing postconflict reconstruction. A simple regulatory fix could encourage many permanent residents to return home for extended stays by creating a release from their necessary time-in-class requirements for U.S. citizenship. No such waivers currently exist, thus inhibiting U.S. permanent residents from participating in reconstruction and development.

JUMP-STARTING TRADE

Opening domestic markets to foreign exporters, however, should go hand in hand with U.S. efforts to engage foreign businesses in commercial trade ventures. Developing countries are the fastest-growing export markets for the United States and will soon account for 40 percent of global trade.

Breaking down trade barriers in Africa and Asia could provide important incentives to U.S. businesses. Trade initiatives could support significant investment opportunities in such places as the Balkans, East Timor, Angola, or Afghanistan. Today, the U.S. government has ways to grant developing countries increased market access and beneficial trade preferences. For example, Preferential Trade Waivers would be useful in postconflict environments because they offer unilateral trade preferences on exports entering the United States. The Caribbean Basin Initiative (CBI) of 1983 and the African Growth and Opportunity Act (AGOA) of 2000 provide models for duty-free and reduced-duty treatment. CBI and AGOA both seek to expand foreign and domestic investment in nontraditional sectors, to diversify beneficiary country's economies, and to expand those country's export bases.

To jump-start trade with postconflict economies and promote local investment, the United States should:

- Expand the mandate of the Trade Development Agency (TDA) to include specific funding mechanisms to assess the private-sector investment climate in countries emerging from conflict. This task would involve establishing the specific authority for providing information to large international corporations on opportunities and risks in these countries.

- Grant authority to the Small Business Agency (SBA), which currently supports technical assistance to developing nations, to expand its work in postconflict countries, developing specific programs to support expatriates residing in the United States to develop businesses at home. SBA programs could also be expanded to train local entrepreneurs in ways to reach U.S. import markets.

- Authorize and fund a new version of the CBI tailored to postconflict states, using the CBI and AGOA models. Such a fund could have a limited time frame of two years, but would also provide incentives for importers to work with businesses in those sites and help U.S. commercial interests gain access to potential markets. Successful participation in such an initiative could also lead to qualification for beneficial trade preferences through the General System of Preferences program, a medium-term goal.

- Establish a postconflict capacity to address potential investment opportunities for U.S. businesses with the U.S. Commercial Service. The service currently addresses only trade promotion in normal commercial environments and does not have the capacity to address postconflict economic environments.

- Establish a specific subcommittee on postconflict states for addressing trade- and investment-related issues within the Trade Policy Review Group under the auspices of the Office of the U.S. Trade Representative (USTR). This subcommittee should develop a policy framework for the U.S. government for states emerging from war.

ESTABLISHING BASIC EDUCATIONAL SERVICES

Wars disrupt education, thereby reducing a state's long-term capacity to grow economically. In postconflict environments, no consistent approach exists for this type of assistance. During the last decade, education assistance has decreased, relegating it to a minor component of development assistance. The net decline in literacy that accompanies economic downturns and wars demonstrates the need. A state's inability to support basic education also leaves room for religious schools that exclude women or indoctrinate young men to elevate violence as a political means.

Restoring education immediately after conflict sends a signal of hope to families whose lives have been turned upside down. In Haiti, for example, restoring schools in almost every district in 1994 and 1995 sent a powerful sign to Haitians that life had begun to return to normal. Returning children to school also has an important deterrent power. Removing young men from the streets limits opportunities for militias to recruit. Schools also provide employment for many individuals in a community.

To improve the human capital of postconflict societies, the United States should:

the elected leadership delivering indicted war criminals to the International Criminal Tribunal in The Hague.

To condition its aid more effectively, the United States should:

- Increase use of targeted conditionality to ensure that spoilers are hit the hardest through economic restrictions and other types of targeted approaches, such as travel sanctions and asset freezing, that harm only those who pose a threat to reconstruction.

- Review the structural adjustment conditionality that the International Monetary Fund imposes for its impact on U.S. government interests. Both the Treasury and State Departments should work with USAID to measure the impact of these conditions on U.S. development strategies for postconflict societies. The U.S. government should use its leverage to prevent further economic disaster.

Getting Our Own House in Order

The seven conditions noted above require the U.S. government to get its own economic house in order when developing a reconstruction strategy. The U.S. government lacks an overarching vision, speed in responding to economic reconstruction, and adequate emergency credits to stimulate exports and investments. Overcoming these obstacles will require central, coordinated leadership at the highest levels of government. Current U.S. government assistance programs in postconflict reconstruction fall short by not linking short-term economic and social needs with long-term development objectives. Yet, precisely those good-development practices that invest in economic growth within transparent administrative environments will allow an economy to flourish and make the difference between failure and potential growth.

A gap also exists between the onset of emergency programs put in place by U.S. military forces when a conflict has just ended and the start of programs that address transitional economic needs. Inadequate information sharing, resource gaps, and a lack of systematic procedures complicate transference to the private sector, to the U.S. government, or to other bilateral development programs. Too often, the overwhelming nature of rebuilding a country that has been at war for a number of years has far outpaced the U.S. government's capacity to respond in any holistic way. Emergency humanitarian assistance that saves lives or quick economic-impact projects that create jobs and some community credit may exist but these short-term programs are often not sustainable. Success will depend on integrating the skills and capacities of different U.S. government civilian agencies. Without this comprehensive, long-term approach to social and economic well-being, external assistance is unlikely to prevent the recurrence of future conflict.

Since September 11, the U.S. government has recognized the ease of money transfers intended for nefarious purposes. Diasporas have frequently provided a resource that has fueled conflict in war-torn states and also supported terrorism. Foreign remittances have not only supported families in need of assistance, but also provided money to purchase weapons and salaries to sustain fighters in places such as Kosovo, Somalia, Northern Ireland, and Croatia. In light of recent events in Afghanistan, much remains to be done to limit diaspora money that helps support and sustain fighting.

To strengthen the effectiveness of its economic assistance programs, the United States should:

- Create an economic rapid-response capacity for economic recovery housed at the NSC. An Office for Economic International Security would help bring together all the relevant tools of the U.S. government in a timely manner, including a roster of private companies prepared to work in postconflict emergency environments. It would facilitate coordination between international financial institutions; the State, Treasury, and Commerce Departments; USAID; USTR; the TDA; EXIM; and OPIC to provide centralized and coherent responses to the immediate reconstruction needs.[7]

- Establish a regulatory mechanism within the Treasury Department to oversee the international distribution network for remittances. Such an office would provide citizens of foreign countries with a more reliable and secure means of receiving funds from accredited agencies while also preventing money from reaching the hands of illegal organizations from the outset.

- Create a memorandum of understanding between the Treasury and Defense Departments to monitor ongoing economic crises jointly. In postconflict environments, the U.S. military is often left to extract U.S. nationals from an economic meltdown. Working with the Treasury Department to establish an early warning system for economic crises would help the Defense Department plan for potential hot spots where a military operation might be necessary.

Conclusion

Crisis is part of the development process, and man-made disasters have often set back development gains. Integrating humanitarian programs with programs that look toward more stable and sustainable development is thus the best approach to recovery and reconstruction. U.S. leadership is needed to support programs that achieve sound economic governance and address the immediate needs of countries emerging from conflict. Effective measures to start a country's economic engines will ultimately prevent conflicts and help restore social capital. As the events of September 11 made apparent, the United States ignores the social and economic well-being of postconflict states at its peril.

Robert Orr

Governing When Chaos Rules: Enhancing Governance and Participation

In many cases after a conflict, a country has neither a legitimate government in place nor agreement on how to arrive at a process to determine what constitutes a legitimate government. Even if a government is in place and many of the country's citizens deem it legitimate, war and the attendant chaos often render its ability to deliver services to the population virtually nonexistent. At the same time, many citizens are hesitant to become overly involved in the political rebuilding process, having been conditioned by wartime realities to defer to individuals who exercised authority through the barrel of a gun. In addition, potential spoilers—those with an interest in undermining both a peace accord and the development of a new order—abound.

Arguably, the single most important factor that determines the success or failure of a postconflict reconstruction effort is the extent to which a coherent, legitimate government exists—or can be created. Having such a government is key to providing essential security, justice, economic, and social functions and to channeling the will, energies, and resources of both the indigenous population and the international community. Because little in the way of legitimate, capable government often exists in the wake of conflict, however, the international commu-

Robert Orr is a senior fellow at CSIS and codirector of the Post-Conflict Reconstruction Project. A white paper version of this article has been submitted to and reviewed by a bipartisan Commission on Post-Conflict Reconstruction sponsored by CSIS and the Association of the United States Army.

The Washington Quarterly • 25:4 pp. 139–152.

The Battle for Hearts and Minds

nity must find ways to support this indigenous self-governing capability. The effort involves at least three sets of activities: (1) helping to support a process for constituting a legitimate government; (2) enhancing the government's capacities; and (3) helping to ensure broad participation in the government and the reconstruction process. All these steps are crucial to the political process of maintaining peace by identifying and progressively isolating potential spoilers and their independent bases of power.

While seeking to build up local governance and participation capacity, the international community must observe the cardinal rule of governance: indigenous ownership of the process is key. Even when local actors are disorganized and disempowered in the wake of conflict, they must be given a leadership role in the rebuilding process. Likewise, even when international actors must assume certain functions temporarily, they should always train and empower indigenous counterparts.

Unfortunately, the international community's existing instruments for undertaking activities to enhance governance and citizens' participation are poorly adapted to the special requirements of postconflict environments.

Governance and Participation

Good government requires an interactive two-way process between the government and the governed. The first challenge is to ensure that the government has the ability to deliver the security, economic, social, political, and justice goods that the population demands—the top-down process that will be called "governance" in this paper. As the term is used here, the definition of governance is consistent with definitions used by the U.S. Agency for International Development (USAID) and the United Nations Development Program (UNDP). According to USAID, "Governance issues pertain to the ability of government to develop an efficient and effective public management process ... [that is able] to deliver basic services."[1] According to the UNDP, "Governance is the exercise of economic, political, and administrative authority to manage a country's affairs at all levels and the means by which states promote social cohesion, integration, and ensure the well-being of their populations. It embraces all methods used to distribute power and manage public resources, and the organizations that shape government and the execution of policy."[2] The UNDP definition contains an additional quality, one that can be considered the essence of participation: "It encompasses the mechanisms, processes, and institutions through which citizens and groups articulate their interests, exercise their legal rights, meet their obligations, and resolve their differences."[3] The World Bank's definition of governance—"the manner in which power is exercised in the management of a country's economic and social resources"—is significantly narrower than the one used in this article.[4]

In postconflict situations, building the capacity for governance involves a broad range of tasks.[5] Frequently, fundamental agreement on how the political system should be structured, or even who should have a say in helping to design it, is lacking. In these cases, "national constituting processes" are often key—whether they are called a national dialogue, a constitutional convention, or a *loya jirga*. In some cases, governance may require creating a transitional administration to exercise power before a new legitimate regime can take office. Another set of governance tasks consists of strengthening institutions, either in the executive branch or the legislative branch, that deliver goods to the population at the national or local level. A final major challenge involves ensuring transparency in the delivery of goods and services. Indeed, unaddressed corruption can severely undermine all other efforts.

The second essential component of good government is the ability to enable citizens to make their views heard and to act on those views—a bottom-up process referred to as "participation" in this article. Participation encompasses the processes that give the population a voice through formal governmental mechanisms such as elections and political parties and through the development of a vibrant civil society, including the generation and exchange of ideas through advocacy groups, civic associations, and the media.

Even though the top-down process of governance and the bottom-up process of participation can be separated analytically, in practice they are intimately related. Transparent, effective governance is difficult to achieve if participation is insufficient to ensure that government programs respond to the will and needs of the people and remain channeled toward public, not private, ends. Likewise, participation produces little if a government is incapable of delivering basic security, economic, social, justice, and political goods to the population. Only through encouraging sufficient participation and ensuring effective governance can a government establish a degree of legitimacy and stability over time.

Current U.S. Approach and Capabilities

During the last decade, attention to governance and participation has expanded dramatically. Bipartisan recognition that democracy is consistent with U.S. values and interests has led to explicit programming to promote democracy, with a budget approaching $1 billion annually. (The Bush administration has requested $963.3 million for democracy and governance activities in fiscal year 2003: $200 million for USAID democracy and governance programs, $251 million in Economic Support Funds used for similar activities, $277 million in democracy and governance-oriented assistance for Eastern Europe and the Balkans, and $236 million for similar assistance in the independent states of the former Soviet Union.) Even though the United States initially led the charge, programs to promote governance and democracy have also emerged among a number of European donors, at the UN, and at some regional organizations such as the Organization of American States. On the developmental side, the World Bank and other multilateral development banks are increasingly integrating governance concerns into their development programming.

This activity has vastly improved the capacities of the United States and the international community to engage in these issues. That said, the international community is rather poorly prepared to address the special challenge of governance and participation in postconflict settings. As indicated by where most U.S. "democracy" money is spent, the democracy promotion paradigm was developed over the years principally in Eastern Europe and Latin America. Not only do most of today's postconflict challenges take place in environments quite different from those formerly Communist and authoritarian regimes, but they also lack the greater institutional capacity and resources upon which those regions could draw. In addition, current challenges inhibit resolution of a whole range of additional problems arising from the legacy of protracted armed conflict.

All too often, governance efforts in postconflict settings have boiled down to supporting formal election processes (allowing the international community to leave after a legitimate government has been elected), complemented by inchoate attempts to build civil society by funding a wide range of nongovernmental organizations (NGOs). From Cambodia to Angola to Haiti, this minimalist approach to governance as an exit strategy has led to crucial reversals of peace processes, costing thousands of additional lives and wasting millions of international dollars, time, energy, and credibility. Establishing a comprehensive approach to governance and participation, one that addresses the full range of institutions and tasks and presupposes support that will last beyond the first election, is necessary.

Addressing Key Capability Gaps and Shortfalls

If peace is to be sustainable in more cases, outside assistance for governance and participation activities must be improved in five areas:

- supporting national "constituting processes";
- mobilizing broad peace constituencies and civil society actors to progressively marginalize spoilers;
- building state capacity, particularly civil administration;
- addressing corruption; and

- crafting a coherent system of conditionalities to support good governance and peace.

SUPPORTING 'CONSTITUTING PROCESSES'

As violent conflict comes to a close, establishing the forthcoming order usually requires resolving a number of fundamental questions: What should the new political structure be? How is power to be shared or administered during the transitional period? Who are the citizens of the country? What are the rights and responsibilities of citizens and of former combatants? Sometimes, a peace accord at least partially answers these questions; in other cases, peace accords create or call for processes to answer these questions; in still others, existing political structures are expected to work out the uncertainties. Regardless of the form of the peace process in question, some sort of "constituting process" is always needed to answer these fundamental questions.

The role of outside actors in these processes can be decisive. Choosing which actors to recognize, which ones to work with, and what processes and projects to support can tilt the balance of power either toward or away from a stable peace. Although choosing sides in internal power struggles does not generally produce the desired consequences, establishing clear ground rules and acting accordingly can often have a strong positive effect. Ultimately, for a new government to survive and thrive, its own citizenry and the international community will need to perceive it as legitimate. This outcome involves a careful balancing act of attempting to conform to two different sets of standards—international standards of respect for the peace agreements, the rule of law, and a range of other international norms and practices; and local standards based on recent history, traditional political practices, the local balance of power, and acceptability of working with outside players.[6]

Despite the fundamental importance of outside actors in many constituting processes, external assistance for these types of activities is paltry, and what exists is currently handled in an uncoordinated, ad hoc manner. Special envoys are often dispatched without clearly articulated mandates, training, or any significant means of supporting the political processes. Coordination among envoys is left to happenstance. Little direct linkage exists between the individuals who negotiate the hard political questions and those who support the long-term political and economic developmental process that will implement the solutions. Expertise in this highly specialized area of nation design is widely dispersed, with few mechanisms for retaining it on call. Additionally, following negotiations to end a conflict—a process that tends to be highly centralized—finding the same level of coherence among the international actors to implement agreements among the parties or between the parties and the donors is rare.

Given these realities, the United States should:

- Create new "director of reconstruction" (DR) posts responsible for directing U.S. efforts in specific countries in which the United States has intervened (i.e., a "U.S. director of reconstruction for Afghanistan"). Unlike traditional special envoys who negotiate or shepherd political agreements, these DRs would be responsible for implementing large, multidisciplinary U.S. government programs after an agreement has been reached and, as such, should be people with significant operational experience. The posts would be lodged in the Department of State but the logistical and operational authorities and capabilities of USAID and the Department of Defense would support them. Interdepartmental memorandums of understanding and standard operating procedures should be drafted and approved so that they are all in place prior to the appointment of a specific DR.

- Create an integrated mechanism within the State Department and USAID to support special envoys and DRs. This action would require a line item in the State Department budget (initially set at $5 million) to fund the operations of various special envoys and DRs and the establishment of a small support unit under the secretary of state's auspices to provide functional expertise to these posts, as well as to serve as a repository of lessons learned and a link to standing capacity within the system (i.e., the State Department's regional bureaus and Legal Affairs Office; USAID's regional bureaus and Bureau of Democracy, Conflict, and Humanitarian Assistance; and the Defense Department's logistical operations).

- Develop and maintain on-call lists of people with experience in negotiating settlements, designing new political orders, and writing new constitutions. Within the U.S. government, this responsibility should be vested in the support unit for special envoys and directors of postconflict reconstruction identified above.

- Streamline State Department and USAID disbursement processes for monies required to support the initial establishment of governments constituted by legitimate processes.

- Increase support for ongoing initiatives to strengthen the roles and capabilities of the UN special representatives of the secretary general (SRSGs) and build broad support for them among UN member states. This step would involve authorizing a more direct, more central, and better-funded role for SRSGs in postconflict countries. They can no longer be expected simply to pick up UN agency scraps as they try to establish a coordinated international position on sensitive political questions.

MOBILIZING DISENFRANCHISED SECTORS OF THE POPULATION

Peace and democratic development depend on incorporating marginalized constituencies into a new political order. Armed conflict tends to heighten political exclusion of all but certain political elites and armed combatants. Enabling disenfranchised groups to begin to play a role in determining the country's direction and mobilizing them to defend a new peaceful order not only facilitates democratic development but also provides the means to progressively squeeze armed combatants, warlords, and other spoilers out of the picture.

Previously marginalized noncombatants stand to gain the most from peace. Mobilizing "peace constituencies" (often including women and politically disenfranchised groups), however, is difficult. Armed combatants, warlords, and political elites frequently strive to protect their privileged positions by keeping political decisionmaking processes highly circumscribed. The disenfranchised groups often hang precariously on the edge of being able to sustain themselves; they therefore focus on immediate survival needs rather than on political participation. In addition, wartime conditions have often so beaten down these constituencies that they are bereft of hope.

Mobilizing the disenfranchised requires, first and foremost, providing them a concrete basis for hope as well as incentives for participation. Their material needs far outstrip the ability of the local government or international community to meet them in their entirety; as a result, initial programs need to target top priorities for these constituencies and provide for processes whereby these individuals themselves determine how international monies are spent in their communities.

In recent years, both USAID's Office of Transition Initiatives (OTI) and the World Bank have developed programs and methodologies for getting small amounts of money to villages quickly. By making the money available for any type of development priorities, as long as the village pursues an inclusive participatory process in determining those priorities, OTI and the World Bank (at least in some cases) have been able to show results quickly, broaden participation, and build support for peace. The challenges now are to extend these programs to reach more local communities, to find ways to translate participation at the local level into comparable participation at the national level, and to mesh them more effectively with longer-term development programs.

To mobilize the disenfranchised sector of the population, the United States should:

- Enhance support dramatically for quick-disbursing community-based approaches that can immediately reach grassroots constituencies and provide them with the means to enhance the participation of marginalized actors at the local level. The easiest way to accomplish this goal is to increase OTI's budget for this purpose.

- Charge OTI with ensuring linkage of these local processes to a national peace implementation strategy (created by the government, in conjunction with donors) through funding the participation of local actors in national constituting and peace implementation processes, including paying for their transportation, lodging, and other types of logistical and administrative support.

- Instruct the U.S. executive director to the World Bank to request a study of community-based approaches used by the World Bank. Based on the study's conclusions, the U.S. government should be prepared to increase support for participatory models for World Bank and other multilateral development bank programs by working out cooperative agreements at the country level. Given the lack of field presence by the World Bank and multilateral development banks, these programs should be implemented through NGOs. Doing so is not only likely to improve immediate success rates and free the World Bank to focus on its comparative advantages, it may also help to build crucial institutional links between these programs and long-term development programming.

- Develop a strategy and capacity within USAID civil-society promotion programs for designing and funding projects that enhance the standing of disadvantaged groups at the earliest possible stage of the reconstruction process. This effort should involve, but not be limited to, bolstering political parties through NGOs such as the National Endowment for Democracy, the International Republican Institute, and the National Democratic Institute; ensuring free information flow; and targeting the marketing of at least some programs and opportunities to these groups.

BUILDING SUSTAINABLE CIVIL ADMINISTRATION CAPACITY

In the wake of conflict, states, if they exist at all, tend to have very little ability to deliver goods of any kind to the bulk of their population. Any new government must earn the support of its people—enabling it to marginalize spoilers and supplant parallel power structures—by building sufficient state capacity to begin delivering basic security, justice, economic, social, and political goods to the citizenry. Although security and justice are essential for establishing fundamental order, they are not sufficient. The state's legitimacy and effectiveness also depend on its ability to provide a simple set of rules and structures that help to organize basic political, economic, and social life. No institution is more central to providing this structure than plain civil administration at the district, provincial, and national levels.

U.S. democracy and governance programs have four principal objectives: (1) to strengthen the rule of law and respect for human rights; (2) to develop more genuine and competitive political processes; (3) to foster the development of a politically active civil society; and (4) to promote more transparent and accountable government institutions.[7] Even though these goals are laudable, consideration of the more fundamental question facing postconflict societies—building basic state capacity to deliver essential public goods—is largely absent. Programs intending to strengthen local government exist, but are quite limited and not complemented by any similar focus on enhancing the capabilities of the executive branch of central government.

The other major players in this arena—the multilateral development banks—do have programs dealing with civil administration; these tend to concentrate on reforming public administration, however, with a focus on cutting bloated bureaucracies to save on government costs. For example, the focus of the World Bank's 169 operations to reform civil service in 80 countries between 1987 and 1998 "has been and remains on addressing fiscal concerns ... [by] reducing wage bills, compressing salaries [and] reducing employment."[8] This approach does little for postconflict settings, where the primary concern is building enough government capacity to deliver basic services. One critical area where the World Bank has made a significant contribution is that of reforming tax systems—one of the key elements of revenue-generating capacity necessary to sustain the ability of a state's public administration to function effectively. In fact, during the 1990s approximately 120 of the World Bank's loan operations in 67 countries had components involving the reform of some aspect of the tax system, at an outlay of about $13.9 billion.[9] Despite extensive experience, however, a comprehensive study of these programs concluded, "Background work is essential to improve Bank assistance for revenue administration [and] a strategy needs to be articulated for the Bank."[10]

To help build a sustainable civil administration capacity in postconflict states, the United States should:

- Create a mechanism for fielding U.S. civil administration experts, including seconding federal government employees, and recruiting and paying state and local officials. The United States should also build a mechanism for assembling interagency, interdisciplinary teams that specialize in building civil administration capacity. Because this activity is primarily developmental with a focus on building indigenous capacity, USAID should establish and Congress should support a line item for these activities, and USAID should develop a core of specialists to lead the U.S. government's civil administration efforts. The USAID civil administration unit should also work with other donor governments whose civil administration systems and capacities may be different than our own. In some cases, working with another government whose system is more like the one of the postconflict country may be more productive.

- Instruct the U.S. executive director to the World Bank to urge the Bank to enhance the capacity-building elements of its civil-service reform programs and to develop a strategy for reforming tax systems and building them from scratch in postconflict countries.

ADDRESSING CORRUPTION

Corruption is endemic in virtually all postconflict societies. Weak institutional structures, patterns of behavior exacerbated by war, a semilawless environment, and a shortage of well-paying jobs combine to create a hothouse environment ripe for corruption. The prospect of infusions of new money from the outside world during peacetime only heightens the challenge and the stakes. In addition to threatening economic reconstruction, corruption jeopardizes the country's political stability and its prospects for peace. Corruption not only siphons money from needed government services, it scares off investment, inhibits economic development, empowers spoilers, and leads to a dangerous lack of confidence in the new order.

Since 1994, the international community has begun to talk about corruption much more openly. The UN, the World Bank, the U.S. government, and many other donors have developed programs to combat corruption. New international NGOs aimed at eliminating corruption—Transparency International, for example, with local chapters in more than 90 countries—have come into their own.

No single solution exists to combat corruption; a comprehensive approach is required. Different institutions have approached this dilemma in various ways, but at a minimum, the anticorruption package should include (1) serious self-policing among donors; (2) building anticorruption institutions (inspector generals, ombudspersons, civil service training); (3) passing legislation; (4) developing rule of law programs; (5) establishing strong enforcement mechanisms; (6) monitoring; (7) developing free media and civil-society mobilization; and (8) improving the transparency of the government budgeting processes.

To address the problem of corruption in postconflict states, the United States should:

- Develop a set of procedures with international financial institutions and the UN to share information and collectively sanction entities found guilty of corruption. This effort would involve everything from terminating contracts and sources of financial support to freezing assets and enforcing targeted smart sanctions, as well as pursuing legal cases against individuals and entities guilty of corrupt practices.

- Develop a comprehensive set of resources within USAID's anticorruption programming specifically designed for postconflict countries that have little or no infrastructure. This step will require a significant institution-building component (i.e., establishing ombudspersons and inspector general offices as well as strong civil-service programs).

Through USAID, the U.S. government should also provide more support for a range of local and international watchdog NGOs that keep an eye on corruption by local and international actors and should sponsor information-sharing networks that build the anticorruption movement into a permanent fixture of international society.

- Support the free flow of quality information by building institutional centers like the Center for Public Integrity in the United States, which sponsors the work of investigative journalists; by providing technical assistance for designing and implementing information programs via all means of communication; and by ensuring a capacity to tap into U.S. agency expertise on such important decisions as allocating radio spectrum and television licenses; and, in extreme cases, by blocking "hate" media that has the potential to drive a country back into conflict.

CRAFTING AN APPROPRIATE SYSTEM OF CONDITIONALITIES

Although the international community has long used conditionality on developmental assistance to promote macroeconomic goals and transparent economic-related governance, conditionality related to politics or democracy has been much more controversial. Some analysts have pointed out that good political governance is a worthy objective and is also essential to ensuring the effective use of foreign assistance monies; they have therefore argued that political governance is a legitimate target for conditionality. Others have argued that politics is the sole province of the citizens of the country in question and thus should not be subject to conditionalities of any sort.

As debate in the United States intensifies about targeting foreign assistance to "deserving countries" that meet performance indicators—particularly those related to the substantial new funds that the proposed Millennium Challenge Account will make available—bipartisan concurrence by the executive and legislative branches on the role for governance conditionality is important. Governance conditionality is an important tool both to ensure U.S. taxpayers that their money is well spent and to leverage difficult policy decisions. Because sovereign rights related to governance are so jealously guarded, however, the United States and other outside parties should work firmly but humbly in this area. Where possible, the United States should work to see governance conditionality included in agreements among the parties to conflict themselves so that outsiders are seen to be helping the peace process rather than imposing a "foreign" system of governance.

"Peace conditionality," more broadly, a system of conditionality to ensure that peace agreements are respected, is crucial.[11] Another area where conditionality is likely to be most useful relates to the issue of corruption. Tailoring "microconditionality" to individuals and organizations to ensure transparency and to punish those who violate anticorruption norms not only improves the odds of getting an honest government but also enhances locals' views of the international community. Where conditionality is less effective is on the priorities of specific donors. Even on such high priorities as ensuring full participation of women and other marginalized groups in the political process, conditionality can be counterproductive. In these areas, carrots are more likely to produce results than sticks.

Finally, for conditionalities to be effective, donors must tightly coordinate them. If all the donors do not agree on them and if a single entity (an SRSG-type figure or a country team) metes them out, leverage is dispersed and donors run the risk of destroying government coherence by pulling in different directions.

To achieve U.S. objectives in postconflict situations, the United States should:

- Propose a clear set of distinct guidelines on the use of conditionality for postconflict and institutionally weak countries as part of the process establishing the Millennium Challenge Account. The White House, in conjunction with the Treasury Department, USAID, and the State Department, should carefully coordinate this undertaking with the relevant actors on Capitol Hill, such that any enabling legislation for the Millennium Challenge Account (or a new parallel account designed for postconflict countries) includes an agreement on how the government should use conditionalities in postconflict situations (acknowledging that performance indicators in these situations will almost always be very different from those used for top economic performers that are not burdened by conflicts).

- Instruct U.S. foreign assistance administrators and U.S. representatives to the multilateral development banks and the UN to coordinate conditionality tightly through country teams composed of major donors, multilateral development banks, and UN representatives. Leverage is best exercised when those closest to the peace process coordinate their efforts.

The Earlier, the Better

Patterns for governance and participation are not open for discussion during a conflict and are most malleable in the period soon after the conflict ends. For the United States and other international actors to have any hope of affecting these fundamental issues, they must be ready to engage before lines harden. This serious undertaking will require adapting existing democracy and governance mechanisms to postconflict environments and enhancing those mechanisms' flexibility and ability to deploy quickly.

Notes

1. U.S. Agency for International Development (USAID), "Democracy and Governance: A Conceptual Framework," PN-ACC-395, November 1998, http://www.usaid.gov/democracy/pdfs/pnacd395.pdf (accessed July 29, 2002).
2. See http://www.undp.org.
3. Ibid.
4. World Bank, *Governance and Development* (Washington, D.C.: World Bank, 1992).
5. For a comprehensive, systematic listing of potential governance and participation tasks in a postconflict environment, see Commission on Post-Conflict

Reconstruction, *Post-Conflict Reconstruction Task Framework* (CSIS and Association of the U.S. Army, May 2002), http://www.pcrproject.org (accessed July 10, 2002).

6. The author would like to thank Ambassador James Dobbins, who has served as a special envoy in various postconflict settings, for calling to our attention this political balancing act based on different sets of standards.

7. USAID, "Program, Performance and Prospects," *Budget Justification FY 2002*, http://www.usaid.gov/pubs/cbj2002/prog_pref2002.html (accessed July 10, 2002) (Democracy and Governance section).

8. *World Bank Poverty Reduction and Economic Management Notes*, no. 31 (October 1999).

9. Luca Barbone et al., *Reforming Tax Systems: The World Bank Record in the 1990s* (Washington, D.C.: World Bank, 1999), p. 3.

10. Ibid, p. 31.

11. See, for example, James K. Boyce, *Investing in Peace: Aid and Conditionality After Civil Wars* (Oxford: Oxford University Press, 2002).

Part III

Public Diplomacy

Christopher Ross

Public Diplomacy Comes of Age

Since the September 11 attacks on the United States, the nature and role of public diplomacy have been debated more vigorously than at any time in recent memory. A foreign affairs specialty that was once the province of a relatively small number of professionals has suddenly—and quite properly—taken its place in the wide-ranging discussion of national security in which the U.S. population is currently engaged. The growing consensus that the time has come for the United States to rethink, reinvigorate, and reinvest in not just traditional diplomacy but also in the public dimension of the government's overseas presence has been encouraging. I am delighted with the burgeoning recognition that how the U.S. government communicates abroad—and with whom—directly affects the nation's security and well-being.

Yet, what is this art that people call public diplomacy? It is not traditional diplomacy, which consists essentially of the interactions that take place between governments. The practitioners of traditional diplomacy engage the representatives of foreign governments in order to advance the national interest articulated in their own government's strategic goals in international affairs. Public diplomacy, by contrast,

Christopher Ross is special coordinator for public diplomacy and public affairs at the U.S. Department of State. He is a former ambassador to Syria and former coordinator for counterterrorism at the State Department.

Copyright © 2002 by The Center for Strategic and International Studies and the Massachusetts Institute of Technology
The Washington Quarterly • 25:2 pp. 75–83.

engages carefully targeted sectors of foreign publics in order to develop support for those same strategic goals.

Global Changes Affecting Public Diplomacy

The practice of public diplomacy by professionals, including U.S. ambassadors, has changed dramatically with the proliferation of communications technology and the equally remarkable increase in global mobility. A full generation ago, for instance, small teams of U.S. Foreign Service officers drove Jeeps to the hinterlands of Latin America and other remote regions of the world to show reel-to-reel movies to isolated audiences, while U.S. diplomats in capital cities scouted out future leaders and sent them on exchange programs to experience life, society, and democratic values in the United States firsthand. That world now seems impossibly quaint, and the contrast with today's global environment could hardly be more pronounced.

First and perhaps foremost, the number and affiliations of players in public diplomacy have mushroomed. The U.S. government is by no means the only actor on the public diplomacy stage abroad. Nongovernmental organizations (NGOs) and, with increasing frequency, individuals now pursue their goals in public venues around the world, often with skill and success. Even among government agencies, the Department of State is in no way the only actor involved in public diplomacy. Many observers have noted the spiraling rise in the number of federal, state, and local agencies that conduct international activities and frequently have an overseas presence. Less widely appreciated, however, is the on-the-ground fact that most of those agencies and organizations play an ever-larger role on the public stage in the countries with which they are involved.

Communications technology has changed as well, proliferating and constantly extending its reach. The players have changed, in greater numbers with more mobility and increasing skill. The media have changed, with multiple channels and segmented audiences. Not surprisingly, then, the challenge facing government practitioners of public diplomacy has also changed. To take advantage of the resources at hand, they must more often effectively galvanize disparate efforts than command their own limited funds and personnel. They must promote collaboration among all the actors involved inside and outside government. They must stimulate and persuade. They must also exploit their one distinct advantage—they are, after all, the U.S. government's authorized voice to audiences abroad. An NGO spokesperson may make an eloquent case for his or her cause, but only U.S. practitioners of public diplomacy can articulate official policy to foreign publics.

Ways to Communicate the Message

A good portion of the current debate about public diplomacy has focused on decisions made in the past—particularly in the wake of the Cold War, but actually retreating even further in time—that reduced the resources for what Edward R. Murrow called "telling America's story." That kind of collective soul-searching is useful to a point. The September 11 attacks and their continuing global resonance clearly indicate, however, that the United States must focus not on what happened in the past but on the challenges it faces today and will face tomorrow. Ways to describe the challenges are abundant: winning hearts and minds, making friends and influencing enemies, building the policy context, projecting U.S. values. However it is phrased, public diplomacy essentially operates in two separate but closely linked ways.

The first is the communication of policy. Whereas the task is ongoing, intensive, and fraught with difficulties, public diplomacy is basically a short-term effort with a simple goal: to articulate U.S. policy clearly in as many media and languages as are necessary to ensure that the message is received. The practitioner, however, must keep in mind the home truth that it is not what one says, but it is what the other hears that ultimately matters most. This task is the daily work of ambassadors, the press, and information offices in U.S. embassies. Murrow's famous "last three feet"—the distance to be crossed when one person meets another—remain vitally important in the chain of communication that successfully delivers the country's policy message. Direct, face-to-face contact has no substitute. As the United States builds a public diplomacy apparatus equal to the daunting task at hand, the government should frankly acknowledge the need for a robust corps of public diplomacy specialists in the field. The language-capable, media-savvy, policy-wise, accessible, and persuasive Foreign Service officer who understands the country in which he or she is serving has no acceptable replacement.

Equally important, the impact of technology on how public diplomacy work is carried out can scarcely be overstated. One recent example suggests how much things have changed since Foreign Service employees overseas went to work early in the morning to pull down the "Wireless File" and distribute reams of mimeographs or photocopies. Following the attacks on the World Trade Center and the Pentagon, the Department of State's Bureau of International Information Programs (IIP) produced a pamphlet, *The Network of Terrorism*, designed to convey the horror of September 11 to foreign publics and to persuade them not only that terrorism must be fought but also that the coalition required for this effort must be sustained.

While printed copies were being sent around the world, *The Network of Terrorism* was loaded onto IIP's Web site, enabling interested embassies and media abroad to download sections of the document easily and reproduce what they needed to present to local audiences. In practice, the Web site has exponentially expanded the pamphlet's readership. For instance, *Panorama*, Italy's most influential weekly news magazine, reproduced most of *The Network of Terrorism* in its own full-color, Italian-language edition. The State Department's IIP has put translations of the document on its Web site in 14 languages, and, at last count, embassies and others who saw the utility of a document that was visually impressive, clearly presented, and effectively persuasive have produced versions in more than 30 languages. *The Network of Terrorism* is an encouraging example of paying careful attention to that home truth.

More generally, the Internet has become a fundamental medium for communicating State Department policy. The IIP Web site has at-some places, a magazine published by the State Department might be appropriate; in others, carrying the U.S. message to a wider audience by entering into a cooperative arrangement with a respected local publisher to make U.S. government–produced material available may be possible. In unusual or compelling circumstances, the government might even consider buying space in an important foreign publication.

Similarly for languages, English-language publications will cover the State Department's needs in some places; in others, versions in the country's native language are absolutely essential. In all instances, however, the concept undergirding the State Department's return to print publications must be that of Web-based, digitized content made rapidly available for use in any and all media and transmitted electronically to publication centers as individual circumstances dictate.

Programs to Promote Cultural Understanding

As demanding as articulating U.S. policy to foreign publics is, it is only half of public diplomacy's responsibility. The other half is a longer-term effort to develop an overseas understanding and appreciation of U.S. society—the people and values in the United States. As the Fulbright-Hays Act states, the U.S. government must conduct activities that lead to "mutual understanding." Yet how is this task performed? For the most part, the government uses educational and cultural exchange programs, the overwhelming majority of which consists of educational exchanges. Among these, the Fulbright Program remains the flagship government-sponsored exchange, and deservedly so, but cultural programs barely register beyond Fulbright.

Success on the information front can be measured. An op-ed piece signed by an ambassador and placed in a major newspaper is an indisputable triumph, especially when one tracks its influence in changing attitudes. In contrast, gauging the success of exchange programs is more intangible and requires time and patience. In the past, one common mistake was thinking of government exchanges as a kind of frill, a nice undertaking if the resources were available. Today, viewing exchanges as a long-term investment in the national security of the United States is vital. The effects of a young government official's stay in the United States may take years to make themselves felt, but much more often than not they will be felt. The U.S. government will benefit from having exposed that person to U.S. society, values, and the company of U.S. peers. The degree of apparent hostility to the United States and the depth of unfamiliarity with U.S. society—its values, accomplishments, and aspirations—that recent events have brought into dramatic relief have surprised even those who work in foreign affairs. Perhaps the United States should have expected it. In any event, the way forward is clear. The U.S. government must commit the resources, both financial and human, that are required to increase our exchange capacity to a level sufficient to respond to the national security challenge the country faces. The government must recognize exchanges as a high-priority investment, even though the returns will only be apparent over time and, even in the best of circumstances, will be difficult to measure.

As the government invests in exchanges, a number of factors must be considered. First, what types of people should it invite to participate in these programs? In general, participants should be young. They should be individuals whose minds remain open and who would not otherwise have an opportunity to get to know the United States. They should not be the sons and daughters of local elites, people who can visit or study in this country any time they choose, but upwardly striving persons of promise who are likely to make an impact on their own societies, chosen by U.S. embassy officers with a thorough knowledge of the country in which they are serving. An invitation to participate in an exchange program with the United States is not a reward or a favor.

In addition, the U.S. government must think about a judicious expansion of its cultural programs around the world. As widely known, the portrait of the United States that most people absorb through mass culture and communications is skewed, negative, and unrepresentative. A U.S. cultural presence indeed has a place abroad. Done properly, cultural programs are not simply the government's version of art for art's

The Battle for Hearts and Minds

sake. The programs are not a luxury, and they are not the provinces of cultural elites. Cultural programs are, instead, the frank mobilization in the service of national security of what Joseph Nye referred to as "soft power."[1] U.S. culture is dynamic, diverse, and democratic. It already has tremendous appeal around the world. Harnessing its obvious power is another cost-effective investment to ensure U.S. national security.

Much has been written about the virtues of developing public-private partnerships to advance the U.S. cultural presence abroad; these arrangements indeed have a number of built-in advantages. Private-sector partners, however, reasonably expect to see the federal government's financial commitment to the cause in which they are invited to participate. The private sector does not want to be simply tapped for cash. The State Department's unique advantage of maintaining a global network of cultural experts in embassies is invaluable but not by itself sufficient for a partnership. The United States should wisely invest money in cultural programs, perhaps beginning with a few pilot projects in strategically important places, while leveraging the investment with private partners who may be willing to follow the government's lead.

Another mainstay of public diplomacy fell on particularly hard times in the 1990s. American studies came to be viewed as the most expendable luxury—at best, as a kind of sweetener to make the hard truths of policy more palatable. Yet, in a world in which information is power and in which power works by persuasion, American studies can inform and sometimes even persuade some of those whose reaction to the events of September 11 was expressed in the throwaway line, "They deserved it." If the government decides to reinvest in American studies, it cannot revert to the old model of support for foreign universities' literature departments. Rather, the government should direct its efforts at the target audiences it seeks to influence: the media; the NGO community; governments (and not just foreign ministries); academic institutions; and even, selectively, the business community. The founding of the first Department of American Studies in an East European university in Warsaw in the late 1970s was a courageous act by the faculty of Warsaw University. The department's first chairman later became

Poland's foreign minister and graduates of the program have become prominent in international commerce and politics.

A Paradigm for the Future

Finally, as the United States begins to rebuild the government's capacity to conduct public diplomacy, considering a new paradigm would be useful. Throughout the Cold War, public diplomacy efforts ran essentially one way. Programs and activities were pushed out to target audiences. Given the bipolar international political environment of the time, that approach was appropriate and, indeed, successful. (The obvious exception, the exchange programs, was predicated on mutual exchange.)

In today's world, the United States is more likely to meet with success if it structures activities in ways that encourage dialogue. Although the wording of recriminations varies—ranging from hegemony to multilateralism to cultural imperialism—the United States, as the world's dominant power, will inevitably be accused of heavy-handedness and arrogance. It will inform and influence public opinion effectively only if it changes the paradigm of the past and establishes a two-way approach that builds credible dialogue. To arrive there, the United States should experiment and take a few chances, developing programs that encourage two-way engagement with the people it seeks to influence. Some efforts may fail, but others will succeed; the U.S. government can use those successes to shape a sustained future effort.

Terrorism has changed the way people think about public diplomacy. Today, no serious observer can deny the link between perceptions of the United States and the country's national security. Some of those perceptions range far beyond U.S. control. Some of them, however, depend on how the United States talks to the world. All the pieces matter: the U.S. policy message itself, the channels of communication the United States selects, the tone of voice in which it speaks, and its familiarity with the environment in which it is speaking.

The United States will never persuade its sworn enemies. The surprisingly muted reaction to the quick U.S. military success in Afghanistan, however, suggests that more people might be able to be persuaded than we originally thought. Certainly, most people will back a winner. The United States is winning and, because it is resolute, it will continue to win. Nevertheless, great numbers of people reject terror and hope for themselves, their families, and their societies exactly that for which the United States is known: democratic governance, tolerance, and freedom to prosper. In their complexity, their remoteness, and their distrust of U.S. leadership, such people are the target audience for the United States. Is anybody out there listening? The answer is yes. Let the United States engage them.

Note

1. Joseph S. Nye Jr., *Bound to Lead: The Changing Nature of American Power* (1990).

Lamis Andoni

Deeds Speak Louder Than Words

The collapse of the twin towers like a deck of cards symbolized the collapse of U.S. foreign policy in the Arab and Muslim worlds. The tragic loss of thousands of innocent U.S. lives, and those of other nationals, exposed the fragility of security and safety for a superpower involved in policies that perpetuate inequities and exacerbate regional conflicts. Wars that the United States has been waging in the region, through the bombing of and embargo against Iraq or through support for Israel's occupation of the Palestinian territories, have reached the United States. Ultimately, U.S. military prowess could not stop the continued bleeding in the Middle East from spilling onto U.S. shores. Neither U.S. control over the flow of news, nor the efforts of Pentagon and Madison Avenue spin doctors, can ease the resentment of U.S. policies and actions that have affected the lives, hearts, and minds of the people of the region.

Of course, the United States does not see itself or the terrorist attacks of September 11 this way—despite the prevalence abroad of this perception of the United States. In the era of "us against them" and the absolute battle between "good and evil," the United States has no room for another worldview and little if any inclination to consider the victims of U.S. economic, political, and military dominance. Most alarmingly, the United States fails to realize that a foreign policy based solely

Lamis Andoni, a Middle East analyst, is widely published in Western and Arabic newspapers.

Copyright © 2002 by The Center for Strategic and International Studies and the Massachusetts Institute of Technology
The Washington Quarterly • 25:2 pp. 85–100.

grievances of the people are not seriously acknowledged. In the rare times that these concerns are mentioned, albeit vaguely, such acknowledgment falls short of recognizing the U.S. role in practicing or supporting violence through its allies, such as Israel, against Arabs. For example, although Secretary of State Colin Powell announced, "The occupation must end," he exclusively blamed the violence on the Palestinians without taking accountability for the U.S. military support of the Israeli occupation army. "Whatever the sources of Palestinian frustration and anger under occupation, the Intifada is now mired in the quicksand of self-defeating violence and terror directed against Israel," Powell said in the short-lived administration's "peace proposal" for a Palestinian state. In the few paragraphs regarding the Israeli-Palestinian conflict, Powell used the words "terror" or "terrorists" six times exclusively describing Palestinian actions.[3]

The Failure of U.S. Policy

U.S. policy has been an utter failure in the Arab and Muslim world. In his September 20 speech to the nation, Bush defined the U.S. attitude to the rest of the world—but particularly toward Arabs and Muslims—in unequivocal terms. "Either you are with us or with the terrorists," Bush warned the rest of the world in his speech to a joint session of Congress. No spin can camouflage or sweeten such threatening words that carry the weight of U.S. military, political, and economic might. Such a polarized view of the world leaves no room for dialogue or for a search for a middle ground that addresses the threat of terrorism and the underlying problems of political and economic inequities. Accordingly, the world is strictly divided between Washington and "terrorists," between "good" and "evil." The only middle road tolerated, albeit temporarily, is when a country renders some support for the U.S. war effort. The United States, however, demands that countries go "all the way" in their support, or threats against them may resurface. A case in point is Iran, which allowed the United States to use Iranian aircraft to transfer military equipment and troops to Afghanistan, but was nevertheless accused by Bush in his State of the Union address of being part of "an axis of evil [along with Iraq and North Korea], arming to threaten the peace of the world."[4]

The United States places individuals, leaders, and even nations who oppose its policy in the "other" camp that will be bombed or whose governments will be toppled. In a message meant for any country that supports terrorism, Deputy Defense Secretary Paul Wolfowitz declared, "You are setting yourselves up to suffer the same as Afghanistan."[5] In a press conference shortly after September 11, Wolfowitz talked of the necessity "of ending nations" that sponsor terrorism and, although Powell reportedly opposed his hard line, the world heard the message loud and clear.[6]

I deliberately place "terrorists" in quotes because the word has come to describe all enemies or opponents who resist U.S. policies or those of its allies. (The State Department mainly applies it to groups that practice violence against civilians to attain their goals, but any definition of state-sponsored terrorism against civilians, especially that perpetuated by the United States or its allies such as Israel, is absent.) The selective political use of the term by the United States to justify its policies and actions has generated distrust and resentment among Arabs and Muslims. Such a stark division of the world at once marginalizes and even demonizes the voices of discontent. As a result, a combination of the U.S. exercise of power and of Arab rulers' suppression of political dissent, a suppression that the United States often backs, has always ignored and eventually drowned out popular sentiments in the Arab world.

An examination of U.S. foreign policy throughout and since the Persian Gulf War gives a clear glimpse into how the United States relies on sheer economic and military power to impose its policies in the region. At no point did Washington stop to give serious consideration to the message of the millions of Arabs who protested against the war on Iraq and the continued bombing and sanctions against that beleaguered country. U.S. public diplomacy focused only on demonizing Saddam Hussein, while ignoring the increasingly angry protests in the Arab and

Muslim world over the suffering of ordinary Iraqis. Saddam was not by any means the credible spokesman for legitimate Arab and Muslim concerns, but public policymakers in the United States decided to kill the message with the messenger.

Public policy strategists, it seems, never noticed that demonizing Saddam has never succeeded in either marketing the war or the sanctions or in quelling growing resentment toward the United States in the Arab world. U.S. military force, accompanied by a public policy of denial of concerns of "the other," only deepened the feeling of humiliation, despair, and powerlessness among Arabs and Muslims.

The continued saga and death in Iraq is a daily reaffirmation of U.S. hostility and aggression against an Arab nation. Blaming Saddam for the death of children due to the most stringent economic sanctions ever imposed may play well in Washington, but the receptive Arab and Muslim audiences are small. The notion of a collective punishment of Iraqi civilians for their leaders' deeds is not only unacceptable among Arabs and Muslims, but a reaffirmation of the U.S. disregard for Arab lives. Former secretary of state Madeleine Albright's infamous response in a U.S. televised interview—when asked whether the deaths of thousands of Iraqi children was "worth it" to keep sanctions in place, she responded with an unqualified "yes"—is etched in Arab memory.

If Albright's blunt language was a diplomatic blunder, however, the U.S. role in the Israeli-Arab peace negotiations shows the limits of positive spin when the actual policy does nothing to improve the lives of the people on the ground. In a March 1990 speech, President George H. W. Bush seized the moment of U.S. victory against Iraq to make a grand gesture to the Arab world. His commitment to bring about peace in the region indicated that Washington was aware that only a resolution of the Palestinian-Israeli conflict could ease the impact of the crushing Iraqi defeat on the Arab world and ensure stability.

The great wheels of U.S. statecraft, in the wake of which scores of pundits followed, churned out endless messages of peace, security, and even prosperity for the region. The message for public consumption in the West was that the ruins of war would lead all to grasp for the olive branch. In the realpolitik behind this facade of U.S. public policy, U.S. arm-twisting convinced Arab leaders to enter the process. In the end, a state of shock, defeat, and humiliation coerced a skeptical Arab world to accept the U.S.-imposed terms for negotiations with Israel while their interests were effectively dismissed. The United States and Israel rejected Arab demands for an Israeli commitment to stop settlement building, home demolition, expropriation of lands, and detention and deportation of Palestinians, although all are prerequisites under the 1949 Fourth Geneva Convention. Demands that talks lead to the clear establishment of a Palestinian state and the end of Israeli occupation of Arab lands were also denied, plunging Arabs into an open-ended process.

Although Arab rulers had every reason to ingratiate themselves with the supreme power in return for economic and military dividends, the reaction of the Arab people was a combination of resentful submission and a desperate hope to survive their crushing defeat after the Gulf War. Even those governments that allied themselves with the United States during the war found a deaf ear in Washington. Israel summarily rejected their attempts to improve the terms of negotiation as coming from the "losing" camp. Many clutched to the promise of prosperity as compensation for lost dreams, while Palestinians looked for a flicker of freedom.

The euphoria that accompanied the signing of the 1993 Oslo accords between Israel and the Palestine Liberation Organization (PLO) was a statement, particularly by Palestinians in the West Bank and the Gaza Strip, of a yearning for independence. The excitement and support, however, was based on false expectations, manipulated by some PLO officials and world leaders, of the beginning of freedom and peace. Throughout my travels in the Palestinian territories in the two years that followed the Oslo signing, the Declaration of Principles was largely interpreted as a guarantee of an independent and sovereign Palestinian state with East Jerusalem as its capital. Refugees were less enthusiastic, feeling that the PLO leadership had betrayed them because the Oslo agreement did not address the right of return.

As effective Israeli control over the Palestinian territories continued, it became clear that expectations built up by the historic handshake did not stand the test of time. Israeli governments continued expanding settlements and refused to release most Palestinian prisoners. Israel continued to control freedom of movement, including that of PLO leader Yasir Arafat. In the wider regional context, the key to U.S. aid— as well as entry through the gates of globalization, such as the World Trade Organization (WTO)—was presented as acceptance of peace agreements with Israel. In the case of Jordan, it was free-trade zones that qualified for exemption of import duties. The caveat for entry into these global "clubs" has been and remains Arab consent to "normalization" with Israel.

The Oslo accords, however, and the Jordanian-Israeli peace treaty— each with their promise of an economic "peace dividend"—were not enough to win popular support for normalizing ties with Israel. The United States overlooked the obvious: no broader economic and cultural ties could emerge as long as the Israeli occupation of Palestinian territories, Syria (the Golan Heights), and Lebanon (until its withdrawal in 1998) continued. Incremental Israeli redeployments from the occupied areas, and sustaining the negotiation process through waves of violence, were not enough to facilitate the broadening of peace ties in the region.

In Arab eyes, the tale of the peace process has become a definitive reaffirmation of how one-sided and pro-Israeli U.S. policies and objectives have become. From then–Secretary of State James Baker's to then-President Bill Clinton's stance in Camp David and finally Bush's support for Ariel Sharon, Washington's consistent policy has been to guarantee Israeli military superiority and security goals. Increased U.S. military support of Israel, security demands the United States made to the Palestinians, and the U.S. blind eye to expanding Jewish settlements contradicted public statements in support of Palestinian rights.

On the international level, Washington blocked many attempts by the United Nations (UN) to enforce an end to settlement building. In 1999 the United States successfully thwarted a UN resolution to con-

vene a meeting for the contracting parties to the fourth Geneva Convention, scheduled for July 15, regarding the Jewish settlements in occupied Palestinian Arab lands. In testimony to the Senate Committee
on Foreign Relations, David Welch, assistant secretary of state for international organizations, boasted of the then-ongoing efforts. "The
[United States] voted against this resolution. ... We have worked strenu-
ously in the days since its adoption—up to and including today—to
cancel or delay this ill-conceived conference."[7]

The Camp David talks of July 2000 ultimately shattered any remaining illusions and hopes for the Palestinians. Camp David may continue
to be heralded in the United States as a missed historic opportunity,
but with the exception of the elite among pro-U.S. allies, Camp David
is seen in the Arab world to represent the bankruptcy and incredibility
of U.S. foreign and public policy. The myth created around Camp
David serves the U.S. and Israeli objective of blaming the Palestinians.
If judged by the future it provided for the Palestinian people, however,
that interpretation does not withstand scrutiny. The alleged offer from
Israel's then–Prime Minister Ehud Barak boiled down to a noncontigu-
ous "state" devoid of sovereignty in the West Bank and the Gaza Strip.
The Barak proposal involved a division of East Jerusalem, as opposed to
the Palestinian vision of two capitals in East and West Jerusalem. The
offer would have kept the city under Israeli sovereignty, and Israel would
have retained control over Palestinian borders and freedom of movement and the area's vital water resources. Hardly any Palestinian could
have accepted this offer; indeed, Arafat told Clinton during the tense
hours of negotiation that, if the Palestinians accepted, the U.S. president would soon be attending the funeral of another Arab leader.

The Arab world saw full-fledged U.S. support for the Israeli proposal
and the consequent vilification of Arafat for refusing it as proof that
Washington had never envisioned freedom for the Palestinians. The
fact that the proposal fell far short of the minimum provided by UN
resolutions reinforced the Arab view of U.S. double standards and disdain for international law when applied to the Israeli-Palestinian conflict. Clinton's two farewell letters to the Palestinian and Israeli people

removed any doubt about his administration's bias against the Palestinians. Clinton opened his letter to the Israeli peoples by pointing out, "I have expanded our special strategic relationship and helped protect and enhance your security." He announced that he had recommended that Israel become "among the first, if not the first" foreign buyer of the advanced F-22 fighter aircraft when it became available for sale. He concluded by pledging, "I will be standing with you as strong and faithful a friend as I am today."[8]

Clinton's underlying argument that Israeli security comes first and foremost is, ironically, consistent with the Arab view that the so-called peace process is little more than a security operation to control the Palestinian population. In the two important agreements brokered by the Clinton administration—the 1997 Hebron Protocols and the 1998 Wye River Memorandum—this position was, in fact, consolidated as a policy and function of the "peace process." The gist of U.S. policy was summarized in the letter of assurance that then–Secretary of State Warren Christopher sent to Israel and that was included in the addendum of the Hebron Protocols:

> The key element in our approach to peace, including the negotiations and implementation of agreements between Israel and its Arab partners, has always been a recognition of Israel's security requirement. Moreover, a hallmark of our policy remains our commitment to work cooperatively to seek the needs that Israel identifies.[9]

The next day, Prime Minister Benjamin Netanyahu told the Knesset that the Hebron agreements clarified that implementation of redeployments (of Israeli troops) must be an Israeli decision and that "this decision must comply with Israel's security considerations as Israel sees fit."[10]

Behind the scenes and away from public diplomacy, the U.S. team entrusted with mediation was emerging as a bidder for Israeli positions in a manner that astounded even the most lenient Palestinian negotiators. Most notable among these bidders were the former special envoy for the Middle East peace process, Dennis Ross, and Martin Indyk, who rotated as ambassador to Israel and assistant secretary of state for Near Eastern affairs during the Clinton years.

The recruitment by Clinton almost immediately after his inaugura-
tion of Indyk, a former official for AIPAC (the American Israel Public
Affairs Committee) and head of the pro-Israel Washington Institute for
Near East Policy from 1985 to 1992, gave many in the Arab world a bad
premonition of the administration policies to come. Ross, an old hand
in the State Department, was a behind-the-scenes silent type with well-
known sympathies for Israel. Palestinian frustration with Ross's open
bias was the subject of tens of articles in the Arab media throughout
the negotiation process. Since their departure from public office, both
men have been leading and outspoken apologists for Israeli policies in
public forums and the media.

In retrospect, public policymakers seem to have confused grand gestures
with actual policies. For example, the fact that Clinton often received
Arafat in the White House was used to illustrate the administration's
open-mindedness to, if not sympathy for, the Palestinians. Yet, for some
Palestinians watching Arafat in the White House and Camp David, the
hard facts of U.S. pressure on the Palestinian leader to crack down on its
militants while Israel continued its punitive measures against the Palestinians soon replaced the initial excitement.

This lack of evenhandedness is seen as an act of open hostility in the
Arab world. During the last decade, U.S. officials have at most expressed regret at Israeli killings of Palestinian civilians, but have never
offered condolences to their families (as compared to the families of Israeli victims of suicide bombers) much less condemned Israel for these
actions. Instead, this U.S. exoneration of Israel is taken as further evidence of intentional U.S. humiliation of the Arab world.

Same Story, Different Century

During the 2000 presidential campaign, both Bush and Vice President
Al Gore seemed oblivious, if not indifferent, to the message they were
sending to Arabs and Muslims as they competed to outbid each other
in support of Israel during the annual conference for AIPAC. The
very fact that major presidential candidates' appearances could take

The Battle for Hearts and Minds

place at such a biased forum is itself an example of the entrenched U.S. establishment.

This animosity had become more open and strident since the beginning of the current Intifada in September 2001. The Intifada had effectively undermined the whole premise behind the U.S.-led peace process that emphasized Israeli security as its driving force preceding an end to the occupation—proving that the first goal cannot be attained without achieving the latter. The U.S. response—officially and through its pundits—initially dismissed the Intifada as violence that should be stopped and finally condemned it as a "campaign of terror." In contrast, statements regarding Israeli army violence have reflected U.S. understanding or, at most, calls for "restraint." Even when the administration intervened to get Sharon to withdraw tanks from the areas he recaptured, the United States did not condemn Israel when it took its army 10 days to begin pulling out.

Such policies go far beyond bias. In fact, they sanction violence by an occupying force while delegitimizing resistance by the people under occupation. In the Middle East, these actions are interpreted as denouncing Palestinian violence as "terrorism" while refusing even to acknowledge state terrorism practiced by Israel against people under occupation. No campaign to "improve the U.S. image" in the Arab world could change this perception. In an interview with Al Jazeera television, Ross confirmed Arab perceptions by insisting that suicide bombers "are murderers of children" and that Israel does not deliberately target civilians. Such pronouncements utterly contradict the findings of major international human rights organizations, including Amnesty International, Human Rights Watch, Physicians for Human Rights, and the respected Israeli group B'tselem, that Israel has used excessive force, causing the death and maiming of Palestinian protesters and stone throwers. According to these organizations, Israeli soldiers were using high-velocity bullets and aiming at protesters in situations where the soldiers' lives were not threatened. With the exception of a few reports in the U.S. press, both the media and the government ignore the conclusions of human rights reports, again reaffirming the perceived notion of disrespect for Arab lives.

Getting Worse, Not Better

In the aftermath of September 11, the gap between the United States and the Arab and Muslim world reached unprecedented proportions. Overestimating the damage done by Bush's description of the declared war on terrorism as a "crusade" is difficult. In one word—its later retraction carried far less weight—Bush conjured deep-seated feelings of resentment and anger that had been built up against the legacy of the bloody European Crusades. For many in the region, it underscored Western colonialism, Israeli occupation, and the current U.S. domination. Ironically, Bush confirmed what extremist Islamic fundamentalists and many disgruntled Arabs and Muslims have claimed for decades: the United States represented latter-day crusaders against Muslims. Even Christian thinkers in the region who were pioneers in Pan-Arab and leftist ideologies had always denounced and warned against Western colonialism and Western animosity toward Islam as a pillar of Arab culture. Especially after the start of the bombing of Afghanistan, the stepped-up threats to attack Iraq and other Arab countries, the unequivocal endorsement of Sharon's position, and the naming of Palestinian organizations as targets in the war against terror, the damage control that followed Bush's gaffe had limited effect.

The Arab world has watched the detention of thousands of Middle Eastern men in the United States and the demonizing of Arabs and Muslims in the U.S. media with alarm and anger and as indications of growing U.S. hostility. A review of post–September 11 foreign and public policy shows that the United States has lost more Arab and Muslim hearts and minds than it has gained, aggravating an already simmering resentment.

The only apparent foreign policy shift was very short-lived and did not stand the test of wavering U.S. credibility. Few in the Arab world believed that the United States was preparing a policy initiative regarding the Palestinian-Israeli conflict prior to the September 11 attack. Yet many, mostly Arab, governments and some media col-

Bin Laden's Role

In his first taped broadcast since the September 11 attacks, aired on Al Jazeera on October 6, Osama bin Laden captured the depth of the sense that the United States devalues the lives of "the other." Bin Laden started by invoking the memory of victims of the atomic bombs dropped on Hiroshima and Nagasaki, then drew on an Arab proverb that roughly translates, "Massacres committed by the powerful against the weak are justified acts while reactions by the oppressed are acts of crime." These words express the sentiments of many average Arabs and Muslims, including those who loathe bin Laden. In its campaign to censor bin Laden tapes, the U.S. government was missing the point: bin Laden himself does not muster a majority following in the Arab and Muslim world, but his articulation of grievances felt across the region echoes feelings that Washington continues to ignore.

Like Saddam before him, bin Laden is not a legitimate spokesman for Arab and Muslim causes, even less so than Saddam. Yet, both men were able to seize moments of focused attention—regardless of the cynical motivation behind their actions—and give public voice to people's grievances. Thus, while most Arab leaders are struggling to appease U.S. interests, any voice raised in opposition to oppressive U.S. and Israeli policies resonates widely in the region.

The typical U.S. reaction is that of Rumsfeld's dismissal as propaganda of bin Laden's claims in his last videotape that U.S. bombings had inflicted high Afghan civilian casualties. When a respected Lebanese-American writer, Assad Abu Khalil, a declared atheist and opponent of religious extremism, tried to explain on MSNBC that bin Laden's reference to Afghan victims of the bombing rings true to Arab and Muslim ears, the host asked him pointedly, in a question reminiscent of Joseph McCarthy, if Abu Khalil was himself a bin Laden sympathizer. These official and media tactics of vilification of dissenting voices may succeed in the short term to drown out Arab and Muslim grievances. In the long run, they will only serve to deepen a sense of injustice and humiliation.

Attempts to link Arab and Muslim opposition voices with bin Laden and terrorism is another manifestation of myopic U.S. public policy. The United States must understand that it cannot win by delegitimizing deep-rooted concerns in the region that are the heart of Arab and Muslim disaffection, which is exactly how the U.S. government and most of the media have responded since September 11. Countless pages in the press and hours on television and radio, with some exceptions, were dedicated to interpretations that trivialize these grievances and justify the fundamental assumptions of past and current U.S. policies and actions.

Apologists for Hegemony

Two examples of these rationalizations, promoted by the most influential pundits, need to be dissected and refuted. The first is that repressive Arab governments deliberately foment hatred of the United States and Israel to deflect criticism of their own corruption and incompetence. Accordingly, animosities portrayed by Arabs and Muslims are largely a function of systematic brainwashing by the state-controlled Arab media. Although Arab rulers have used the Arab-Israeli conflict to avoid democratization, reforms, and accountability, this fact does not minimize the intensity of Arab and Muslim resentment of the Israeli occupation and U.S. policies. For starters, most Arab and Muslim opposition parties, as well as critical intellectuals, repeatedly attack Arab governments for their subservience to U.S. policies and inaction toward Israel. In most cases, criticism of Israel and the United States reflects disenchantment with, if not an indictment of, pro-U.S. states in the region.

More significantly, Arab governments, especially U.S. allies, have often suppressed political and press freedoms to curb criticism of their own support for U.S. policies. For example, since the beginning of the Intifada and the consequent increased calls for annulling Jordan's peace treaty with Israel, the Jordanian government has imposed severe restrictions on demonstrations, rallies, and political meetings. After Jordan declared its support for the U.S. "war against terror," the noose was tightened, as the government banned demonstrations and introduced draconian penal codes to prosecute journalists who "damage the country's reputation." The wording is understood to mean punishment for those who raise doubts in the West about Jordan's commitment to U.S. objectives.

Since September 11, more columnists and television and radio analysts are blaming the United States for supporting repressive regimes in the Arab and Muslim worlds, but they fail to question U.S. pressure on leaders to defy the will of their peoples. U.S. coercion has rarely failed in getting already authoritarian and insecure Arab governments to curb popular dissent to appease U.S. and Western demands. These leaders are equally accountable—even considering the expected U.S. punishment that comes with defiance—for choosing their own survival at the expense of their people's aspirations.

Arab leaders' disregard of public opinion, however, has always endeared them to Washington, while any minimal attempt at a balancing act—as we are witnessing now—brings the wrath of the U.S. government and media. Analysts and talking heads ironically proceed to attack repression in Saudi Arabia and Egypt while expressing anger at these governments' inability to silence opposition to Israel and the United States. The epitome of U.S. hypocrisy was its intervention with Qatar to censor Al Jazeera, accompanied by a disparaging and slanderous media campaign to discredit a forum for free statement in the Arab world. The eventual bombing and destruction of the station's office in Kabul on November 20, 2001, which could not have been a "mistake," symbolized for the region the true U.S. position on freedom of speech and the press. The United States has no tolerance for any narrative other than the one disseminated by U.S. media, which has come to echo the official line.

Another irony of the media-distorted portrayal of Arab and Muslim views is the way the United States uses the region's lack of democracy and prevalence of social inequity to exonerate its foreign policy. Poverty and lack of participation and representation are indeed a failure of Arab and Muslim states; the best thinkers in the region have repeatedly said that these phenomena help breed extremism. Most Western apologists for U.S. hegemony, however, ignore two important factors, the first being the U.S. collaborative role with some Arab and Muslim governments in fomenting and funding Islamic fundamentalist and even fanatic movements—not only having mobilized resistance to the Soviet occupation of Afghanistan but also in countering and weakening secular nationalist and leftist movements across the region. The U.S. Cold War mentality, with its determination to crush leftist and communist trends, created an uncontrollable monster of fanaticism that feeds on the despair of the poor and the oppressed. The second factor that pundits ignore is that U.S. policies have not encouraged redistribution of wealth or other means of bridging the gaps. By focusing on controlling the flow of cheap oil and prodding Arab governments to endorse International Monetary Fund, World Bank, and finally WTO prerequisites, Washington has aggravated the problems of poverty and deprivation. Its heralded programs to finance small businesses with microcredits are a drop in a bucket; they do not compare with the benefits of using vast resources for genuine development. How would the same pundits react if a progressive, democratic ruler took power in Saudi Arabia? A representative government in such a key country would more likely reflect popular demands to adopt a different policy regarding the oil flow and the wealth generated from it. Would the United States react by supporting such a government, or back a coup similar to the one that overthrew Salvador Allende in Chile?

Public policymakers must think hard before appearing on Arab television networks and proceeding with plans for U.S. government–funded Middle East television and radio networks to promote U.S. policies and repeat claims about Washington's commitment to justice, equality, and human rights. The targeted audience will be evaluating the words not in terms of the eloquence or proficiency of the speaker's Arabic but in terms of present and past U.S. actions.

Notes

1.   Thomas Friedman, "A Manifesto for the Fast World," *New York Times*, March 28, 1999, sec. 6, p. 40. Friedman repeats the argument in his book *The Lexus and the Olive Tree* (New York: Anchor Books, 2000), p. 50.

2. Fareed Zakaria, "Why Do They Hate Us," *Newsweek*, October 15, 2001, pp. 22–40 ("What to Do?" section can be found on pp. 36–40).

3. Colin Powell, McConnell Center for Political Leadership, University of Louisville, Ky., November 19, 2001.

4. The campaign started in the second week of January and continues in the press to the date of this writing.

5. Associated Press, December 4, 2001 (dispatch from MacDill Airforce Base, Tampa, Fla.).

6. Warren P. Strobel, "Bush Given Conflicting Advice; Some Aides Want U.S. to Topple Governments," *Seattle Times*, September 18, 2001.

7. For more details, see Welch's full testimony from July 14, 1999, on the Web archives of the Department of State, www.state.gov.

8. Bill Clinton, "Open Letter of President Clinton to the People of Israel," January 19, 2001, www.usembassy.ro/USIS/Washington-File/500/01-01-19/eur505.htm (accessed January 20, 2002).

9. Warren Christopher, "Letter to Be Provided by U.S. Secretary of State Christopher to Benjamin Netanyahu at the Time of Signing of the Hebron Protocol," www.mfa.gov.il/mfa/go.asp?MFAH00qo0 (accessed January 20, 2002).

10. Benjamin Netanyahu, "Statement to the Knesset by Prime Minister Benjamin Netanyahu on the Protocol Concerning Redeployment in Hebron," January 16, 1997, www.israel-mfa.gov.il/mfa/go.asp?MFAH00t60 (accessed January 20, 2002).

Antony J. Blinken

Winning the War of Ideas

U.S. success in Afghanistan will count for little if the United States loses the global war of ideas. That war has produced a growing gap between much of the world's perception of the United States and the U.S. perception of itself. If this gap persists, U.S. influence abroad will erode, and the partners the United States needs to advance its interests will stand down. The few real enemies the United States faces will find it easier both to avoid sanction and to recruit others to their cause.

The United States remains powerfully attractive. Most people around the world hold a favorable view of the United States, considering it a land of opportunity and democratic ideals while admiring the country's technological and scientific achievements.[1] Millions of the world's citizens desire to move to, become educated in, do business with, or visit the United States. When people vote with their feet, the United States wins in a landslide.

Yet, the United States tends to disregard an increasingly potent mix of criticism and resentment that is diluting its attraction: anti-Americanism. Admittedly, anti-Americanism is a recurring refrain in U.S. history. A century ago, conservatives in Europe looked across the Atlantic and saw a society plagued by loose mores, bad manners, materialism,

Antony J. Blinken is a senior fellow at CSIS and served on the National Security Council from 1994 to 2001.

and egocentrism. A few decades ago, liberal critics around the world saw a country poisoned by racial strife at home and corrupted by its association with dictators abroad.

Although anti-Americanism is nothing new, its relevance to U.S. interests is emerging in starker relief. The early United States had few ambitions beyond its borders; European disdain was that of old money for new and did not prevent the United States from prospering. In the 1960s, for every person distressed by U.S. deficiencies, dozens more were alienated by Soviet tyranny. Now, the United States has global interests and no ideological rival whose vices remind the world of its virtues. The United States' global pervasiveness makes it a symbol of the status quo and, rightly or wrongly, a potential target for people everywhere who do not like the status quo. The war of ideologies is over. The war of ideas is just beginning.

Critics of the United States cluster in distinct, if overlapping, categories. Some focus on U.S. policies abroad, others on U.S. domestic behavior. Some decry unilateralism and the onslaught of "Americanization"; others fear exclusion from the progress and prosperity that the United States enjoys.

As a result, on the battlefield of ideas, the United States often is on the defensive for what it does or fails to do, as well as for how others perceive it. Some of the criticisms are justified. On other fronts, however, facts have been losing ground to fiction. Many Muslims outside the United States consider the country hostile to Islamic and to Arab interests. In fact, the United States saved tens of thousands of Muslims in the Persian Gulf, Somalia, Bosnia, and Kosovo. Washington brokered a peace offer from Israel that would have given Palestinians 95 percent of the occupied territories and dominion over East Jerusalem. At the request of the government of Saudi Arabia, U.S. troops were deployed there to protect that country's people and Islamic holy sites from Iraq. The United Nations (UN)—not the United States—imposed sanctions against Iraq. The Taliban killed far more Muslims intentionally than the U.S. bombing campaign killed accidentally; the demise of the Taliban will save many more Muslim lives.

Europeans complain about a growing values gap between the West and the United States. They see a country enamored of the death penalty, obsessed with guns and violence, and beholden to unchecked capitalism. In fact, U.S. citizens are questioning the death penalty, not embracing it; violent crime is at a 30-year low; large majorities favor stricter gun control; and the poverty rate is at its lowest level in 22 years. On every continent, some blame the United States for the growing gulf between rich and poor. Yet, the policies the country advocates—democracy and economic liberalism—offer more opportunity than any other nation's policies do.

Why should the United States care that some criticize its policies and others resent its power? Following U.S. military success in Afghanistan, concluding that unilateral might makes right, silencing critics and creating a bandwagon effect among friends, is tempting. As Charles Krauthammer wrote, "We made it plain that even if no one followed us, we would go it alone. Surprise: others followed. ... Not because they love us. Not because we have embraced multilateralism. But because we have demonstrated astonishing military power and the will to defend vital American interests, unilaterally if necessary."[2] Military power remains the foundation of U.S. security; successfully applied, it magnifies U.S. influence.

More than ever before, however, the transnational nature of the problems the United States faces defies unilateral solutions. Globalization is erasing borders that once protected the United States, while empowering its enemies. Thus, trouble on the far side of the planet, such as economic disaster, outbreak of disease, or theft of a weapon of mass destruction, can quickly become a plague on the United States' house. Rogue states, outlaw actors, and religious fanatics use the nation's very strengths—its openness, advanced technology, and freedom of movement—against it, as demonstrated on September 11. U.S. leadership is essential to meet these threats successfully; now more than ever, however, so is followership. Whatever response the United States chooses—engagement, containment, or elimination—requires the help of others.

Consider the long-term war against terrorism. Al Qaeda has cells in dozens of countries. Success will depend as much on multilateral law enforcement and international cooperation on intelligence gathering as on the unilateral projection of force. Military might, no matter how impressive, does not guarantee followership. For example, Spain arrested eight alleged members of Al Qaeda for complicity in the September 11 attacks, but refused to turn them over to U.S. authorities because the Bush administration said that they might face secret trials before military tribunals. This setback in the war against terrorism also establishes bad precedent for the future. "On what leg does the [United States] now stand when China sentences an American to death after a military trial devoid of counsel chosen by the defendant?" asks William Safire.[3]

Similarly, extreme devotion to national sovereignty threatens followership. For example, the Bush administration's opposition to the Comprehensive Test Ban Treaty (CTBT) and to an enforcement mechanism for the Biological Weapons Convention (BWC) is not without reason: the former would tie the United States' hands for future nuclear testing, the latter would subject U.S. companies to intrusive inspections and possible espionage. Both agreements present significant verification shortcomings. Yet, the United States also has a profound interest in preventing other countries from testing nuclear arms and in stopping rogue regimes and terrorists from acquiring biological weapons. Despite their imperfections, the CTBT and the BWC protocol would advance these important goals. If the United States rejects the restraints these agreements impose or declines to negotiate improvements, how can it ask others to embrace them?

The result is what Joseph Nye calls the paradox of U.S. power.[4] Never has a country been more powerful by traditional measures: military might and economic prowess. Yet, never has a major power been so dependent on the active cooperation of others to defeat its enemies and to advance its interests. Left unattended, those who criticize U.S. policies or resent U.S. power today are less likely to stand with the United States tomorrow. In the extreme, a failure to address foreign grievances risks broadening the base from which the country's enemies draw sanctuary, support, and successors. Winning the war of ideas is critical to the United States' future.

The Decline of Public Diplomacy

Many currents of anti-Americanism develop not because the United States is misguided, but because it is misunderstood. The economic sanctions against Iraq are a case in point. Around the world, people believe that the United States single-handedly imposed and maintains these sanctions. In fact, the UN decreed the imposition of sanctions following Iraq's invasion of Kuwait and set specific conditions under which they would be lifted, including (1) the verifiable destruction of Iraq's weapons of mass destruction and the means to produce and deliver them; (2) payment of reparations for Iraq's invasion of Kuwait; and (3) a full accounting of Kuwaiti citizens who are missing in action. Instead of complying with these conditions, Iraqi president Saddam Hussein has spent a decade trying to dodge them. Around the world, people believe that the sanctions apply to food and medicine. In fact, they do not and never did. Likewise, people around the world believe that the sanctions are responsible for the suffering of Iraq's people. Yet in northern Iraq, where the UN and the local Kurdish authorities control the distribution of oil-for-food revenue, the infant mortality rate is lower than it was before the Persian Gulf War, and the average caloric intake is higher. Even luxury goods such as electronics and cars are widely available in that area. Only in the south—where oil exports are back to prewar levels but where Saddam diverts the proceeds to his own ends—are people suffering.[5] In short, pursuing the right policies is not enough. The U.S. government must convince its critics that the United States is right. Enter public diplomacy.

In 1953 President Dwight D. Eisenhower created the U.S. Information Agency (USIA) to be an independent and objective source of information about the United States and its policies. During the Cold War, public diplomacy—the U.S. government's ability to understand, inform, and influence foreign publics—was an effective weapon in the

West's arsenal. It gave confidence to dissident groups of politicians, intellectuals, and artists throughout the Eastern bloc. Public diplomacy put a spotlight on the stark differences between capitalist and command economies, as well as between democracy and despotism, and helped bring about the collapse of communism from within. Having won the ideological war, policymakers began to perceive public diplomacy as an expensive anachronism. They believed that broad access to private media would suffice to carry the U.S. message to the world; they overlooked that these media tilt heavily toward materialistic expressions of U.S. success, rarely deal with foreign policy issues, and do not penetrate some critical parts of the world. As a result, resources devoted to shaping the image of the United States abroad have been in decline. Between 1989 and 1999, the budget of USIA, adjusted for inflation, decreased by $150 million, or 10 percent. USIA was folded into the State Department in 1999, a move born out of a desire to streamline government; public diplomacy now accounts for 8 percent of the State Department's already inadequate budget.

Proponents hoped that consolidation would put public diplomacy closer to policymaking. In practice, integration has proved difficult, as the State Department's culture devalues public diplomacy. For foreign policy professionals, other "policy" priorities are always more pressing; political appointees view public diplomacy as a waste of time because foreigners do not vote. Most senior U.S. government officials rarely grant interviews to foreign media. In a department where making and executing foreign policy are considered more substantive endeavors, officers responsible for public diplomacy feel like second-class citizens and find themselves subject to burdensome bureaucratic rules and procedures.[6]

Particularly in the Arab and Muslim world, U.S. ambassadors who engage actively and frequently with the local media, students, nongovernmental organizations (NGOs), and religious leaders are the exception, not the rule. Ambassadors, who are political appointees, often do not speak the language of the country to which they are assigned. Especially in difficult languages such as Arabic, a dearth of fluent senior Foreign Service officers means less-than-effective spokespersons for the

United States. Embassy public affairs teams are also understaffed and underfunded. The process of receiving clearance to use policy talking points in public is often so onerous that the points are irrelevant by the time approval is granted.

The State Department retains important communications assets, including the Voice of America (VOA). At its peak during the Cold War, VOA, together with Radio Liberty and Radio Free Europe, reached 50 percent of the Soviet populace every week and between 70 and 80 percent of the population of Eastern Europe. Today, a mere 2 percent of Arabs hear VOA. It is time for the United States to rediscover its voice.

Rebuilding the Power to Persuade

Bolstering public diplomacy will take time and require a sustained effort. President George W. Bush's administration wisely created a 24-hour crisis response team to fight the short-term information war in Afghanistan. The real test will be whether the administration will support a permanent public diplomacy campaign that will endure long after U.S. troops return home.

The president and secretary of state should appoint a bipartisan commission to evaluate the state of the country's public diplomacy and make concrete recommendations for improving its development and delivery, especially to Arab and Islamic audiences. The commission should include experts in communications from the private sector (e.g., television programmers, film writers and directors, and advertising specialists) and academics with a thorough understanding of the Arab and Islamic worlds. The commission should build on the important work of the U.S. Advisory Commission on Public Diplomacy. The president and secretary of state should review the commission's findings promptly, decide which recommendations to accept, and order periodic progress reports on their implementation.

To Prevail: An American Strategy for the Campaign against Terrorism[7] lays out a number of ideas and initiatives worthy of consideration by such a commission, including:

The Battle for Hearts and Minds

- *Prioritize public diplomacy in the foreign policy process.*

Officials responsible for public diplomacy should be included as a matter of course in high-level meetings at which foreign policy is debated and formulated to enable these officials to inform policymakers of the likely impact of U.S. policies on public opinion abroad and to communicate the U.S. government's policy more effectively. Senior government officials should receive periodic media training and should be encouraged to brief foreign media regularly at the Foreign Press Center or in individual interviews. The president and cabinet-level officials should regularly grant interviews to the foreign media in advance of, and during, foreign trips and when "rolling out" policy initiatives. Simply including the foreign media in press conferences or in pressroom briefings does not suffice; exclusive or limited pool interviews garner significantly more airtime for the interviewee.

- *Strengthen research on public opinion.*

Foreign public opinion should not dictate foreign policy, but awareness of other views is vital in helping policymakers shape and explain policy. Funding for research on foreign public opinion remains low—about $5 million a year—and has declined in real terms during the past decade, despite new opportunities to conduct opinion polling in more open societies. The proposed commission should consider increasing funding for public opinion research.

- *Develop a rapid response capability.*

Technology makes possible the scouring of international, national, regional, and local media; academic publications; and Web sites and chat rooms for critical or erroneous commentary about U.S. policies. The commission should consider developing a rapid response program to correct or clarify distortions of U.S. policy. A team of public affairs officers could be assigned to respond to misinformation or one-sided opinion in real time. Ideally, no false charge in a major or influential medium would go unchallenged. The commission should also look carefully at the system used to formulate and clear talking points for senior officials at home and abroad. The United States needs to be able to act within news cycles, not in their wake.

- *Empower ambassadors, embassies, and Foreign Service officers.*

In an era of high-speed communications and direct contacts between foreign capitals, some believe that ambassadors have become obsolete. In fact, their relevance is greater now than ever before, but their role should be refined to focus more on public diplomacy. In selecting ambassadors and senior embassy officials, greater consideration should be given to language and presentation skills. These government officials should receive regular training in use of the media. Senior embassy officials should be encouraged to engage in the public debate in the countries to which they are assigned. These representatives should also consider a core function of their jobs to be granting interviews, writing opinion pieces or letters to the editor in the countries' newspapers, participating in televised debates and radio call-in shows, and cultivating writers of editorials and opinion pieces in newspapers published in the countries where they serve.

For effective communication, listening is as important as talking. U.S. envoys should devote more time to a broad cross-section of groups and individuals, including religious leaders, NGO representatives, students, professionals, and union members, not just their counterparts in the host country's Ministry of Foreign Affairs. In recruiting and training new Foreign Service officers, the State Department should focus more on communications skills. The department should place higher priority on the public diplomacy "cone" through which it trains officers and civil servants in the international dissemination of information and public diplomacy. The commission also should consider whether the U.S. government could improve the training it offers in foreign languages.

- *Create U.S. presence posts outside of foreign capitals.*

In many countries, regional media reach more people than do newspapers and television and radio programs that are based in the capital

This effort must become a foreign policy priority. The United States should clearly communicate to governments that control their countries' media and educational systems that broadcasting lies and teaching intolerance will have consequences for foreign assistance, political support, and military aid that the United States provides. So will double-talk behind the back of the United States. The United States should promote reform of the media and educational systems in these countries and support independent media around the world. Such efforts might include helping to draft media laws and academic curriculums, supporting watchdog groups, and providing financial and technical support to independent media. Such assistance could be directed in the first instance to independent NGOs to avoid charges of U.S. tampering.

Over time, technology and trade, both of which are needed for countries to succeed in a globalized economy, can help forge a new marketplace of ideas. Satellites, computers, televisions, and cellular phones will be the messengers of the twenty-first century. Technology carries with it ideas and information that can break up government monopolies and overcome intellectual biases. By exposing governments to rules, standards, pressures, and scrutiny and forcing them to be less arbitrary, corrupt, and autocratic, trade can remove barriers that keep individuals locked in and ideas locked out. The United States should deploy technology and trade as strategic weapons in the war to win hearts and minds around the world.

Smart Power

Rebuilding the power to persuade and remaking the marketplace of ideas can help the U.S. government counter critics of its policies. Yet, Washington must also address those who resent its power. The end of the Cold War was supposed to mark the end of history. Instead, it signaled the true beginning of U.S. hegemony: the preponderant influence and authority of one nation above all others. By most measures of hard and soft power, the United States' global dominance is extraordinary. Throughout history, hegemons have provoked envy and resentment.

Challengers arise to put hegemons in their place, and coalitions form to contain them. Thus far, the United States has escaped the fate of past hegemons. The post–World War II generation reined in U.S. power in order to extend it. U.S. citizens created international institutions— NATO, the International Monetary Fund, the World Bank, the UN, and the World Trade Organization, for example—that provided friends and allies fora in which to voice their views and vehicles for influencing the actions of the U.S. government. Europeans and Japanese accepted U.S. hegemony more easily because they were allowed to shape it.[8] During the Cold War, concern for Soviet tyranny trumped criticism of U.S. clout. The U.S. defeat of communism and its overwhelming power have dissuaded frontal attacks from other countries. So has the benign nature of U.S. hegemony; the imperial reach of the United States is primarily a function of the free will of the conquered, not the force of the conqueror. Now, however, those who find fault with the way the United States wields its power sound a useful warning that the country has begun to take its hegemony for granted and therefore risks losing it.

Some critics complain about unilateralism. According to this view, the United States disregards the interests of others and promotes international norms and treaties, only to flout them when they do not advance U.S. interests. This perception results as much from style as it does from substance. Those governments that are upset with Washington for certain policies—its failure to embrace the Comprehensive Test Ban Treaty, the International Criminal Court, a treaty on land mines, and the Kyoto Protocol; its lack of interest in UN mandates; or its imposition of extraterritorial sanctions against Cuba, Iran, and Libya—are bothered as much by the process (in which they perceive the United States as a country that ignores other views and dismisses compromise) as by the result.

Others fault the United States for its perceived failure to use its power at all. One billion people live in poverty, 110 million children go without schooling, seven million children die from neglect every year.[9] Meanwhile, the gap between the United States and much of the rest of the world is widening, even as more people than ever before are escaping poverty. In the poorest countries, people have incomes of $100–200 a year, whereas U.S. incomes average more than $30,000 a year. Thanks to technology, the have-nots are more aware of this gap today than they ever were before.

The first step toward smart power is to defuse the complaint that the United States acts unilaterally. The default approach of the U.S. government should be to work with others whenever it can and to act alone only when it must. This strategy requires building coalitions, sustaining alliances, and forging compromises. It requires listening to others. It requires sensitivity to concerns about cultural Americanization. It requires strengthening international institutions whose rules foster stability, create credibility, and enshrine U.S. norms. This approach also requires working on, not walking away from, difficult issues such as climate change, the biological weapons protocol, the nuclear test ban treaty, and the International Criminal Court, lest the United States alienate its friends and give moral ammunition to its foes.

The second step toward achieving smart power is to win over those who resent the United States' success—and the perceived U.S. failure to exercise its power on their behalf. The United States should become the champion of sustainable modernity. As the most prosperous country on earth, the United States bears a special responsibility—and a profound self-interest—to help spread the benefits and share the burdens of a globalized world. The country must become and be seen as an enthusiastic leader, not a reluctant follower, in international development, poverty alleviation, educational reform, debt relief and trade barrier removal for poor countries, as well as bridging the digital divide, preserving local cultures, combating the spread of infectious diseases, and promoting good governance. It also must reconsider its previously understandable support—in light of Cold War necessities and other strategic interests—of regressive regimes. Only then will the silent majority around the world believe that it has a stake in joining and supporting the status quo that the United States leads. Only then will the silent majority not vent its frustrations on the United States and its citizens.

The war of ideas will help determine whether the new century, like its predecessor, is an American century. The United States brings powerful weapons to the battlefield: freedom, opportunity, and tolerance. The nation's enemies can counter only with repression, regression, and fanaticism. Critics of the United States have useful corrections but no alternative system of values and practices that offers as much progress and possibility as the U.S. system does. The war of ideas is the United States' to win. The United States must approach it seriously.

Notes

1. See Pew Project on Global Attitudes, Washington, D.C., December 19, 2001.

2. Charles Krauthammer, "Unilateral? Yes, Indeed," *Washington Post*, December 14, 2001, p. A45.

3. William Safire, "Kangaroo Courts," *New York Times*, November 26, 2001, sec. A, p. 19.

4. Joseph S. Nye Jr., *The Paradox of American Power: Why the World's Only Superpower Can't Go It Alone* (Oxford and New York: Oxford University Press, 2002).

5. See Michael Rubin, "Sulaymaniyah Dispatch: Food Fight," *New Republic*, June 6, 2000.

6. See United States Advisory Commission on Public Diplomacy, "Consolidation of USIA into the State Department: An Assessment after One Year," October 2000, Washington, D.C.

7. Kurt M. Campbell and Michèle A. Flournoy, *To Prevail: An American Strategy for the Campaign against Terrorism* (Washington, D.C.: CSIS, 2001).

8. C. John Ikenberry, *After Victory: Institutions, Strategic Restraint and the Rebuilding of Order after Major Wars* (Princeton: Princeton University Press, 2001).

9. Global Economic Prospects and Developing Countries 2002, www.worldbank.org.

Edward Kaufman

A Broadcasting Strategy to Win Media Wars

Some have argued that using military means in the war against terrorism might ultimately make the problem worse by helping the opposition cast the campaign as a legitimate clash of civilizations.[1] In modern, post–Cold War international conflicts, we must pay attention not only to our military response to conflicts and crises but also to the role that information and media play in creating and feeding these conflicts. For instance, low-tech "hate radio" in hot spots such as Central Asia, Serbia, the West Bank, and Gaza has whipped up emotions and motivated the killing of thousands of people. Military power alone is often insufficient to resolve modern conflicts and will likely be unable to end this current war against terrorism. Effective broadcasting to "win hearts and minds" strengthens the traditional triad of diplomacy, economic leverage, and military power and is the fourth dimension of foreign conflict resolution. Particularly in times of crisis, the United States must deliver clear, effective programming to foreign populations via the media. How does one win modern media wars? All eyes now are on Afghanistan, but the impact of international media has not yet been measured in that war-torn country.[2] For a more complete case study, we have to look a little farther back—to the Balkans.

Edward Kaufman is a senior lecturing fellow at Duke University's School of Law and Fuqua School of Business. He has been a member of the Broadcasting Board of Governors since its inception.

Copyright © 2002 by The Center for Strategic and International Studies and the Massachusetts Institute of Technology
The Washington Quarterly • 25:2 pp. 115–127.

'Spinning' in Belgrade

In 1993, Senator Joseph Biden (D-Del.), then-chairman of the Foreign Relations Committee's Subcommittee on European Affairs, visited the Balkans to investigate what he could do to help end the genocide in Bosnia-Herzegovina. Staffers at the U.S. embassy in Belgrade warned Biden that Slobodan Milosevic would use Yugoslav state media to leverage the senator's visit to build his own popularity and support among the people of Serbia. They predicted that Milosevic would want to have a press conference after the meeting at which he and the senator could address the press. The state radio and television would not use what Biden said, but would use a voice-over saying that this important U.S. government official had come to Belgrade to pay homage to Milosevic, an influential player on the world scene. Biden made his meeting with Milosevic conditional on no press attendance.

U.S. embassy staff said Milosevic had used his control of state-owned radio and television to inflame the Serbian people. They thought that one of the reasons that the Serb soldiers had committed their crimes in Bosnia and Croatia was because of the daily broadcasts of the manufactured atrocities of the Bosnian Muslims, provoking a desire among the Serbs to seek revenge. They said that Serbian state television and radio had reported that the hated Croats and Muslims were raping nuns and killing babies. The media appeared to be escalating the conflict toward genocide.

Biden said he learned many things about Milosevic and the Balkans during his visit, the most important thing being how media can be misused to start and feed religious, ethnic, racial, and regional conflicts. If the United States is to deal with these problems in the future, he concluded, we have to move beyond military, political, and economic weapons.[3] We must learn how to fight the media war.

Biden became intimately involved in the effort to consolidate all U.S. international broadcasting after that trip. His legislation, the United States International Broadcasting Act of 1994, created the Broadcasting Board of Governors[4] (BBG) composed of eight private citizens—

four Democrats and four Republicans—and the director of the U.S. Information Agency (USIA). He did this to assure the integrity of the journalists in the organization and to maintain their ability to operate under the Voice of America (VOA) charter.[5] The government-funded BBG became an independent federal entity in October 1999 when the U.S. secretary of state replaced the USIA director on the board.

Forget Fire—Fight Media with Media

In an effort to resolve the Kosovo conflict, the United States intensified its existing economic sanctions on the Serbs and initiated a number of diplomatic efforts from 1998 to 1999 without success. The news media extensively covered the subsequent U.S. bombing campaign, beginning in 1999, to destroy Serbian heavy military equipment and compel the Serbs to exit Kosovo. What many U.S. citizens do not know is that the United States also instituted the most concentrated media focus directed toward a single foreign country in our history. The campaign used a plethora of different media methods and platforms, making the media a full-time partner of our military, economic, and diplomatic efforts to win the battle for Kosovo.

U.S. government broadcasters had been broadcasting into the Balkan region for years. VOA had been broadcasting in the local languages since 1943, and Radio Free Europe/Radio Liberty (RFE/RL) created its South Slavic Service in 1993. In mid-1998, VOA and RFE/RL, using shortwave transmitters, sent more than 40 transmitter-hours[6] of programs daily in Albanian, Bosnian, Croatian, Serbo-Croatian, and Serbian to the region. Local AM and FM affiliates added coverage in many areas. Surveys at the time showed VOA to be the number one international radio broadcaster with a regular listening audience of 14 percent in the targeted regions. As hostilities began, Milosevic pulled the plug on international broadcasters by shutting down their access to local affiliates, but this obstruction did not deter the VOA or RFE/RL. They expanded their broadcasting through external shortwave, medium-wave, and Internet transmissions and worked with the U.S. Department of

State and the U.S. Agency for International Development to bolster FM broadcasting in the area that became known as "the ring around Serbia."

The level of U.S. broadcasting increased dramatically in late 1998. RFE/RL expanded its South Slavic broadcasts and Internet service, added a new Albanian Service to Kosovo in February 1999, and by mid-March had increased shortwave and medium-wave broadcasts to a full 13.5 hours per day. RFE/RL also provided a number of publications by fax and e-mail, including the weekly *Balkan Report*, which was widely recognized as one of the best analyses of events in the region. At the same time, VOA began live streaming of both audio and video programming over the Internet. BBG transmission stations in Morocco, Germany, Spain, and Greece, as well as leased stations in Albania, Bulgaria, Hungary, Romania, and the United Kingdom, combined to bring total transmission hours to a peak of 80 transmitter-hours per day.

At the same time, RFE/RL began broadcasts via Commando Solo, a fleet of planes developed by the Defense Department to give almost instant surge-broadcasting capability during times of conflict. The BBG had worked out an agreement with the Defense Department that RFE/RL would be broadcast on a dedicated frequency under BBG control.

Contemporary Encirclement

The final piece of the puzzle was "the ring around Serbia." In March 1999, shortly after Milosevic shut down VOA and RFE/RL access to affiliates in Serbia, BBG directed a team of engineers to place a ring of FM broadcast transmitters in the countries around Serbia. Preconflict information indicated that more than 50 percent of the Serb audience received their news from local FM stations. Because FM signals travel in line-of-sight patterns and are therefore most effective broadcasting over short ranges and serving densely populated areas on flat landscapes, the mountainous terrain and longer distance presented challenges for the engineers.

The BBG first assembled a coalition of U.S. government agencies, U.S. embassies, and equipment suppliers, as well as host-country broadcasters, and then surveyed the sites; negotiated agreements; and selected, ordered, and shipped transmitters, antennas, shelters, generators, towers, satellite receivers, and other broadcast equipment. Finally, they installed the equipment and began to operate. By July 1999, three new FM stations were on the air in Bosnia, Croatia, and Romania. A fourth was added in northern Kosovo in October 1999 once conditions on the ground permitted. Transmitters were maximized for coverage of Belgrade.

The results achieved by this U.S. international broadcasting foray were striking. A nationwide survey in October 2000 found that international radio had played a major role in informing the Serbian people during the crisis.[7] Forty percent of Serbian adults tuned to RFE/RL and VOA for news during the elections and the beginning of the massive street demonstrations between September 24 and October 4, 2000. During this time, more Serbs listened to RFE/RL (37 percent) than to the main state radio station, Radio Belgrade (31 percent). On October 3, the crucial day before the start of demonstrations that overthrew Milosevic, 25 percent of Serb adults tuned in to RFE/RL and 20 percent to VOA. A majority of listeners to RFE/RL and VOA were young, blue-collar workers.

These results only bolstered what BBG already knew from a May–June 1999 survey of 448 Kosovar refugees who had fled to Albania during the conflict. That survey showed that international radio broadcasts were the primary source of news for Kosovar refugees in Albania during their expulsion from the embattled Serb province. Some 94 percent of refugees used international radio or television as a primary means of staying informed about the unfolding events in the NATO campaign against ethnic cleansing in Kosovo. The other major sources of information were Albanian media reports (89 percent) and word of mouth (76 percent). VOA's Albanian programming was the leading service, drawing 83 percent of adult refugees on a weekly basis. Deutsche Welle (55 percent) and the British Broadcasting Corp. (BBC) (50 percent) followed VOA. RFE/RL's Albanian Kosovo service also drew a

sizeable audience, attracting 31 percent of the adult refugee population weekly.[8]

This extraordinary outcome was achieved because all U.S. international broadcasting had been consolidated under the single authority of
the BBG. The single structure facilitated coordination with the Departments of State and Defense and enabled quicker decisions on allocating
transmitter time among the stations. Coordinated international broadcasting was as crucial as military, economic, and diplomatic efforts to
advance the U.S. agenda in the Balkans. Sadly, the results in other regions of the world, particularly where hate radio is used, have not been
as positive.

Battling Hate Media

From the days of the Nazi and Soviet propaganda machines, a particularly powerful form of media warfare, known as hate radio, has been a
favorite tool of tyrants and rebels alike. Hate radio keys up emotions
among part of the local population and incites violent conflict against a
target group by providing rationales for, and legitimizing, violence. It
relies on distortions of the truth; misreporting of events; and long, ven-
omous diatribes. Hate radio is a deadly but effective use of media.

In Rwanda and Burundi, hate radio drove genocide. Rwanda's Radio
Mille Collines is probably the most notorious example. Its broadcasts,
which disseminated hate propaganda and incited the murder of Tutsis
and of opponents to the Rwanda regime, greatly contributed to the
1994 genocide of almost one million people. Mille Collines, aided by
Radio Rwanda, the government-owned station, called on the Hutu majority to destroy the Tutsi minority. The programs were relayed to all
parts of the country via a network of transmitters owned and operated
by Radio Rwanda. "What are you waiting for? The graves are empty.
Take up your machetes and hack your enemies to pieces," according to
one reported broadcast.[9] Four years later, during the 1998 conflict between Democratic Republic of Congo authorities and their army on
one side and Rwandan soldiers and Congolese ethnic Tutsis on the

other, Radio Candip, a state broadcaster of the Democratic Republic of Congo, openly called for killing Tutsis, saying, "[B]ring a machete, a spear, an arrow, a hoe, spades, rakes, nails, and truncheons ... barbed wire, stones, and the like, in order, dear listeners, to kill the Rwandan Tutsis."[10]

Several international stations, including VOA, which rebroadcast via several FM stations locally, attempted to counter hate radio but with little effect. Probably too few hours of broadcast material were delivered locally to make much of an impact against the local media onslaught, but the transmissions did get the attention of the Rwandan government. Rwandan state television accused VOA and other international stations of "giving alarming information that the attackers have been making advances within the national territory ... as part of a vast campaign aimed at diverting the sons and daughters of this country from their noble mission of defending the fatherland." The television quoted one Kinshasa resident as saying he was "disgusted by the kind of mind-poisoning methods used by the VOA." The lesson learned was that, if international broadcasting is to impact locally delivered programs, it must be on the air more than just an hour or two per day.[11]

The United States must develop a better strategy for combating hate media because, as in both the Balkan and Rwandan massacres, hate radio is having a powerful, insidious effect in the West Bank, Gaza Strip, Afghanistan, and Pakistan. In these conflicts, newspapers and media other than radio also contribute to the intractable tensions in this region. Clearly, combating hate radio or the broader problem of hate media more effectively will not solve these conflicts. The Intifada, for example, has confounded policymakers for 14 years,[12] but hate media contributes to the problem. An article in an October 2000 edition of the Egyptian newspaper *Al-Ahram*, for example, concluded with the following paragraph:

> The bestial drive to knead Passover matzos with the blood of non-Jews is [confirmed] in the records of the Palestinian police where there are many recorded cases of the bodies of Arab children who had disappeared being found, torn to pieces without a single drop of blood. The most reasonable explanation is that the blood was taken

to be kneaded into the dough of extremist Jews to be used in matzos to be devoured during Passover.[13]

These days, hate propaganda goes beyond radio and newspapers. Television too is being used to convey escalatory messages. Around the Muslim world, the terrorists' September 11 message of hatred of the United States fit perfectly into the local news. Commentary that the United States was arrogant, anti-Muslim, and pro-Israel frequently accompanied the awful scenes of the collapsing trade towers on television and in local newspapers. Al Jazeera, the influential CNN-like Arab satellite television seen by 10 million people across the Middle East, was anything but evenhanded in its coverage.

Finally, a Response

Finding the truth in the Middle East can be difficult. BBG has fought for years for funding to obtain a real media presence in the Middle East. Only now is that effort being realized through the 2002 creation of the Middle East Radio Network (MERN).

MERN will be unique in the Middle East: a 24-hour-a-day, 7-day-a-week Arabic language service broadcasting news, analysis, editorial comment, talk, and music for the emerging generation and news seekers of all ages. Produced in the Middle East and in Washington, D.C., MERN breaks the mold of traditional international broadcasting. Its programming format throughout the day will aim to appeal consistently to a particular target audience and will not vary from hour to hour. Its target audience will be under-30 Arabs, who constitute more than 50 percent of the population throughout the region. Using a combination of powerful medium-wave and FM transmitters, as well as popular regional satellites, it will both broadcast to the region as a whole and generate individually targeted programs for Jordan, the West Bank/Gaza Strip, Iraq, Egypt, the Persian Gulf, and Sudan. Other targeted programming may be added in the future. MERN will thus appeal to audiences as a local station concerned for, and involved in, their daily lives. At the same time, MERN will better acquaint its listeners with the United States and make U.S. policies clearer.

A Growing Role for International Broadcasting

Combating hate radio and hate media is just one example of the need for a strong international broadcasting policy. In many places around the world, simply clarifying U.S. purpose and policy, not combating hate media, requires new initiatives. China is a good example where a flexible, creative system is needed to provide the U.S. point of view to the Chinese. As China's role in East Asia and the world grows, a disturbing 68 percent of urban Chinese consider the United States to be their nation's number one enemy.[14] Perceptions change when outside information challenges certain assumptions. Providing such information is vital to the well being of the United States, particularly in places where the flow of information is restricted. Currently, the Chinese government jams international broadcasting, blocks Internet sites, and tightly controls domestic media.

Beijing is especially good at giving visiting Western policymakers and businessmen the impression of a free press in China. CNN and the BBC are available at most first-class hotels, and the *International Herald Tribune* and the Asian edition of the *Wall Street Journal* are available in the lobby. None of these media sources, however, are available to the vast majority of Chinese. Chinese radio, television, and newspaper options exist, but the government tightly controls all of them. Although many are now "independent" business entities fighting each other for advertising, the government closely monitors their news and analysis.

Because the Internet could provide a new means to transmit information, Beijing still fears this medium's threat to their information monopoly, even though the Chinese government recognizes the Internet's economic and educational importance.[15] The government has instituted draconian regulations and conducts widespread electronic blocking of particular Web sites, usually international news sources. Once again, the government choreographs all this activity beautifully. When

President George W. Bush visited Shanghai to attend the meeting of Pacific Rim nations in October 2001, the Chinese government stopped blocking a number of Internet news sites including CNN, the BBC, Reuters, and the *Washington Post*.[16] The blocks were reactivated following Bush's departure.

As a result of all these governmental measures, the Chinese people are woefully short of objective information on the United States and its people. Ironically, they believe that they understand the United States quite well from syndicated sitcoms, movies, and music videos—a major problem for the development of a healthy, long-term Sino-U.S. relationship. In the short term, it is a policy disaster. The Chinese people's responses to the May 1999 bombing of the Chinese embassy in Belgrade and the April 2001 captured spy-plane incident are notable. The Chinese government's monopoly of information media enabled it to orchestrate Chinese public reactions to both incidents. In May 1999, rock-throwing demonstrators attacked the U.S. embassy; in April 2001, Chinese domestic media presented a one-sided version of what happened to the U.S. spy plane but deliberately toned down its rhetoric, and demonstrations were minimal. Finding anyone in China who has heard the U.S. version in either case is difficult. Ultimately, in a time of crisis with China, the U.S. president has no way to communicate directly to the Chinese people. The United States cannot afford to have 1.2 billion people, about 18 percent of the world's population, so ill-informed.

In order for the president to have what is needed to fight the media war, U.S. international broadcasting must adapt to this modern world and turn the media tide. How can the United States do this?

How to Make International Broadcasting More Effective

Some specific solutions can improve international broadcasting. With regard to China, Bush must first use his diplomatic leverage at the presidential level. Gaining permission to establish shortwave and particularly cross-border, medium-wave transmitters within range of the United States' high-priority target areas for international broadcasting in the Far East is essential. Fearing the Chinese reaction, local governments in several countries in the region have locked Radio Free Asia (RFA), whose stock-in-trade is coverage of domestic news in the target countries, out of logical transmitter sites. Yet, although China jams VOA and RFA broadcasts and Internet sites, the United States allows Chinese radio and television broadcasters on U.S. cable systems. China government television, CCTV, can be found on many cable systems in the United States and will soon be on many Time/Warner systems, including those in the major media markets of New York City, Los Angeles, and Houston. China government radio, China Radio International, also broadcasts unjammed on shortwave and can be found on a number of affiliated AM and FM radio stations in the United States. Officials at the highest levels of the U.S. government must demand reciprocity.

Beyond China, though, the United States also needs leverage with governments in countries where it wishes to have its own broadcast frequencies or local affiliates. Several years ago, the BBC set the objective to have FM stations in 100 of the world's national capitals by the end of 1999. They achieved 110 by that date and aim to have world service in 135 capitals by 2003.[17] One method the British used to accomplish this goal was having the prime minister contact national leaders in these countries to reinforce the priority the British government places on obtaining these frequencies.

Second, in important media markets, the BBG should own local broadcasting stations. Local censorship and market constraints apply to affiliate stations owned by the host country. Affiliates also do not put a high priority on U.S. broadcasts, and controlling what precedes and follows the U.S. programs on such stations is impossible. BBG ownership helps combat these problems. At the same time, prudence demands backup delivery via shortwave to places where government interference might occur.

Third, the BBG needs more access to modern equipment and satellites. Money can solve most of this problem. The BBG has the programming, but needs more satellite time and modern television production facilities and equipment, not only in the United States but also in regional centers overseas, to combat biased stations such as Al Jazeera.

Television is wildly popular in Iran, India, Indonesia, and China. In closed societies such as Iran and others in the Middle East, satellite dishes will be more accessible in the future. In more open societies such as Indonesia, Russia, Kosovo, Albania, the Philippines, Nigeria, and the countries of sub-Saharan Africa and Latin America, where satellites are accessible now, the BBG needs Congress to appropriate more funds for satellite time and satellite dishes for local affiliate stations to download programs for rebroadcast.

Fourth, existing shortwave transmitters must be refurbished. Shortwave and cross-border medium-wave are used for two purposes. They are still the media of choice in regions such as sub-Saharan Africa, south central Asia, and Eurasia. They are also needed almost everywhere for surge broadcasting in times of regional and international crises. In troubled times, the first thing that despots such as Milosevic do is block access to local affiliates. In those cases, the BBG must be able to rely on shortwave.

Many of the BBG shortwave transmitters are about 30 years old. Because of jamming and the recent crises in the Balkans and now throughout the Middle East, these transmitters now broadcast many more hours per day. Some of them have been on the air 24 hours a day broadcasting to the Middle East since September 11. Refurbishing these shortwave transmitters to extend their life would cost approximately $50 million in a one-time capital improvement expenditure.

Fifth, the key to success of international broadcasting continues to be the credibility of its broadcasts. The BBG must continue to have editorial independence to produce and deliver accurate, objective, and comprehensive programming. People will listen to the broadcasts only if they believe them. Real effectiveness absolutely needs the continued support of the Congress and the administration in maintaining the firewall between the BBG and outside governmental influences.[18]

Sixth, the BBG with congressional help must continue the reforms it started. The BBG's enabling legislation mandates that the board "at least annually" review broadcast languages for additions and deletions and that it evaluate the effectiveness of programs. In its first two Language Reviews, the board has made difficult decisions that have seen resources moved in the post–Cold War period from areas such as Central and Eastern European to grossly underfunded but higher priority areas such as the Middle East. It must continue to use its Language Service Review process to assure the allocation of resources to the proper language services based on the priorities of U.S. foreign policy. Even though resources for research increased fivefold in recent years, the BBG must use more surveys, focus groups, expert panels, and other methods to help broadcasters know what is working. The BBG should continue to assure that U.S. international broadcasting adheres to the highest standards and fulfills the individual, complementary missions of the broadcast entities. It also must start a twenty-first century advertising and promotion effort so that those in the client countries know when and how to access their programs.

Finally, since the BBG was created in 1994, its budget has declined by about 12 percent in real dollars, from $573 million to $507 million. Part of this deterioration stems from the logical consolidation of duplicate radio and engineering services after the end of the Cold War. Yet the challenges that U.S. international broadcasting faces are greater and more varied today than ever before. The number of languages broadcast today is higher than during the Cold War, even though the use of a number of languages used during the Cold War broadcasts, such as Polish, Hungarian, Bulgarian, Czech, Slovak, and Brazilian Portuguese, have either been reduced or eliminated.

In the twenty-first century, the U.S. president will continue to face many kinds of international problems. If events at the end of the twentieth century are any indicator, ethnic, religious, racial, and regional conflicts will cause them. Hate media sponsored by individuals, groups, or states will escalate many of them. Military, economic, or diplomatic tools will be insufficient to prevent or solve them. Democracy, freedom, and a civil society require constant advocacy. International broadcasting must return to the front page of the U.S. foreign policy agenda. Media is a big part of the problem and, therefore, the president must have a strong and prominent media solution.

Notes

1. Rob de Wijk, "The Limits of Military Power," *The Washington Quarterly* 25, no.1 (winter 2002): 90.

2. A 1999 survey of Afghan males (the Taliban would not permit interviews with women) by the Afghanistan Media Research Center in Peshawar, Pakistan, found that Voice of America (VOA) and British Broadcasting Corp. (BBC) broadcasts each attracted about 80 percent of the male listening audience on a weekly basis. The impact of the war on the listening rate remains to be seen. Another survey of the population will occur in the spring of 2002.

3. Sen. Joseph Biden, interview by author, Wilmington, Del., December 27, 2001.

4. The BBG oversees all U.S. nonmilitary international broadcasting, including VOA, which broadcasts in 53 languages around the world; Radio/TV Marti, which broadcasts to Cuba; Radio Free Europe/Radio Liberty, which is a private corporation funded by a grant from the BBG and which broadcast in 25 languages now but will soon add Dari and Pashto broadcasts to Afghanistan as "Radio Free Afghanistan"; grantee Radio Free Asia, established by the BBG in 1996, which broadcasts in nine languages to Asia; and Worldnet Television, a global satellite-delivered program soon to be merged with VOA. All entities are entirely U.S. government–funded.

5. VOA's legal requirement under Public Law 94-350 to broadcast "accurate, objective, comprehensive" news has on a number of occasions put the organization at odds with policymakers and U.S. ambassadors. The BBG's "firewall" function isolates VOA and other entities from direct interference.

6. One transmitter broadcasting for one hour produces one transmitter-hour. Typically, international broadcasters use at least three transmitters for each program on shortwave to ensure at least one clear frequency at any given time.

7. The Institute of Social Sciences, University of Belgrade, conducted a nationwide survey of 1,104 face-to-face interviews for the Intermedia Survey Institute (ISI). ISI used a short questionnaire designed for a crisis situation that would allow quick turnaround and would measure the audience for radio and television. The questionnaire was distributed October 3, 2000, with results presented three days later.

8. ISI organized a survey of ethnic Albanian refugees from Kosovo at the request of the BBG. BBSS Gallup from Sofia, Bulgaria, and Index Albania from Tirana, Albania, conducted the fieldwork. The survey was conducted with 448 refugees in Kukes, Tirana, Durres, Shkoder, Fier, and Lezhe. In addition, 36 in-depth interviews utilizing detailed, open-ended questions were conducted with refugees who listened to international radio before and after their

departure from Kosovo. Dr. Robert Austin of the University of Toronto monitored the fieldwork and provided analysis of the in-depth interviews.

9. A version of this quote is now the title of a book on the subject. See Bill Berkeley, *The Graves Are Not Yet Full: Race, Tribe, and Power in the Heart of Africa* (New York: Basic Books, 2001).

10. Radio Netherlands Wereldomroep Web site, www.rnw.nl/realradio/dossiers/html/hateradioafricame.html.

11. VOA programs did, however, facilitate reunification of more than 3,000 (mainly Tutsi) families who had been dispersed during the genocides.

12. "Intifada" literally means "uprising" in Arabic. The earlier Intifada (1987–1993) consisted of stone-throwing Palestinian youths facing Israeli troops who were using tear gas and rubber-covered steel bullets. Thirteen people died. The current uprising is much more violent, with more than a thousand deaths so far and the level of weaponry employed virtually that of wartime.

13. Translated and reported by Middle East Media Research Institute, which further pointed out, "*Al-Ahram* is not a fringe publication; it is the *New York Times* of Egypt and has the largest circulation of any Egyptian paper. The Egyptian government funds *Al-Ahram* and its editor is appointed by the president of Egypt."

14. Per a September 2000 survey ISI conducted in three large Chinese cities. The second-ranked country was Japan, which drew 10 percent.

15. Internet use in the September 2000 survey of the three Chinese cities ranged from 8.2 percent to 12.3 percent. Of those Internet users, 77.5 percent reported using the medium to read news and 35.7 percent reported using it to listen to news.

16. Clay Chandler, "China Again Censoring Web," *Washington Post*, October 23, 2001, p. E1.

17. BBC 1999–2000 annual report.

18. The "firewall" function is one of the board's most important responsibilities. It is based on the statement in the 1998 act (Sec. 305(d)) that "The Secretary of State and the Board, in carrying out their functions, shall respect the professional independence and integrity of the International Broadcasting Bureau, its broadcasting services and the grantees of the Board." On March 10, 1998, in the conference report on the Foreign Affairs Reform and Restructuring Act, Congress specified that the bill did not alter the consolidation of U.S. international broadcasting achieved in 1994, but did prevent the board and the broadcasting entities from being merged into the State Department with the rest of what was then USIA. The report gave two reasons for this mandate: to provide "deniability" for the State Department when foreign governments complain about U.S. broadcasting and to provide a firewall between the department and the broadcasters to ensure the integrity of the journalism.

Lael Brainard

Compassionate Conservatism Confronts Global Poverty

On March 22, 2002, President George W. Bush announced his intention to request an increase of $5 billion per year over current foreign assistance levels of $12.5 billion through the creation of a bilateral development fund, the Millennium Challenge Account (MCA). The MCA presents an enticing opportunity to transform U.S. development policy. Because the MCA is being crafted at a time when national security has returned to the forefront of the nation's consciousness, however, there is an acute risk that the MCA will instead further add to the confusion of overlapping U.S. programs and criteria for developing nations. In announcing the program, Bush stated explicitly, "We fight against poverty because hope is an answer to terror."[1]

To implement the program, the administration has recommended the creation of an independent agency, the Millennium Challenge Corporation (MCC), to allocate the new funding based on objective selection criteria measuring a nation's commitment to "governing justly, investing in people, and encouraging economic freedom."[2] Yet, numerous aspects of the MCA's internal design and operation that will prove

Lael Brainard is the New Century Chair at the Brookings Institution in Washington, D.C. This article is part of a joint Brookings Institution/Center for Global Development project on the Millennium Challenge Account under the auspices of the Brookings Global Poverty Reduction Initiative. The author wishes to thank Allison Driscoll for excellent research assistance.

The Washington Quarterly • 26:2 pp. 149–169.

crucial to its ability to meet these goals still have to be developed. On what kinds of programs will the MCA focus? Will the established methodology to select countries yield the types of recipients intended, or will geopolitical imperatives influence the allocation?

Moreover, the MCA should not be designed in a vacuum, or it will fall prey to the tension between foreign policy and development goals that chronically afflicts U.S. foreign assistance programs. The president's decision to establish a new agency to administer the MCA was a clear vote to design around the 7,000-strong U.S. Agency for International Development (USAID), established in 1961 with the mission of "promoting sustainable development," rather than confront the messy challenge of reforming it. Nevertheless, a successful transformation of U.S. development policy requires a concrete plan for how the efforts of the two organizations can complement each other.

Congress must also be a committed partner if the MCA is to break new ground on development assistance. The unprecedented flexibility sought for the MCA will only be possible if the design contains adequate self-executing safeguards and is presented in the context of a coherent foreign assistance strategy.

The proposed expansion of U.S. assistance to combat global poverty in nations committed to reform is ambitious and exciting. There is a risk, however, that this administration-led initiative will fall short of expectations unless many critical, remaining decisions are made, and soon, so that MCA funding does not follow the fruitless path of much of U.S. aid during the Cold War; so that the MCA and USAID can avoid bureaucratic redundancies that lead to waste; and so that the MCA can enjoy the kind of congressional and national support it will need to succeed—and positively transform U.S. foreign assistance efforts at large.

Potential Promise and Pitfalls

At best, the MCA could transform U.S. policy toward the poorest countries over time—driving greater coherence among U.S. trade, aid, and investment policies and helping to rationalize existing programs. With clear criteria and substantial sums of money made available on enticing terms, the MCA could create incentives for governments to improve economic policies and governance while helping strong performers sustain growth and improve investment climates. By establishing a record of success, the MCA could earn both the trust of Congress and a measure of independence from political meddling by the executive branch, freeing it from burdensome restrictions and procurement requirements faced by other agencies. A successful MCA could also have salutary ripple effects on other U.S. aid programs by strengthening public support, clarifying missions, and leading to greater overall coherence. Such a best-case scenario could strengthen USAID, helping it to focus more clearly on challenges the MCA does not address: humanitarian crises, transition in postconflict countries, and social investments in weaker performing states.

Unfortunately, darker scenarios are at least as plausible, wherein the MCA becomes one more pot of money among a morass of overlapping U.S. programs and conditions. At one extreme, by maintaining too high a degree of purity, the MCA might remain beyond the reach of most poor nations. It would thus become the more marginal player in development assistance rather than the key player, relevant only for the few stellar performers with substantial local capacity to formulate and implement proposals, while USAID would remain the main source of U.S. funding for the far more numerous, less capable countries.

At the other extreme, the MCA could become the preferred fund not only for the best performers but also for geopolitically salient countries. This outcome could very well emerge if the increased demand for assistance associated with security imperatives and the rapidly deteriorating budgetary environment conspire to undermine the MCA's purity. If this scenario evolves, the lines between the MCA and other forms of assistance would blur, and Congress might feel compelled to constrain the MCA as it currently constrains existing assistance programs.

In fact, the administration's November 2002 decision to expand the MCA pool of eligible countries to include not just the poorest but also lower-middle–income countries moved in precisely this direction, taking development advocates completely by surprise. With this change, the eligibility pool encompasses nations already among the largest beneficiaries of politically directed U.S. assistance but which do not qualify for concessional lending from the World Bank, such as Russia, Jordan, Egypt, Colombia, Peru, and South Africa. In fiscal year 2002, these six nations received $1.25 billion in U.S. economic assistance—one-fifth of all foreign economic assistance for nondisaster programs.

The deteriorating budget outlook raises the stakes. In the words of the director of the Office of Management and Budget, Mitch Daniels, "Unexpected new defense and homeland security spending is needed to protect America from new threats. Given these two developments, it is absolutely essential that we set aside business as usual and keep tight control over all other spending." Within the context of the overall discretionary spending increase cap of four percent, and in light of the increased demand for security and defense spending, finding room in the budget for the MCA and the additional $1 billion in HIV/AIDS funding pushed by Congress and promised by President Bush has proven difficult. In fact, the FY 2004 request for the MCA totals just $1.3 billion—20 percent less than the illustrative funding level of $1.66 billion suggested by a White House fact sheet released after the MCA proposal.[3]

U.S. Foreign Assistance: A Servant to Two Masters

To shape the success of the MCA requires a clear understanding of why previous programs have failed. More often than not, development policy and foreign policy have pulled U.S. foreign assistance programs in two different directions. Too often, U.S. economic assistance is equated with development assistance, contributing greatly to aid's discredit. The history of U.S. assistance is littered with tales of corrupt foreign officials using aid to line their own pockets, support military buildups, and pursue vanity projects. It is no wonder that few studies show clear correlations between aid flows and growth.

It makes little sense, however, to measure the return on investment in economic terms when aid dollars were allocated according to geopolitical criteria in the first place. In some cases, aid has yielded the desired geopolitical outcomes while failing to yield economic gains; in other cases, it has failed on both fronts. Most examples of aid lost to corruption, waste, or diversion—as was the case in Zaire, Liberia, Sudan, and Somalia—involved aid allocated according to Cold War logic. The billions of aid dollars poured into Egypt since the Camp David peace accords may have achieved their goals even though they have been criticized for failing to produce durable economic or political modernization. On the other hand, even politically motivated assistance can yield impressive economic dividends when recipients are committed to reform and have sound economic policies, as happened in Taiwan and South Korea.

It is important to distinguish between the principles that guide the allocation of U.S. aid among countries and the purposes for which aid is spent in those countries. Strictly speaking, for assistance to have the greatest impact on a nation's development, funds not only must be spent on economic development but also must be allocated on the basis of development worthiness. The fact of the matter is that the majority of what is considered "economic assistance" in the U.S. budget is actually directed to countries based on political considerations, even though the money itself is used for economic purposes. Only about a third of existing FY 2002 U.S. bilateral economic assistance (and an even smaller portion of overall aid) is allocated among countries based on developmental priority, and in contrast to the MCA, much of this aid is not based on performance but rather on assessed needs as well as on the political and economic objectives of the United States.

To make this distinction clearly, table 1 shows a taxonomy of various interests and objectives that U.S. assistance intends to promote.[4] (This taxonomy implicitly assumes a set of disqualifying political criteria, such as demonstrating inadequate respect for human rights or engaging in activities contrary to U.S. or international security interests such as proliferation.)

In principle, pure development assistance should be allocated to the investments with the highest potential social value, which generally re-

Table I: Foreign Policy Goals of U.S. Assistance

Type of Beneficiary	Objectives/Interests of U.S. Foreign Policy	Examples
Strategic Partner	• To maintain goodwill or provide a political reward deemed vital to U.S. interests.	Egypt
Quid Pro Quo	• To secure cooperation on a particular activity (e.g., counternarcotics and counterterrorism measures). • Mainly targeted at cooperative activity but may encompass development assistance.	Colombia
Regional Linchpin	• To help maintain the economic stability of a country that serves as a critical regional anchor whose instability could have ripple effects throughout the region. • Targeted at development.	South Africa
Failing/Postconflict	• To avoid a vortex of instability that poses risks in the region or more generally through external intervention.	Afghanistan
Salient, Stable	• To maintain the support and goodwill in multilateral arenas of countries where the United States has moderate to negligible direct interests in their economic development.	Senegal
Afflicted with Humanitarian Crises	• To address humanitarian emergencies, regardless of the development worthiness of the affected countries.	Hurricane Mitch

flects a combination of the extent of need and the local policy environment. Typically, U.S. development assistance is conditioned on the beneficiary's policy performance and on per capita income levels, with the poorest countries receiving the most generous assistance. Unlike the existing USAID Development Assistance and Child Survival and Health funds, which are allocated to countries whose development needs are most compelling, the MCA would attempt to isolate the highest potential investments by targeting only the best performing poor countries.

The figures in table 2 show that less than one-third of the administration's FY 2003–requested U.S. foreign assistance budget of roughly $18 billion[5] is actually devoted to development assistance, in the strict sense that both the eligibility criteria and the programmatic impact focus on development. Another quarter of the foreign assistance budget is directed toward economic ends but is allocated according to political criteria, and the remainder is provided for security and humanitarian assistance and contributions to international organizations. Of the $5.9 billion in development assistance, $2.7 billion, or slightly less than half, is for bilateral development assistance; and the remaining development assistance is for multilateral organizations, food aid, the Peace Corps, and U.S. export and investment programs. Two striking comparisons emerge from these numbers: The proposed $5 billion magnitude of the MCA is nearly double the size of existing U.S. bilateral development assistance programs, but the United States currently spends very little on bilateral development assistance—only about half the level of bilateral economic aid for political purposes. The president's budget request for FY 2004 would increase the share of the foreign assistance budget devoted to bilateral development aid by half—from 15.0 percent to 22.6 percent—reflecting the new funding for the MCA and the Global AIDS Initiative.

In contrast with the majority of U.S. foreign assistance, the MCA's allocation criteria, based solely on economic performance and governance, would be the closest to a development purist's blueprint for aid that the United States has ever attempted. In many respects, the MCA is precisely the sort of fund that development advocates had hoped would emerge as the Cold War wound down. Instead, in the absence of the aid imperative associated with the threat of communism, development assistance declined through much of the 1990s until initiatives on debt relief and HIV/AIDS were funded at the end of the decade. Paradoxically, the MCA, which would be the largest single increase in pure development assistance, was announced only a few months after the tragedy of September 11, 2001.

Security experts were puzzled by the proposal to sharply increase pure development assistance at a moment of greatly increased need for political funding to reward allies in the antiterrorism coalition, shore

Table 2: U.S. Foreign Assistance and Development

TYPE OF ASSISTANCE	FY 2003 REQUEST (IN $ BILLIONS)	% OF TOTAL	LEAD AGENCY
TOTAL	18.7	100	
DEVELOPMENT AID	5.8	31.0	
Bilateral Development Assistance^A	2.8	15.0	USAID
Food Aid for Development^B	0.6		State, USAID
Multilateral Development Programs	1.4		Treasury, State
U.S. Export, Investment Programs; Peace Corps and Development Foundations	1.0		Independent agencies
POLITICALLY ALLOCATED ECONOMIC ASSISTANCE	5.1	27.3	
Economic Support Funds (ESF)	2.5		State, USAID
Assistance for Eastern Europe & the Baltic States (SEED)	0.5		State, USAID
Assistance for the Independent States of the Former Soviet Union (FSA)	0.8		State, USAID
International Narcotics Control and Law Enforcement (INCLE)^C	0.9		State
Nonproliferation, Antiterrorism, Demining, and Related Programs (NADR)^C	0.4		State
HUMANITARIAN ASSISTANCE	1.6	8.6	
Migration and Refugee Assistance (MRA)	0.7		State
Disaster Assistance	0.3		USAID
Emergency Food Aid (Title II, P.L. 480)	0.6		USAID
SECURITY ASSISTANCE	5.0	26.7	
Foreign Military Finance (FMF)	4.1		Defense, State
International Military Education and Training (IMET)	0.08		Defense, State
Peacekeeping Operations and International Peacekeeping	0.8		Defense, State
INTERNATIONAL ORGANIZATIONS AND PROGRAMS^D	1.2	6.4	State

Notes

A   Although the majority of these funds are bilateral, this category includes some funds for regional or global programs as well as contributions to some international agencies.

B   The table includes Public Law 480, Title II (nonemergency and humanitarian assistance) food aid. Roughly another $0.6 billion in food aid should be available through Public Law 480, Title I (concessional sales) programs and Section 416(b) surplus commodity programs. Because these are budgeted through and administered by the Department of Agriculture, they are not reflected here.

C   In fact, less than half of the counternarcotics assistance is devoted to development. The remainder, which is devoted to interdiction, may fit better conceptually in the security assistance category; this is also the case for the NADR spending.

D   Includes both assessed and voluntary contributions.

The Battle for Hearts and Minds

up "front-line" states, and stabilize failed states. In fact, few such countries could meet economic performance and governance tests, even though Bush used this rationale when he announced the MCA, declaring, "We also work for prosperity and opportunity because they help defeat terror. ... When governments fail to meet the most basic needs of their people, these failed states can become havens for terror."[6]

Through 2003, there had been an enormous increase in terrorism-related assistance—on the order of $3.3 billion in FY 2002,[7] but development assistance has remained flat, despite compelling needs on infectious disease and education. With requirements for security-related assistance increasing and with an overall budget crunch, the risk is high that MCA funding could be diverted to strategically important countries or that USAID funding for critical health and education programs in weaker but just as needy nations could be squeezed.

Critical Design Elements

Whether or not the MCA is transformational for U.S. development policy hinges in great part on its design and operation. As of the end of 2002, the Bush administration had developed details on three elements of its design. First, the MCA would be administered by a new government corporation—the MCC—overseen by a board composed of cabinet-level officials, and chaired by the secretary of state. Second, the MCC would have a staff of roughly 100 on limited-term appointments. Third, extraordinarily detailed information has been provided on performance indicators—the criteria for selecting countries. In contrast, the administration has made no statement on several critical operational questions:

• What types of programs would the MCA fund?

• Would the MCA support expenditures not currently funded by USAID, such as budget support and sectoral support, as well as capital projects and recurrent costs?

- How would monitoring and evaluation be performed?
- What is the division of responsibilities between the MCA and other U.S. agencies, such as USAID and the Overseas Private Investment Corporation (OPIC)?

The theory animating the MCA appears akin to a take-off model, according to which foreign assistance plays a catalytic role at an initial, critical stage, helping a country with good policies to attract investment and trade, thereby graduating after a relatively short time. In the president's words, "Countries that live by these three broad standards—ruling justly, investing in their people, and encouraging economic freedom—will receive more aid from America. And, more importantly, over time, they will really no longer need it, because nations with sound laws and policies will attract more foreign investment."[8]

Most development experts would expect this process to take decades rather than the several-year horizon that the MCA architects have suggested. Nonetheless, many outside observers support the emphasis on strong policy environments and hope that the MCA's focus on the best performers will produce concrete results and thereby win political support from Congress and the public over time.

Although research elsewhere provides more detailed recommendations for the MCA design,[9] the ultimate success or failure of the MCA initiative largely hinges on what decisions are made on a few critical issues.

Selection Criteria

The administration has highlighted the selection criteria as the defining aspect of the MCA. The decision to fund only the best performers not only intends to create good incentives for reform but also is the underlying rationale to provide both the beneficiaries and administering agency a greater sense of ownership as well as more flexibility in the use of funds. Getting the selection criteria right is, therefore, absolutely critical. Although compelling in theory, however, the data are unlikely to be up to the task in practice, creating greater scope for discretion than might be hoped.

Countries must meet per capita income criteria, which rise progressively over the first three years. In the first year, only countries eligible to borrow from the International Development Association (IDA) and having annual per capita incomes less than $1,435 (the historical IDA threshold) will be considered. In the second year, the pool will expand to include all countries with annual per capita incomes less than $1,435, regardless of IDA eligibility. In the third year, all countries with per capita incomes up to $2,975 a year—the World Bank threshold for lower-middle–income countries—will be included.

Selection will be based on scores on 16 data indicators, grouped in three broad areas: (1) governing justly (six indicators), (2) investing in people (four indicators), and (3) promoting economic freedom (six indicators). To qualify for assistance, a country must score above the median overall on at least half of the indicators in each area and specifically on the "controlling corruption" indicator. Countries with annual per capita incomes less than $1,435 will be scored against the median in their group while those with incomes between $1,435 and $2,975, when they become eligible in the third year and beyond, will be evaluated separately.

On the surface, this approach is as analytical and objective as one is likely to find in the realm of policy. The method is appealing insofar as it lays out a transparent methodology, against which the actual results can be compared to check for fairness and objectivity. In principle, the data should measure those variables that empirical research has shown to be the best predictor of poverty reduction and growth. In practice, the Bush administration's indicators—emphasizing responsible fiscal and monetary management, investments in basic health and education, and accountable and efficient governance—conform to this approach. Most economists would also support the inclusion of efficient levels of regulation and economic openness, although the role of trade openness in contributing to growth has been contested.[10] Finally, including indicators measuring political rights and civil liberties is important for winning U.S. domestic political support.

In effect, however, this approach produces some surprising outcomes, as evidenced by a dry run undertaken by Steve Radelet.[11] The most notable result is that both China and Egypt would qualify quite comfortably under this methodology, despite China's severe human rights deficiencies and Egypt's history of wasting vast quantities of aid.

There are several reasons why this approach risks yielding results that do not comport with common sense. First, the quality of the data varies enormously. Indicators for a country's policies on health and education can be measured with numerical precision, as is the case for fiscal and monetary performance in general; but indicators for trade openness, the regulatory climate, and most of the governance data are surveys or composites of a variety of statistics, which are measured with a high degree of error.[12] Further, even though the administration's proposed inclusion of data on the number of days to open a business has intuitive appeal, the data series is in fact new, and its contribution to growth is yet unproven.

Second, the methodology tends to magnify rather than correct data deficiencies. Because countries are required to score above the median on half the indicators in each category, and the categories contain several indicators that are highly correlated, some countries achieve eligibility despite what might seem a disqualifying weakness in the remaining subset of indicators. Thus, Egypt, which has a terrible record on overregulation and trade protection, nonetheless gets a passing score on economic freedom on the basis of the macroeconomic indicators alone, which are likely to be interrelated. China qualifies on governing justly despite the country's terrible human rights record because China scores above the median on the half of the indicators relating to governance and corruption, which are highly correlated, rendering the remaining indicators that measure political and civil rights in the governing justly area irrelevant. Finally, the MCA's emphasis on virtue relative to need is starkly evident in that eligible countries are home to only 12.8 percent of the population of sub-Saharan Africa—the poorest region in the world.

Political Discretion or Political Bias?

Problems inherent in the selection methodology, combined with significant lags and incomplete coverage in the data, are bound to leave a large role for subjective judgment. This in itself is not surprising and need not bias the selection process, but in allowing more room for discretion, such problems could contribute to greater geopolitical bias, given the administration's decisions to designate the secretary of state as the lead on the MCC's board of directors and to expand the eligibility pool to include politically salient countries in the third year of operation.

In particular, although the effect that including lower-middle–income countries in the MCA would have on poverty reduction and growth remains open for debate, one cannot deny that this approach is essential for bringing strategically significant countries such as Jordan, Egypt, and South Africa into the tent. Table 3 shows the amount of foreign economic assistance that currently goes to countries likely to qualify for the MCA in the first three years. The expansion of eligible recipients, associated with the inclusion of the lower-middle–income countries, considerably expands the potential for overlap between the MCA and funding under existing assistance programs, especially those allocated according to political considerations. Lower-middle–income countries that could qualify for the MCA account for 34 percent of current Economic Support Fund aid and 24 percent of development assistance for counternarcotics programs. Overall, these countries account for almost $1 billion in current aid—nearly double the assistance received by likely MCA countries with lower per capita incomes.

With the inclusion of the lower-middle–income group, countries receiving one-quarter of current U.S. economic assistance would be eligible for the MCA. By themselves, the low-income countries account for 8 percent of existing assistance—or $0.5 billion—which is only one-tenth of promised MCA funding levels. A central issue, therefore, is whether the MCA funding would constitute additional funding for these countries, free up existing assistance to be allocated elsewhere, or effectively substitute for this assistance eventually.

Table 3: Current U.S. Economic Assistance for Likely MCA Countries (FY 2003 Request, $ Millions)

MCA-Eligible Countries	Development Assistance	ESF	SEED/ FSA	INCLE Development	Total
Total: Low-income countries (less than $1,435)	326	64	115	42	547
Percent of Total	12	3	9	14	8
Total: Lower-middle–income countries ($1,435–2,975)	121	775	28	69	993
Percent of Total	4	34	2	24	15
Total: MCA-eligible countries	447	839	143	111	1540
Percent of Total	16	37	11	38	23
Total: All countries	2740	2290	1250	291	6571

Sources: The list of likely eligible countries is based on Steve Radelet, "Qualifying for the Millennium Challenge Account," Center for Global Development, December 13, 2002, app., www.cgdev.org/nv/Choosing_MCA_Countries.pdf (accessed January 22, 2003). Estimates of foreign assistance are from the U.S. Department of State "FY 2003 International Affairs (Function 150) Budget Request, Account Tables," February 4, 2002, www.state.gov/documents/organization/9194.pdf (accessed January 22, 2003).

Overlap with Trade Preferences and Debt Relief

For U.S. development policy to achieve maximum effectiveness, it should develop an integrated approach toward meritorious countries, combining aid with the powerful tools of trade, investment cooperation, and debt relief. Thus, an important question is whether the incentives associated with MCA eligibility are closely aligned with eligibility for complementary U.S. trade and debt relief programs for developing countries. The overlap turns out to be strikingly low.[13] The Heavily Indebted Poor Countries (HIPC) program targets those countries whose

The Battle for Hearts and Minds

debt burdens are deemed an impediment to poverty reduction and growth. HIPC includes fairly stringent selection criteria on income and the degree of a country's indebtedness and openness. The program further requires that a significant portion of the proceeds be devoted to the same types of social investments included in the MCA selection criteria. Remarkably, only 7 of the 27 countries that have been approved for HIPC are likely to be eligible for the MCA, while the remaining 16 countries likely to qualify for the MCA are not HIPC eligible.

The United States has several trade preference programs for developing nations; these programs provide favorable access to the U.S. market through zero tariffs (and quota relief in some textile and apparel areas). The African Growth and Opportunity Act (AGOA), Caribbean Basin Initiative (CBI), and Andean Trade Preference Act (ATPA) programs provide the most generous terms in their respective regions. The regional programs have selection criteria on per capita income, corruption, and trade openness—similar to the MCA's criteria—and include additional conditions on workers' rights. The AGOA program also requires progress on the same types of social investments in basic health and primary education that the MCA emphasizes. Still, the overlap is slim. So far, 38 countries have been approved for AGOA benefits; of these, only six are likely to qualify for the MCA initially, and one other country that meets the MCA selection criteria has not been approved for AGOA benefits. There is a similar mismatch with the CBI program: only 3 of the 24 CBI countries are likely to meet MCA criteria initially. For the ATPA program, two of the four eligible countries are likely to meet MCA criteria.

Country Ownership and Accountability

A core tenet of the MCA proposal is the recipient country's sense of ownership of the funded programs and accountability for achieving results. This approach accords with a growing international consensus that development investments perform better when they are formulated by the beneficiary government through a transparent and participatory process as part of an integrated development strategy. Indeed, the notional MCA process would appear to push this approach further than other bilateral aid organizations do. Notionally, governments that meet the selection criteria would submit funding proposals of their design, rather than reserve the responsibility for formulating proposals in the aid agency, as is currently the practice with USAID. To ensure accountability, a rigorous monitoring and evaluation process would accompany the greater flexibility accorded to beneficiaries.

The administration's rhetoric surrounding the MCA suggests the foreign aid analogy of the domestic welfare-to-work initiative, but those familiar with the messy realities of development in the field wonder whether the program will look so neat in practice. Will the limited capacity of governments in poor nations to formulate and implement acceptable grant proposals ultimately push the MCA to revert back to the current USAID model, whereby the U.S. government relies on an army of U.S. consultants and nongovernmental organizations to design the project and submit proposals? Will the complicated contracting procedures required by Congress necessitate a much greater field presence than envisaged?

With a staff of only 100, can the MCC effectively administer $5 billion in grants a year, including a rigorous, initial proposal review process and an even more rigorous monitoring and evaluation process? As table 4 (assistance-to-staff ratios for a number of bilateral aid agencies) shows, the administration's design implies a disbursement rate of $50 million per staff member annually, which is an order of magnitude greater than that for other aid agencies.

Program Areas

Finally, the administration has provided little information about the MCA's programmatic emphasis. What programs will be funded?

Presumably, certain program areas would be designated for MCA consideration at the outset. Clearly, there is broad support in the administration and Congress as well as at the international level for social

The Battle for Hearts and Minds

Table 4: Annual Assistance Flows Relative to Staff for Select Bilateral Aid Agencies

Country/Agency	Total Staff	Net Official Development Assistance (ODA) ($ millions)	Net ODA/Total Staff ($ millions)*
MCA (proposed)	100	5,000	50.00
USAID	7,920	10,172	1.28
Luxembourg	14	83	5.93
Canada	1,286	2,032	1.58
Denmark	338	1,434	4.24
Finland	185	321	1.74
Belgium	360	644	1.79
United Kingdom	1,077	3,315	3.08
European Community	3,219	4,460	1.39

* This figure actually overstates the ratio of ODA to staff for existing agencies. Although staffing figures are provided for the primary aid agency in each country, net ODA is often administered by multiple entities. In a 2002 Development Cooperation report, the Organization for Economic Cooperation and Development found that USAID administers only about half of U.S. net ODA.

Sources: Organization for Economic Cooperation and Development (OECD), "Belgium," *Development Co-Operation Review Series*, no. 23 (1997); OECD, "Canada," *Development Co-Operation Review Series*, no. 26 (1998); OECD, "Denmark," *Development Co-Operation Review Series*, no. 33 (1999); OECD Development Assistance Committee, "European Community," *Development Co-Operation Review Series*, no. 30 (1998); OECD, "Finland," *Development Co-Operation Review Series*, no. 31 (1999); OECD, "Luxembourg," *Development Co-Operation Review Series*, no. 32 (1999); OECD, "United Kingdom," *Development Co-Operation Review Series*, no. 25 (1997); OECD, "United States," *Development Co-Operation Review Series* (2002); U.S. Department of State, briefing on the "Millennium Challenge Corporation," Washington, D.C, November 25, 2002. All figures converted to 2001 dollars.

investments in areas such as basic health, primary education, and sanitation. Environmental and energy programs, however, do not appear to be priorities for the administration, despite support in Congress and the emphasis on sustainable development in the Millennium Development Goals adopted at the United Nations in September 2000 for achievement by 2015.[14] Conversely, various administration officials have emphasized support for private-sector development and have focused on infrastructure investment even though poor performance led USAID to abandon the infrastructure business long ago.

A second question is whether a particular amount would be set aside for each program area or if there would be other mechanisms to steer MCA funds toward investments the United States considers high priorities within a beneficiary country. Clearly, it would be more in keeping with the beneficiary-driven approach for MCA funding to be allocated strictly on the strength of beneficiary priorities. Yet, what happens if a country that the U.S. government, through the auspices of USAID, has deemed to be a high priority for HIV/AIDS prevention programs applies to the MCA only for infrastructure financing, for instance, to develop industrial capacity?

These critical questions about the internal MCA structure and practice will need to be answered if the MCA is to achieve its goals and win congressional approval. To minimize duplication and maximize the effectiveness of U.S. foreign economic cooperation, those answers can only be provided while considering existing programs.

What about USAID?

Over the past 30 years, every administration has tried to reform USAID. The Bush administration has decided instead to design its proposals around it. Even though development experts advocated from the beginning that an institutional home for the MCA should be created as an autonomous entity within USAID, it is revealing that most of the internal administration debate revolved around either housing it within the U.S. Department of State or establishing an independent corporation overseen by that department.[15] With the proposed creation of the MCC and the Department of Homeland Security, Bush will have earned the double-edged distinction of creating more new government agencies than any president since Jimmy Carter. One can only imagine that administration officials found it uncomfortable to choose between a near doubling of the budget of the much-maligned USAID or creating yet another bureaucracy.

Far from rendering USAID irrelevant, however, the MCA proposal has placed it squarely in the spotlight. To transform U.S. development policy successfully, the proposal must articulate a clear division of labor between the MCC and USAID as well as other programs for developing nations, such as OPIC and the Trade and Development Agency (TDA), or further exacerbate mission drift and duplication. In considering the MCC's relationship to USAID, it is useful to focus separately on those current USAID beneficiaries that qualify for the MCA and those that just miss being MCA eligible.

As explained earlier from data in table 3, the MCC would likely operate initially in countries that currently account for one-quarter of USAID's core development assistance and a high share of politically directed assistance that the State Department allocates and USAID manages. One could imagine a variety of scenarios regarding MCC and USAID coordination within these countries. At one end of the spectrum, MCA qualification could mean that USAID would pack up its bags and move elsewhere—the cleanest distinction between their missions. In a more realistic scenario, the MCC might provide funding for the local government's top priority programs while USAID maintained programs in areas of high priority to the United States, such as child survival and health and HIV/AIDS prevention. Indeed, local officials might game the system, applying to the MCC for program support in other areas, knowing that USAID would continue providing funds for U.S. priorities. Instead of a division along programmatic lines, responsibilities might be divided according to the differential budget authorities of the two agencies, with USAID continuing to invest in nonrecurring expenses such as teacher training and technical assistance while the MCC specialized in capital expenditures such as school buildings and recurring costs such as teacher salaries. Another alternative would have USAID continuing to focus on social sectors while the MCC became more focused on the private sector.

All of the scenarios where USAID and the MCC both operate in the same countries blur the sharp identification of the MCC with the best performers. Moreover, from a practical standpoint the administration has not yet determined what would happen to USAID mission staff in those countries where the MCC is likely to operate. Certainly, it would be wasteful to duplicate staff presence in the field; but USAID staff's assistance with both the preparatory work and with contracting for, monitoring, and evaluating MCC programs would suggest a troubling misalignment of USAID staff's incentives and responsibilities as well as heavy MCC dependence on USAID.

Additionally, for those near-miss countries that fail to qualify for the MCA by virtue of one or two indicators or are just below the median on several indicators, it is not clear whether the MCC or USAID would take lead responsibility. This question is particularly important because it is in precisely such near-miss countries that the promise of vastly increased foreign assistance could be catalytic in encouraging policy reforms (in contrast to poorly performing states, where the government is unlikely to possess the capacity to close the gap). Moreover, this category is likely to include some developmentally important countries, such as Uganda, which has become a poster child for developmental virtue, with the glaring exception of governance. One possible solution for near-miss countries is that limited MCA funding could initially be made available to address areas where performance is below the median but evaluated separately and managed through USAID on the presumption that the arrangement would require greater oversight and involvement than normal MCA grants would.

The current proposal has some bizarre implications even for the clearest hypothetical structure, in which the MCC operates in high-capacity countries and USAID works only in low-capacity countries. Assuming that USAID is left with three core missions—providing humanitarian assistance; helping postconflict countries through transitions; and addressing basic health, education, and governance challenges in poorly performing states—a greater preponderance of USAID programs would be directly related to foreign policy than ever before,[16] while in principle, the MCC's mission should be relatively free of foreign policy considerations. Yet, ironically, the administration's proposal gives the State Department the lead role on the board overseeing the pure development–oriented MCC while doing nothing to strengthen the department's input into USAID's increasingly foreign policy–oriented decisionmaking.

Important questions also arise about coordination among U.S. development programs more generally. Most obviously, the more the MCA moves in the direction of funding infrastructure and enterprise funds, the more it raises questions about overlap with OPIC, the Export-Import Bank, and TDA. Furthermore, U.S. development assistance will not achieve maximal efficiency and impact unless the aid is part of a coherent approach across all U.S. development programs, such as debt relief, U.S. trade preferences, and the credit-rating process.

The eligibility analysis described above makes clear that the creation of another independent agency with its own idiosyncratic conditions threatens to add to the confusion. It greatly increases the need for a strong mechanism to force interagency coherence, which does not exist currently. Moreover, smart development policy would encourage convergence toward a single hierarchy of eligibility criteria across programs over time, so that the most reform-oriented poor nations would automatically qualify for the most flexible terms on trade access, debt treatment, development assistance, and export and investment programs. Unfortunately, the obstacles are high, including jurisdiction problems across agencies within the executive branch and across committees in the legislative branch.

Congressional Oversight

Finally, Congress must be a committed partner if the MCA is to break new ground on development assistance. Only by striking a considered balance of obligations and authority between the executive and legislative branches will it be possible to pioneer a new approach centered on objective selection criteria, beneficiary-driven program design, and unprecedented funding flexibility. In short, for the MCA to succeed, it must forge a more effective partnership with Congress than USAID has. The MCA will be able to win such trust only if its program design contains adequate self-executing safeguards.

Many of USAID's inefficiencies stem from its interpretation of requirements imposed by Congress during the budget process. USAID shoulders one of the heaviest burdens of congressional earmarks—requirements setting aside specific amounts of its budget for particular purposes such as child-survival and health programs.[17] The agency is also subject to numerous policy directives—274 at last count.[18] In the colorful words of Senator John McCain (R-Ariz.), "Peanuts, orangutans, gorillas, neotropical raptors, tropical fish, and exotic plants also receive the committee's attention, though it's unclear why any individual making a list of critical international security, economic, and humanitarian concerns worth addressing would target these otherwise meritorious flora and fauna."[19]

Asked for the single best way to improve their performance, most USAID employees would opt for "notwithstanding authority"—the kind of flexibility that allows the Office of Foreign Disaster Assistance to move money rapidly to support newly identified needs. The "notwithstanding authority" approach makes it possible to bypass time-consuming contracting requirements and procurement regulations that often seem more focused on economic stimulus in the United States than in the beneficiary nation. Others have also emphasized the value of appropriating funds on a "no-year," or several-year, advance basis to avoid the poor incentives associated with a yearly "use it or lose it" funding cycle.[20]

To ask Congress to be judicious in applying its key instruments of control, however, the administration will have to put forward a design that builds in comparable self-restraint—for instance, on political interference—and self-executing safeguards against the misuse of funds. The combination of transparent and rigorous selection criteria, which limits eligibility to the best performers, and strong accountability through continuous monitoring and periodic evaluations moves in this direction but may prove insufficient.

In addition, the unpredictable nature of the congressional oversight process on foreign assistance may make it particularly difficult to craft such a procedural deal. In contrast to the normal reauthorization cycle of one to five years for most programs, the mammoth Foreign Assistance Act of 1961 has not been reauthorized since 1986. Although a handful of new assistance programs have been authorized since then, they have been accomplished through piecemeal legislation, and attempts at a more systematic overhaul have failed. Various reasons have been given, including deep ideological differences between key members on the committees that oversee foreign relations and the perception that foreign aid votes can only cause trouble for a member and never win favors.[21] Because Congress must vote on appropriations bills each year, much of the oversight normally assumed by the congressional authorizing committees has fallen to the appropriators instead.

Presumably, the administration would secure the best chances of achieving the desired procedural quid pro quo on MCC "flexible authorities" by showing appropriate deference to the authorizing committees. Although reauthorizing the Foreign Assistance Act would provide the best vehicle simultaneously to address the particulars of the MCA and to accomplish the vital task of clarifying the complementary mission of USAID, recent history suggests that a less ambitious, piecemeal approach has a far better chance of passage.

No Second Chances

The proposed creation of a $5 billion annual fund to promote growth in reform-oriented developing countries holds tremendous promise. At best, it could transform U.S. development policy, directing money to the highest-yielding social investments and forcing greater clarity of roles and missions among the many existing U.S. programs for developing nations. The pitfalls of such a plan, however, are sobering. If the selection process is overlaid with a geopolitical screen, if the MCA adds to the confusion surrounding USAID's mission, or if the MCA design does not contain adequate self-executing safeguards, the program will fall short of its goals. The negative repercussions could be as great as the positive potential would be.

A failed Millenium Challenge Account would quickly become yet another example—and the most expensive one—of the wasted aid cited by critics, and it could undermine political support for foreign assistance for decades to come. With this in mind, it is extremely important for the United States get it right the first time.

Notes

1. George W. Bush, remarks to the United Nations Conference on Financing for Development, Monterrey, Mexico, March 22, 2002.
2. "The Millennium Challenge Account," www.globalhealth.gov/mcafactsheet.shtml (accessed January 24, 2003) (fact sheet).
3. See *United States Leadership Against HIV/AIDS, Tuberculosis, and Malaria Act of 2002*, 107th Cong., 2d sess., S. 2525 (sponsored by Senator John Kerry [D-Mass.] and cosponsored by Senator Bill Frist [R-Tenn.] and others; introduced on May 15, 2002); George W. Bush, State of the Union Address, January 28, 2003.
4. This discussion owes a great deal to Gayle Smith's input as part of the Brookings Institution/Center for Global Development project.
5. This amount includes funds from the "150 account," the budget account for International Affairs, but excludes other important categories of U.S. aid such as military assistance and some forms of food aid and infectious disease–related assistance funded through the Departments of Agriculture, Health and Human Services, and Defense.
6. George W. Bush, remarks at the Inter-American Development Bank, March 14, 2002 (hereinafter Bush IADB remarks).
7. David Weiner, "U.S. Foreign Assistance and the War on Terrorism," working paper by the Center for Global Development, July 2002.
8. Bush IADB remarks.
9. American Council for Voluntary International Action, "The Millennium Challenge Account," May 2002, www.interaction.org/library/millenium.html (accessed January 24, 2003) (hereinafter InterAction Policy Brief); Larry Nowels, "The Millennium Challenge Account: Bush Administration Foreign Aid Initiative," CRS *Policy Brief*, April 29, 2002; Steve Radelet, "Qualifying for the Millennium Challenge Account," Center for Global Development, December 13, 2002, www.cgdev.org/nv/Choosing_MCA_Countries.pdf (accessed January 24, 2003).
10. Dani Rodrik and Francisco Rodriguez, "Trade Policy and Economic Growth: A Skeptic's Guide to the Cross-National Evidence," in *Macroeconomics Annual 2000*, eds. Ben Bernanke and Kenneth S. Rogoff (Cambridge: MIT Press and National Bureau of Economic Research, 2001).

11. See Radelet, "Qualifying for the Millennium Challenge Account."

12. Daniel Kauffman and Art Kray, "Governance Indicators, Aid Allocation, and the Millennium Challenge Account," World Bank, December 2002, www.worldbank.org/wbi/governance/pdf/gov_indicators_aid.pdf (accessed January 24, 2003) (draft paper).

13. For the list of countries likely to be eligible for the MCA, see Radelet, "Qualifying for the Millennium Challenge Account."

14. For greater detail on the UN Millennium Development Goals, see United Nations Department of Economic and Social Affairs, "Millennium Indicators Database," December 19, 2002, http://millenniumindicators.un.org/unsd/mi/mi_goals.asp (accessed January 24, 2003).

15. InterAction Policy Brief; Steve Radelet, "Beyond the Indicators: Delivering Effective Foreign Assistance through the Millennium Challenge Account," Center for Global Development, September 10, 2002, www.cgdev.org/nv/MCA_indicators.pdf (accessed January 24, 2003) (working paper).

16. This point was brought to my attention by Gayle Smith of the Brookings Institution/Center for Global Development project.

17. Nowels, "The Millennium Challenge Account."

18. David Weiner, "A Portrait of the U.S. Development Assistance Program," Center for Global Development working paper, July 2002.

19. John McCain, statement on the foreign appropriations bill for fiscal year 2002, October 24, 2001.

20. Carol Lancaster, "The Devil Is in the Details: From the Millennium Challenge Account to the Millennium Challenge Corporation," Center for Global Development, December 11, 2002, www.cgdev.org/nv/Devil_in_the_Details.pdf (accessed January 24, 2003).

21. Carol Lancaster, *Transforming Foreign Aid: United States Assistance in the 21st Century* (Washington, D.C.: Institute for International Economics, 2000).

Steve Radelet

Will the Millennium Challenge Account Be Different?

In March 2002, President George W. Bush proposed establishing a Millennium Challenge Account (MCA), beginning in fiscal year 2004, that would provide substantial new foreign assistance to low-income countries that are "ruling justly, investing in their people, and encouraging economic freedom."[1] The MCA promises to bring about the most fundamental change to U.S. foreign assistance policy since President John Kennedy introduced the Peace Corps and the U.S. Agency for International Development (USAID) in the early 1960s. The significance of the proposed program lies partly in its scale: the proposed $5 billion annual budget represents a 50 percent increase over the $10 billion annual foreign aid budget in FY 2002 and a near doubling in the amount of aid that focuses strictly on development objectives.

Perhaps even more important than its size, however, is that the MCA brings with it the opportunity to improve significantly the allocation and delivery of U.S. foreign assistance because, as currently planned, it will differ from existing programs in four critical ways.[2] First, it will have narrower and more clearly defined objectives, aimed solely at supporting economic growth and development and not other foreign policy goals. Second, it will provide assistance to only a select group of low-income countries that are implementing sound development policies,

Steve Radelet is a senior fellow at the Center for Global Development in Washington, D.C., and was deputy assistant secretary of the treasury for Africa, the Middle East, and Asia from January 2000 through June 2002.

Copyright © 2003 by The Center for Strategic and International Studies and the Massachusetts Institute of Technology
The Washington Quarterly • 26:2 pp. 171–187.

The Battle for Hearts and Minds

making the aid funds sent to those countries more effective. Third, the administration hopes that the MCA will have lower bureaucratic and administrative costs than current aid programs. Toward that end, it has proposed establishing a new government corporation called the Millennium Challenge Corporation (MCC) to administer the program. Fourth, the administration plans to give recipient countries a greater say in program design, implementation, and evaluation to improve program efficiency and effectiveness.

The MCA is a very promising new aid program. Many of the details on how it will operate, however, remain uncertain. As of January 2003, the administration has announced only its plans for selecting the eligible countries and for housing the new program in the MCC.[3] For example, it has not yet made clear its plans for operations on the ground in recipient countries, how programs will be evaluated, or how the MCA will coordinate its programs with other existing U.S. aid agencies, particularly USAID. These and other program elements will be worked out with Congress during the first half of 2003, with the aim of initializing operations in October 2003.

Moreover, even when these details are worked out, the MCA will constitute only one part of an overall foreign assistance program because it is designed to operate in a relatively small number of developing countries. To date, the administration has not developed clear foreign assistance strategies for countries that do not qualify for the MCA or for failed states that might be the breeding grounds for terrorism and transnational crime. Similarly, it has not developed a plan for addressing critical transnational problems, most importantly, the HIV/AIDS pandemic.

Sharpening the Focus

U.S. foreign assistance programs suffer from the attempt to do too many things at once. They have multiple objectives and purposes, often leading to a lack of coherence in everything from broad strategic planning to specific programs on the ground. The U.S. Foreign Assistance Act of

1961, as amended, specifies a remarkable 33 different goals and 75 priority areas. Carol Lancaster has classified these goals into six different broad purposes:[4]

- *Promoting security.* For many years, significant amounts of U.S. assistance were aimed at containing communism and supporting countries on the U.S. side of the Cold War. Since the late 1970s, and especially since the Camp David accords of 1979, a growing share of aid has focused on peacemaking. Israel and Egypt have long been the two largest recipients of U.S. foreign assistance, together typically receiving close to 20 percent of all U.S. aid. Since September 11, some foreign assistance has been used to support the war on terrorism, especially U.S. aid to Afghanistan and Pakistan.

- *Promoting development.* A core objective of U.S. assistance since the end of World War II has been to help poor countries finance investments in infrastructure, health, education, and a wide variety of other activities aimed at raising incomes, reducing poverty, and improving standards of living. The MCA is most closely aligned with meeting this objective.

- *Providing humanitarian relief.* The United States has long been a leader in providing relief in cases of both natural disasters and civil conflicts.

- *Supporting political and economic transitions.* Since the collapse of the Soviet Union, substantial amounts of aid have been directed toward supporting transitions to free markets and democracies in former socialist economies. The magnitude of aid for this purpose has begun to decline in recent years.

- *Building democracies.* Since the late 1980s, the United States has helped promote and strengthen democracies, both as an end in itself and as a means toward other ends, such as the protection of human rights and the cessation of civil conflict.

- *Addressing transnational problems.* Some programs focus on problems that arise in one country that affect people in other countries, including high population growth, food insecurity, and health problems such as HIV/AIDS and malaria. Fighting these problems requires different approaches than those problems contained within the borders of one country.

These objectives are all legitimate goals for U.S. foreign assistance and foreign policy more broadly. Problems arise, however, when a single program attempts to meet more than one of these objectives at the same time. For example, the United States provided Pakistan with $600 million in assistance in late 2001 in the aftermath of the conflict in Afghanistan to help gain that government's support in the war on terrorism, with the objective of strengthening regional and global security. Some of the aid is being used to fund health and education programs, among other activities, with the objective of supporting economic growth and poverty reduction. These two objectives could easily come into conflict if the aid-financed social programs show weak results, which under other circumstances might lead to cutting that aid and redirecting it elsewhere. To continue receiving the full support of the Pakistani government, the United States might have to compromise on its goal of making its aid money as effective as possible in fighting poverty. Similar tensions can arise between other objectives, such as providing humanitarian assistance and building democracies. The United States regularly provides humanitarian assistance to nondemocratic governments facing natural disasters, which can have the unintended consequence of helping those governments strengthen their legitimacy and power base.

The MCA's sharper focus on economic growth and poverty reduction should help reduce these tensions, although they can never be fully eliminated. As a result, the MCA will be more able to define specific goals, ensure that resources are better allocated to meet those goals, and allow for stronger and clearer evaluation of results. This should help ensure that both recipient countries and the American public get better outcomes from our foreign assistance program.

Choosing the Right Countries

A central idea of the MCA is that aid can be more effective if it is focused on nations with governments that are committed to establishing policies and institutions conducive to economic growth and poverty reduction. Unfortunately, too many leaders in low-income countries are more interested in consolidating their power and enriching themselves than in fighting poverty, and aid programs in these countries suffer as a result. At one level, this difference is a matter of simple common sense: foreign assistance will go much further in countries where governments are committed to building better schools and clinics, creating good jobs, and rooting out corruption. Foreign assistance yielded great results in Korea and Botswana, where governments placed a high priority on growth and development. For example, aid complemented government efforts by building schools and training teachers while the government developed sound education curriculums and introduced policies that helped create jobs suitable for school graduates.

Aid proved to be a huge waste, however, in countries such as Zaire (now the Democratic Republic of Congo) under Mobutu Sese Seko and Nigeria under its succession of military rulers. These governments and others like them funneled aid into their own coffers and did little to provide the population with the opportunities necessary to pull themselves out of poverty. Because of Cold War politics, the United States and other donors were willing to look the other way and provide funds to buttress these leaders even though aid produced few results. Recent statistical research, for the most part, supports the idea that aid generally has a positive effect on growth in countries with good macroeconomic and trade policies, strong investments in health and education, good governance, and less corruption, while it tends to have little or no effect on growth in countries with weak policies and high corruption.[5]

It is easy to see the difference between Korea and Zaire. The problem, however, is that most developing nations are somewhere in between, with a combination of good and bad policies and a mixed commitment to development. The challenge for donors is to distinguish between countries where aid is most likely to be effective and those where it is less likely. This challenge lies at the root of Bush's call for the MCA to provide aid to countries that are "ruling justly, investing in their people, and establishing economic freedom." How, precisely, can the United States measure these three broad components of a country's development strategy?

The administration has proposed using 16 specific indicators for this task (Table 1), grouped into the president's three broad categories. Countries must score above the median (measured against all broadly eligible countries) on half or more of the indicators in each of the three groups to qualify for the MCA. That is, they must surpass the median

Table I. Eligibility Criteria for the MCA

INDICATOR	SOURCE
I. Ruling Justly	
1. Control of Corruption	World Bank Institute
2. Rule of Law	World Bank Institute
3. Voice and Accountability	World Bank Institute
4. Government Effectiveness	World Bank Institute
5. Civil Liberties	Freedom House
6. Political Rights	Freedom House
II. Investing in People	
7. Immunization Rate: DPT and Measles	WHO/World Bank
8. Primary Education Completion Rate	World Bank
9. Public Primary Education Spending/GDP	World Bank
10. Public Expenditure on Health/GDP	World Bank
III. Economic Freedom	
11. Country Credit Rating	Institutional Investor
12. Inflation	IMF
13. Regulatory Quality	World Bank Institute
14. Budget Deficit/GDP	IMF/World Bank
15. Trade Policy	Heritage Foundation
16. Days to Start a Business	World Bank

Source: "Fact Sheet: Millennium Challenge Account," distributed by the administration on November 25, 2002, available at www.cgdev.org.

in three of the six "ruling justly" indicators, two of the four "investing in people" indicators, and three of the six "establishing economic freedom" indicators. In addition, a country must score above the median on corruption, regardless of how well it does on all the other indicators. This proposed methodology is basically sound, with some caveats as discussed below.

Using publicly available data and this methodology on the 16 indicators proposed by the administration, I have produced an illustrative list of countries that might qualify for the MCA during its first three years.[6] It is crucial to note that this list is illustrative, rather than official U.S. policy; data on all 16 indicators will be updated before the program actually starts in late 2003, so the group of top countries will change. Moreover, the administration has stressed that the list produced by the 16 indicators is not the final word—the board of directors of the new MCC, which will be explained below, can add or subtract countries in preparing a list for final approval by the president. Adjustments to the list may be necessary because of gaps, time lags, or other weaknesses in the data; the board will also be able to take into account "other material information, including leadership" in making its recommendations.[7] Despite these possible adjustments, the list determined by today's data provides some useful insight as to how the MCA might eventually develop.

In the first year, the administration has proposed that the pool of countries eligible for consideration for the MCA should be those that have an average annual per capita income less than $1,435 and are eligible for concessional borrowing from the World Bank. There are 74 countries in this group. Table 2 shows that 13 of these countries might qualify for the MCA during this period, based on data available in late 2002.

The administration proposes expanding the pool of eligible countries slightly in the second year, along with an increase in program funding, to include all countries with average per capita incomes less than $1,435, regardless of their borrowing status with the World Bank. This change increases the total number of eligible countries to 87. The new countries tend to be better off on average than the original 74, so the median values that a country must exceed to qualify rise on most of the

Table 2. Possible Qualifying Countries Using the Administration's Criteria

Year 1: IDA-Eligible Countries with Per Capita Incomes Less than $1,435	Year 2: All Countries with Per Capita Incomes Less than $1,435	Year 3: Countries with Per Capita Incomes between $1,435 and $2,975
QUALIFYING COUNTRIES		
Albania	Bolivia	Bulgaria
Bangladesh	Benin*	Egypt
Benin*	China	Namibia
Bolivia	Honduras	Peru
The Gambia	Lesotho*	South Africa
Georgia	Malawi	
Honduras	Mongolia	
Lesotho*	Philippines	
Malawi	Senegal	
Mongolia	Sri Lanka	
Nepal	Vietnam	
Senegal		
Sri Lanka		
ELIMINATED BY CORRUPTION		
Moldova	Ecuador	
Nicaragua	Moldova	
	Nicaragua	
	Ukraine	
MISSED BY ONE INDICATOR		
Cambodia	Albania	Jamaica
Côte d'Ivoire	Bangladesh	Jordan
Ghana	Cambodia	Tunisia
Guyana	Côte d'Ivoire	
India	The Gambia	
Mali	Georgia	
Mozambique	Ghana	
Vietnam	Guyana	
	India	
	Mali	
	Morocco	

* For Benin and Lesotho, data for the corruption indicator are currently unavailable, so technically they would not qualify. However, these data are expected to become available within the next few months, and these two countries are likely to qualify when the MCA begins in late 2003.
Source: Steven Radelet, "Qualifying for the Millennium Challenge Account," www.cgdev.org.

indicators. As a result, only 11 countries qualify in the second year, including just 7 of the 13 that had qualified the first year.

Perhaps the most interesting qualifier in year two is China. In some ways, China's technical qualification is of little relevance both because it is unlikely to seek MCA funding and because it would be eliminated as a recipient by other statutory restrictions even if it did. Nevertheless, it passes the indicator tests. Because China's performance in economic growth and poverty reduction has been among the best in the world for the last 20 years, perhaps its fulfillment of the requirements should not be such a surprise.

China's qualification by numbers, however, highlights the importance of the administration having the flexibility to adjust the list of country qualifiers before final approval. Allowing for this kind of discretion makes sense, given the weakness in some of the data. Adjustments should be the exception rather than the rule, however, and they should only be made with appropriate justification. The administration must not elevate undeserving countries to the qualifying list simply because they are strong U.S. political allies or demote countries because of a diplomatic scuffle. Too many adjustments would undermine the credibility of the selection process. Congress should require in the MCA authorizing legislation that the administration make publicly available country scoring, any recommended adjustments to country eligibility, and the rationale for those adjustments.

The administration proposes sharply expanding the pool of eligible countries in year three (in line with the increase in annual funding to the full targeted amount of $5 billion) to include the 28 nations with average per capita incomes between $1,435 and $2,975. This group of countries would be judged separately from the 84 countries with average incomes less than $1,435, with separate median scores to assess country qualification. Adding this last group of nations is controversial among development experts and nongovernmental organizations (NGOs) and may not be in the long-term interests of the program. The administration's main reason for including them is that many people in these countries still live in poverty. Yet, as conveyed by Table 3, this

Table 3. Development Status, Resources Flows, and Financing for Three MCA Country Groups (medians)

	IDA-eligible countries with income less than $1,435	Countries with income less than $1,435	Countries with income range $1,435-$2,975
Development Status			
GNI per capita, 2001 ($)	380	460	1965
Adult illiteracy rate, adult total, 2000 (%)	36	33	14
Life expectancy at birth, 2000 (years)	54	56	70
Mortality rate, infant, 2000 (per 1,000 live births)	75	69	27
Resources Flows and Financing			
Aid/GNI, 2000 (%)	10.8	8.5	1.4
Gross private capital flows/ GDP (%)	6.9	8.7	10.3
Tax revenue/GDP (%)	11.7	12.6	21.8
Gross domestic savings/ GDP, 2000 (%)	7.3	8.4	16.2
Number of Countries	74	87	28

Source: Steven Radelet, "Qualifying for the Millennium Challenge Account," www.cgdev.org.

group of nations is far better off than the 87 countries considered in year two, with average incomes more than four times higher, much lower infant mortality rates, and much higher literacy rates. The nations potentially eligible in year three also have much greater access to alternative sources of financing, with higher private capital flows, savings rates, and government revenues. Thus, including this new group of countries would divert aid resources away from countries with greater needs and fewer financing alternatives. In addition, adding this group of 28 nations heightens the possibility that MCA funds will be diverted to support political allies, as the group includes Colombia, Russia, Egypt, Jordan, and Turkey, among others.

Based on data available today, 5 of these 28 nations would qualify in year three if the administration's proposal were adopted, as shown in Table 2. Note that these countries are in addition to those that qualify in year two (not instead of) because they compete to qualify as a separate group. Both because these 28 have access to other financing and because their inclusion in the pool raises the risk of politicizing allocation decisions, this group should be dropped from the MCA. Alternatively, if these nations must remain included, the administration should allocate only a limited portion (a maximum of $1 billion) of the annual $5 billion for them, with the rest reserved for the poorest nations.

Thus, based on the administration's proposal, over the course of the first three years, approximately 18 different countries might qualify for the MCA. More than a dozen other countries miss qualifying by just one of the indicators. Several of these countries could easily qualify within the first few years by improving their scores in that one deficient area. Therefore, it is quite conceivable that 20–25 countries could qualify for the MCA by its fourth or fifth year of operation.

This list of countries is not perfect, but it is a good start. Weaknesses and inconsistencies in the data result in some countries appearing on the list that probably should not qualify, while there are a few nations that just barely miss and have a strong record of using aid effectively (e.g., Mozambique) that should qualify. The existing methodology attempts to be strictly objective, but it is not perfect. Some changes to the criteria (details are beyond the scope of this paper)[8] could improve it. Nevertheless, the proposed system provides a reasonably sensible way to begin distinguishing between nations that show a strong commitment to development and those that do not.

Improving the U.S. Bureaucracy

The U.S. foreign aid system is bogged down by a heavy bureaucracy, overly restrictive legislative burdens, and conflicting objectives. The United States delivers aid in basically the same way in countries with competent, committed governments as in countries with high levels of corruption and poor development policy. The administration wants the MCA to be different. It has proposed that the program be administered through a new government corporation, the MCC, designed to reduce administrative costs and increase effectiveness.

Details on the structure and operations of the MCC are scant and will be developed more fully by the administration and Congress in early 2003 so the corporation can become operational by October 2003. The administration has proposed that the MCC be governed by a cabinet-level board of directors chaired by the secretary of state and managed by a chief executive officer appointed by the president. Staff will be drawn from a variety of government agencies for a limited term. Its biggest advantage would be that an MCC could avoid the political pressures, bureaucratic procedures, and multiple congressional mandates that weaken current aid programs. Its status as separate from any existing department could make it more flexible and responsive as well as allow it to attract some top-notch talent.

Establishing an MCC as proposed, however, entails certain risks. Dividing the U.S. foreign assistance program into two major agencies (USAID and the MCC), in addition to several smaller agencies such as the Peace Corps, could impede coordination and increase redundancy. Furthermore, the administration hopes to keep the MCC small, but its projected staffing of somewhere between 100 and 200 people seems inordinately insufficient for a program with an annual budget of $5 billion. It is also not clear who will represent the MCC on the ground in the qualifying countries. Presumably, it will contract out many services, such as monitoring and evaluation, or it might try to work through USAID staff in each country. Nevertheless, there is a risk that the new agency will be understaffed and thus unable to deliver the high-quality operations that will be expected. In addition, having the secretary of state serve as chairman of the board of the MCC could give the Department of State too much control over qualification and allocation decisions, which could compromise the objectivity of the MCA in favor of other foreign policy goals.

One of the biggest concerns is the impact of the MCC on USAID and the relationship between the two organizations. The MCC is likely to draw staff and resources from USAID, furthering weakening the agency, possibly engendering some resentment, and making cooperation more difficult. Many issues remain uncertain. For example, will USAID continue to operate in the MCA countries, or will it pull out once a country qualifies? On one hand, having both institutions operating in the same country could be very confusing for recipient countries and unnecessarily duplicate services. On the other hand, there may be some projects and programs that USAID is better positioned to administer because of its prior experience and established operations on the ground in MCA countries. This issue could prove particularly tricky for borderline countries that qualify for the MCA for several years, then fail to qualify, then qualify again. Switching back and forth between MCA and USAID programs could be very cumbersome. Similarly, will the MCC operate under new or existing foreign assistance guidelines for procurement of goods and services and other operations? Although more flexible guidelines might seem useful for the MCC, if the two agencies are operating under vastly different rules within the same country, it could lead to serious confusion.

The administration has not yet addressed these questions, and Congress certainly will have strong views that may differ from the administration. If not resolved carefully through strong planning and coordination, the difficulties in operating two foreign assistance programs from two very different parts of the U.S. government are sure to become apparent.

Ensuring Success on the Ground

Regardless of where the MCA is housed, program design, implementation, and evaluation—all of which will be critical—have yet to be developed. Currently, most U.S. foreign assistance is delivered through a country-programming approach in which USAID staff members develop a country strategy, design specific interventions, and evaluate the outcomes. This top-down approach has many shortcomings, including the absence of recipient-nation ownership of specific projects, only partial coordination (at best) with the recipient country's overall development strategy, a heavy requirement of USAID staff, and little competition between proposed projects. This approach, or parts of it, might make sense in countries with weak governments that show little commitment to development, but it makes little sense for the MCA. Because MCA recipient nations will have an established record of good development policies, the administration should give them much more of the responsibility for program design so that MCA-funded programs are more consistent with their national development strategies.

Specifically, the MCA should draw from the approach used by most foundations where recipients write proposals for various activities and only the best ideas actually receive funding. For example, the government of an MCA recipient country could write a proposal to fund a significant portion of its education program. To write a good proposal, the government would first have to develop a strong education strategy—something most developing countries lack. It would need to give careful consideration to budgets, costs, trade-offs, and the various steps necessary over time to achieve success. Proposals would be expected to spell out the specific actions that the recipient would take and the benchmarks by which success would be measured, pushing recipients to establish concrete goals. Government and nongovernment agencies alike, such as private NGOs, clinics, and schools, should be entitled to write proposals and receive funds, as private agencies implement some of the best development programs.

Such an approach would place responsibility for development programs where it belongs—with recipient nations, not with aid agencies. It would ensure that recipient governments and other agencies within MCA recipient countries set their own priorities and develop their own strategies. If such an approach is implemented, the MCA can increase recipient-nation ownership of and commitment to development programs, which should lead to better results. Of course, many MCA countries will initially lack the capacity to develop strong proposals and programs, but the only way they will develop these capacities is if they are given the responsibility to do so, along with some funding for technical assistance in the early years. Obviously, this approach can only work in those countries that have shown and continue to show a real commitment to development.

The key to making the MCA system work is to ensure high-quality MCA-funded programs from conception through implementation. Program design is only the first step. For the program to succeed, the MCC should foster robust competition for funds both within and across countries by soliciting proposals from a variety of government and nongovernment agencies. Proposals should be reviewed through a disciplined process by staff with expertise in both the recipient nation and the substantive area of the program. The MCC should grant funds only for the best proposals, rejecting the weakest and sending back for further development those that are promising but incomplete. To make the proposal process work best, Congress should not earmark MCA funds for specific purposes. Rather, the proposal design, proposal review, and monitoring and evaluation processes should determine where funds are allocated.

The final and perhaps most crucial element is program monitoring and evaluation. Without a much stronger monitoring and evaluation capacity, the MCA is doomed to fail. Effective monitoring and evaluation is critical for keeping funded programs on track to meeting their goals, guiding the allocation of resources toward successful activities and away from failures and ensuring that the lessons learned from ongoing activities—both successes and failures—inform the design of new projects and programs.

Two distinct kinds of monitoring and evaluation are required: financial accountability and progress toward substantive goals. Financial accountability should ensure that funds are spent where they are supposed to be, the project remains within budget, regulations on procurement and payment are followed, and funds are not stolen. Substantive accountability focuses on attaining specified benchmarks, such as purchasing a certain number of textbooks, training a certain number of teachers, building a designated number of schools, increasing test scores by a certain amount, or increasing a school's graduation rate. Monitoring and evaluation must be incorporated into projects and programs from the outset, not added as an afterthought halfway through the process. Both internal (carried out by the grantees) and external (carried out directly by the MCC or a contractor for the MCC) audit will be needed to ensure monitor compliance and high standards.

Of course, providing recipient nations with a greater say in program design, implementation, and evaluation entails some risks. Giving recipients greater flexibility can only work in countries that demonstrate the strongest commitment to development—exactly the countries for the MCA to target. With that greater flexibility, however, should come greater responsibility. Strong results should be expected from the MCA, and grantees should be held accountable for achieving the goals specified in their programs. Programs that achieve results should be funded generously while funds for those that do not should be reduced.

Toward a More Complete Foreign Assistance Strategy

Although the MCA is an exciting new program with enormous potential, only a small number of countries will receive MCA funding. Thus, it is only a partial strategy for U.S. foreign assistance. Because the MCA focuses on those countries with governments that have shown the strongest commitment to development, it essentially deals with the easiest cases among poor countries. The administration has not developed comparable strategies for different groups of nations that fail to qualify for MCA funding, whether they just miss qualifying or are failed states mired in perpetual conflict. Nor has it articulated a strategy for confronting major issues that cut across national boundaries, particularly the HIV/AIDS crisis, which experts within the administration and on Capitol Hill are beginning to realize hold strategic importance.

One extreme position would be to reserve all U.S. assistance for countries that qualify for the MCA. This position would be both negligent and shortsighted, as many non-MCA states, including Afghanistan, Pakistan, India, Israel, Nigeria, Ethiopia, Russia, Ukraine, Colombia, Mexico, and Indonesia, remain central to U.S. foreign policy interests. At the same time, the United States cannot and should not provide foreign as-

sistance to every country, particularly ones whose egregious governments merit no foreign assistance at all. Still, developing a strategy for
how to work with non-MCA nations is essential to a complete U.S. foreign assistance strategy.

U.S. objectives and local circumstances in non-MCA countries
are bound to differ from those in MCA countries, demanding that
a different approach be applied. Consider first the countries that
almost qualify for the MCA but fall short in one or two areas. U.S.
objectives here are broadly similar to those in the MCA countries—economic growth and poverty reduction—but the circumstances on the ground in these countries are not yet strong enough
to allow for the more flexible funding mechanisms envisioned for
the MCA. Because these countries fall outside the MCA, USAID
will play the primary role, implying that the administration needs
to develop a strategy to make USAID more effective on the ground.
USAID programs in these nations should focus on the areas where
the state falls short of qualifying for the MCA, with the aim of
helping them qualify in the near future. As part of these programs,
USAID should allow these nations to take a strong role in designing specific interventions, perhaps even writing proposals for funding as has been proposed for the MCA.

In nations with weaker, more corrupt governments that show no interest in development, USAID should direct funds carefully, with many
activities performed through nongovernment agencies rather than
through the government. The precise methods should be determined
on a case-by-case basis. In some nations with weaker governments—especially new ones or those in postconflict situations, such as Afghanistan for example—working through the government may make sense as
a way to strengthen government institutions and provide a basis for
stronger development policies in the future. The greatest challenge lies
in failed states, where governments are either ineffective or nonexistent and terrorism, drug trafficking, money laundering, and other
transnational crime can easily breed. The Bush administration's 2002
National Security Strategy (NSS), released in September, is notable

The Battle for Hearts and Minds

both for its emphasis on failed states as a foreign policy concern and for the complete absence of a strategy for dealing with them.[9]

Yet another approach is needed to fight the HIV/AIDS crisis. This pandemic has the potential to destroy many fragile societies, leading to generations of weak institutions, political instability, and misrule, with manifold possible negative repercussions for U.S. interests. Western leaders must show much greater leadership in combating HIV/AIDS, working together with leaders of developing nations and international institutions. Stronger efforts are needed across the board: encouraging proactive local leadership, strengthening initiatives to prevent transmission, providing treatment and care for those with the virus and related infections, developing strategies for families and orphans of victims, and pursuing research into vaccines. President Bush announced in his January 2003 State of the Union address his intention to request $15 billion over the next five years for HIV/AIDS funding. If realized, this funding would be a major step forward. The challenge ahead is to convert the funding into an effective strategy to fight the pandemic.

Finally, seriously helping low-income nations establish the basis for robust private-sector activities, sustained economic growth, and poverty reduction requires that the United States rethink some of its other policies affecting these nations—most important, protectionist U.S. trade policies that forbid poor countries from selling their textile and agriculture products in U.S markets. The recent farm bill was a major step backward because it will encourage even greater surplus U.S. agricultural production, thereby artificially depressing world prices further and undermining the incentives and opportunities for some of the poorest farmers in the world to make even a subsistence standard of living. As significant as the MCA is, opening U.S. markets to allow the world's poorest farmers to sell their products on an equitable basis would be far more beneficial to a greater number of poor nations as well as to the U.S. economy.

Similarly, greater debt relief is imperative for some of the poorest countries in the world (Uganda, Ghana, Tanzania) to make the public investments in health and education necessary to provide the basis for economic growth. The United States has already forgiven 100 percent of its claims on these and other low-income countries, including some potentially MCA-eligible countries, through the Heavily Indebted Poor Country (HIPC) Initiative.[10] This was a huge step forward, but the United States should work actively toward finding ways for the International Monetary Fund, the World Bank, and other international institutions to provide more debt relief for deserving countries. More broadly, the United States should ensure that all of its policies toward developing countries are consistent in their objectives and complement one another, rather than conflict with or undermine each other.

Attacking these key problems that lie beyond the reach of the MCA first requires that Congress fully approve the president's plan to allocate $5 billion in annual MCA funds in addition to current foreign assistance spending. The MCA should not be funded by cutting back on these other programs—which are underfunded as it is. U.S. foreign assistance essentially has been level in nominal terms since the mid-1980s and has fallen steadily after adjusting for inflation or the size of the U.S. economy. The United States currently ranks last of 22 industrialized countries in foreign assistance as a share of GDP.[11]

Partly because of its relatively low level of funding, the United States has given up much of its leadership role on foreign assistance in recent years. The MCA provides an opportunity for the United States to reassert this leadership, both because of its size and its (potentially) innovative delivery mechanisms. Nevertheless, simply maintaining or increasing funding for non-MCA programs will not be enough. The United States must formulate new strategies for making its non-MCA foreign assistance programs more effective, which will require both a clear vision for and strong leadership of USAID. The MCA initiative, as currently conceived, is a good start, but the administration and Congress need to work together to develop all of the components necessary for an effective foreign assistance strategy to combat poverty and further U.S. strategic interests around the world.

The Battle for Hearts and Minds

Notes

1. Located at www.whitehouse.gov/news/releases/2002/03/20020314-7.html.

2. For a series of papers and analyses of the MCA, see Center for Global Development, www.cgdev.org/nv/features_MCA.html.

3. For the administration's fact sheet on its proposal, see www.cgdev.org/nv/MCA_FactSheetNov.doc.

4. Carol Lancaster, *Transforming Foreign Aid: United States Assistance in the 21st Century* (Washington, D.C.: Institute for International Economics, 2000).

5. See Craig Burnside and David Dollar, "Aid, Policies, and Growth," World Bank Working Paper #1777, June 1977; World Bank, *The Role and Effectiveness of Development Assistance: Lessons from the World Bank Experience* (2001).

6. See Steve Radelet, "Qualifying for the Millennium Challenge Account," www.cgdev.org/nv/Choosing_MCA_Countries.pdf.

7. For the administration's fact sheet, see www.cgdev.org/nv/MCA_FactSheetNov.doc.

8. See Radelet, "Qualifying for the Millennium Challenge Account."

9. For one approach, see John J. Hamre and Gordon R. Sullivan, "Toward Postconflict Reconstruction," *The Washington Quarterly* 25, no. 4 (autumn 2002): 85–96; subsequent articles.

10. For an analysis, see Nancy Birdsall and John Williamson, *Delivering on Debt Relief: From IMF Gold to a New Aid Architecture* (Washington D.C.: Center for Global Development and Institute for International Economics, 2002).

11. If private contributions were added, the United States would probably move up the list a bit, but it would still rank among the least generous of contributors to low-income countries.

Jennifer L. Windsor

Promoting Democratization Can Combat Terrorism

Can promoting democracy prevent renewed terrorist attacks against the United States? Although cynics may scoff, democratization has gained credence as a counterterrorism strategy in the aftermath of the September 11, 2001, attacks. The underlying logic is that democratic institutions and procedures, by enabling the peaceful reconciliation of grievances and providing channels for participation in policymaking, can help to address those underlying conditions that have fueled the recent rise of Islamist extremism. The source of much of the current wave of terrorist activity—the Middle East—is not coincidentally also overwhelmingly undemocratic, and most regimes in the region lack the legitimacy and capacity to respond to the social and economic challenges that face them.

Although not without risks, and only if pursued as part of a broader strategy, democratization can help reshape the climates in which terrorism thrives. More specifically, promoting democratization in the closed societies of the Middle East can provide a set of values and ideas that offer a powerful alternative to the appeal of the kind of extremism that today has found expression in terrorist activity, often against U.S. interests.

The United States has launched a score of important post–September 11 initiatives to promote democratization in the Middle East. To be

Jennifer L. Windsor is executive director of Freedom House, a nonpartisan organization that promotes democracy and human rights, in Washington, D.C.

Copyright © 2003 by The Center for Strategic and International Studies and the Massachusetts Institute of Technology
The Washington Quarterly • 26:3 pp. 43–58.

The Battle for Hearts and Minds

most effective, the United States must further strengthen diplomatic efforts that demonstrate to the people and the governments that human rights and democratic practices are a U.S. priority and must cohesively integrate those diplomatic messages with foreign assistance strategically directed to strengthen the forces for democratic reform within the region.

Terrorism and Democratization: The Missing Link?

Terrorism resists simplification and easy explanation. Its causes are multifaceted and complex, and any single response to terrorism will yield only partial results. Thus, a comprehensive, dynamic policy response to combat terrorism is necessary. This article focuses on just one important part of that policy: the promotion of democratization. Just as the thesis that poverty causes terrorism has been debunked—the masterminds of the September 11 attacks came from the wealthy and more privileged elements of society—one cannot maintain that the absence of democracy directly explains the causes of terrorism. Countless repressive countries have not generated terrorist movements; conversely, terrorist groups, including Islamic extremists, have emerged in a number of established democracies. The lack of democracy has played a role, however, in creating the conditions conducive to the recent emergence of Islamic extremist movements. As Secretary of State Colin Powell recently noted, "[A] shortage of economic opportunities is a ticket to despair. Combined with rigid political systems, it is a dangerous brew indeed."[1]

This article focuses on the Middle East—the epicenter of the current terrorist upsurge. In addition to being beset by economic difficulties, the Middle East is the least democratic region in the world. With the exception of Israel, none of the countries in the region demonstrates enough respect for political rights and civil liberties to be considered "Free," as classified by Freedom House in its annual survey of freedom around the world. Of the 18 countries in the region, the organization rates 13 as "Not Free"—characterized by severely limited po-

litical rights, political persecution and terror, and repression of free association and peaceful dissent—and four others as "Partly Free." Indeed, Iraq, Libya, Saudi Arabia, and Syria are four of the nine countries
considered to be the most politically repressive in the world.[2]

Whereas almost all other regions have seen unprecedented democratization in the last 30 years, the Middle East has not demonstrated any
significant political progress. The region has been dominated by a range
of authoritarian political systems, including military regimes, monar-
chies, theocracies, and one-party statist regimes. With the exception of
some tactical liberalization, most regimes have resisted efforts to devolve power either horizontally, to other branches of government such
as the parliament or the judiciary, or vertically, by increasing accountability to the people through free and fair elections. In his new book
The Future of Freedom, Fareed Zakaria describes the situation as "an almost unthinkable reversal of a global pattern" in which "almost every
Arab country is less free than it was forty years ago. There are few places
in the world about which one can say that."[3]

Throughout the Middle East, secular opposition parties lack dyna-
mism and a broad base of political support. Civil society is weak as a result of the severe legal restrictions and coercive methods that the
region's regimes use to stifle political expression. Independent media
are largely nonexistent; most newspapers and articles are censored, and
those that exist are seen as serving the interests of the regime or particular political parties. In such societies, severe repression drives all
politics underground, placing the moderate opposition at a disadvan-
tage and encouraging political extremism. Democratic movements and
leaders by nature build support by operating openly and using traditional instruments of peaceful protest such as criticism through the media, public meetings, and mass organizations; but highly authoritarian
societies prevent such activism by interdicting such activities and per-
secuting and imprisoning nonviolent opponents. In contrast, successful
conspiracy is historically linked to authoritarian, top-down systems of
control; to a cult of unity; to the suppression of diversity of opinion;
and to the elaboration of obscurantist theories. Political extremists wel-

come brutal repression because it radicalizes activists and swells their own ranks. In this sense, the net effect of severe repression is to weaken or destroy the moderate elements within society with whom a compromise can be struck and simultaneously to empower those that seek total victory for their extremist cause.

As authoritarian repression creates an environment in which terrorist extremists can thrive, it also erodes public support for the rulers of the region. Globalization has brought an unprecedented level of commercial and cultural penetration of societies, providing populations with ready proof of their comparatively poor economic and social status. Ossified political structures are unable to deal effectively with deteriorating social and economic conditions in the Middle East, which has an annual growth rate lower than that of any region outside sub-Saharan Africa, a double-digit unemployment rate, and declining labor productivity, creating a growing crisis of legitimacy.[4] With little possibility of improving their own lives or channeling their energies toward producing meaningful change in their own countries, the educated but unemployed youth of the Middle East have grown increasingly angry and frustrated.

The reasons behind the progression from frustration with to violence against the United States are many and complex, but certainly the distorted information flow within many Middle Eastern societies plays a role.[5] Regimes that suffer from declining legitimacy have always tended to divert their populations' attention to evils outside their own borders. The closed nature of Middle Eastern societies contributes both to the declining legitimacy of the regimes and to the proliferation of inaccurate, polemical information manipulated for the regimes' own benefit. With populations discouraged by their lack of political and economic opportunities and hungry for a cause with which to identify and for someone to blame, as well as a media that is virulently anti-American, the Middle East is especially fertile ground for the terrorist message.

Over the long term, the establishment of democratic political systems in the Middle East has advantages that can mitigate the great possibilities for recruitment of extremists, including the following:

- *Avenues for peaceful change of government.* Through regular, free and fair elections, the public can bring about a change of policies and can remove leaders without risking widespread political crisis.

- *Channels for dissent and political discussion.* Between elections, legislatures can debate and influence government policies. Independent media and civic society groups allow for a more accurate flow of information between the government and the populace. Local governments can provide an additional level of access and contact. As a result, democratic regimes have better governance structures that can respond to new social and economic needs, and citizens are less likely to feel powerless and unable to affect the decisions that impact their lives.

- *Rule of law.* Leaders are accountable to the law, not above it, and this reduces their incentives to engage in corrupt behavior. Legal restraints also hold the security sector in check. Citizens have access to an independent judiciary to resolve disputes and therefore do not need to resort to violence.

- *Civil society.* In democracies, civil society plays a critical role in checking political power, channeling political participation and aspirations, and encouraging the development of democratic culture. If individuals feel they have meaningful opportunities to effect change in their own countries, they are less likely to channel their energies and animosities against outside actors.

- *Free flow of information.* Democracy also encourages the free flow of information, particularly through the establishment of independent media. The population thus has access to competing sources of information. Governments are able to rely on critical feedback that can help to construct more responsive policies.[6]

- *Strong states.* Democracies tend to be better governed and legitimized by virtue of having been chosen by their own people. They therefore tend to be strong states that do not need to rely on repression and an extensive military apparatus to control their own population and territories. As President George W. Bush noted, "[T]he events of September 11, 2001, taught us that weak states, like Afghanistan, can pose as great a danger to our national interests as strong states. ... [W]eak states [are more] vulnerable to terrorists networks ... within their borders."[7]

- *Sustainable economic and social development.* The latest *Human Development Report*, produced by the United Nations Development Program, bluntly states that democracy is "essential" to human development. "[C]ountries can promote human development for all only when they have governance systems that are fully accountable to all people—and when all people can participate in the debates and decisions that shape their lives."[8] Addressing the looming social and economic crisis, and the psychological toll that the crisis has exacted on the people of the Middle East, is critical to formulating a long-term strategy to reduce political extremism. Political freedom is an integral part of a development strategy focused on maximizing human dignity, and it encourages "individual initiative and social effectiveness," which are the driving forces behind development progress.[9]

- *Needed values and ideals.* Democracy is grounded in certain ideals—tolerance, compromise, respect for individual rights, equality of opportunity, and equal status under law—largely absent in the region. Such values can have a powerful appeal and a revolutionary impact on how individuals view themselves and their relationship to society and government and would thus make them less vulnerable to extremist messages. As Bush asserted, "[S]table and free nations do not breed the ideologies of murder."[10]

Taking Some Risks

Nevertheless, promoting democratization in lands without a tradition of democracy carries certain risks. Democratization assistance is not a silver bullet that could solve the region's problems if we simply tried harder.

First, many of the positive attributes outlined above relate to demo-cratic political systems once they have been established. The actual pro-cess of democratization itself is not necessarily easy and can exacerbate conflict and tensions within societies.[11] Democratization changes the prevailing power structure, threatening the political status and gains of established elites, who then seek to protect their position and access to power. In doing so, they may appeal to religious or ethnic differences to mobilize support or to create a climate of disorder and violence that dis-courages any further change in favor of maintaining the status quo.

Moreover, because elections produce clear winners and losers, they can become political flash points. In cases where most economic and social opportunities lie with the state, elections can lead to violence and fraud as competitors resort to desperate measures to win power and control over resources. A process that seeks to shift the balance of power regularly in the absence of the democratic ideals of participation and inclusion is clearly vulnerable to violence and disorder—a fact that policymakers must bear in mind.

Second, in regions such as the Middle East, fair elections not only risk conflict but also the chance that election winners may be anti-democratic and anti-American. For years, U.S. policymakers have been constrained by the fear that, if Middle Eastern populations are given the chance to choose their leaders, the outcome may be worse than the status quo. The organizational superiority and ideological appeal of Is-lamic extremism was demonstrated in the Algerian elections in the early 1990s, when the Islamic Salvation Front was poised to gain con-trol of the government, and more recently in Bahrain, where the last elections produced significant gains for Islamists. The commitment of these groups to encouraging further democratization is questionable at best, given their platforms and political rhetoric. (The performance of Turkey's new Islamist government, however, may prove that fears that a victory for Islamist parties will automatically lead to "one man, one vote, one time" are exaggerated.)

Zakaria makes exactly this case in his latest book, arguing that the third wave of democratization has produced "illiberal democracies"[12] in which elected leaders have demonstrated a lack of respect for individual freedoms and rule of law. Zakaria would argue that the United States should not support democracy—by which he means elections—in the Middle East but should instead gradually encourage reform of authoritarian regimes by working to put in place the fundamentals of constitutional liberalism, rather than try to establish systems which make the state electorally accountable to its own people.

Zakaria presents an interesting historical analysis and makes a compelling and persuasive case for promoting political systems more likely to yield leaders sympathetic to U.S. interests. His argument is ultimately problematic as a guide to policymakers, however, who are grappling with how to promote a new policy toward the Middle East. First, in both academic and policy circles, the definition of democracy has long evolved beyond merely holding elections. Many of the countries he considers illiberal democracies cannot by current definition be considered democracies at all. Democratization as a process involves building a rule of law, promoting individual freedoms, and strengthening democratic institutions and culture (which Zakaria currently distinguishes as constitutional liberalism), in addition to holding free and fair elections.

Moreover, although elections may in fact be dangerous for short-term U.S. interests, the reality is that elections have become an internationally accepted practice. Of the 192 countries in the world, 121 are considered to be electoral democracies, meaning that they have held largely representative and fair elections.[13] Those individuals who are struggling for reform in repressive societies in the Middle East and elsewhere genuinely desire the right to choose their own leaders. The United States, or any other outside actor, is hardly in the position to dictate to other countries that they are simply not ready for free elections.

Finally, although the United States risks undesirable outcomes in fostering free and fair elections, an alternative method has yet to be found that can predictably confer legitimacy and accountability on a government. The illegitimacy and lack of accountability of the regimes in the Middle East today breeds violent extremism and thus presents the kind of risk that the United States cannot afford to keep taking. Although the world has learned the hard way that it is counterproductive to pressure governments to hold elections prematurely—as the United States did in Bosnia—the greater value of elections cannot be dismissed completely.

Recognizing that promoting democratization, including holding elections, will not necessarily produce regimes that are sympathetic to U.S. policy interests in the short term is crucial for current U.S. policymakers so that expectations are not misguided. As regimes become more accountable to their populations, they may be less willing to back particular U.S. policies. Turkey provided the latest example when its newly elected, more representative, and more energetic parliament rejected U.S. requests for assistance in the war against Iraq.

In short, supporting democratization carries risks that must be taken into account when designing strategies for the Middle East and elsewhere. Arguably, however, there are far greater risks—particularly if one looks beyond the short term—in maintaining the status quo. The current political situation in the Middle East is primarily driven by internal realities, but it also is a reflection of past U.S. policy choices not to support democratic reforms within the region. If the United States persists in supporting friendly tyrants in the Middle East who repress their own people, the region will continue to breed extremists who argue that the United States is perpetuating the misery and frustration that characterize their everyday lives.

The Role of U.S. Foreign Aid

Democratization has always been primarily an indigenous process, often generated and sustained by courageous men and women who push for political change within their societies. Democracy imposed only from the outside rarely succeeds, as the 1990s military invasion in Haiti most recently demonstrated. International actors can play an influential role in encouraging political change, however, as reflected in what has been termed the third wave of democratization in Central and Eastern Europe and Latin America.[14] In particular, international actors can provide resources specifically targeted to supporting democratization, giving valuable support to those struggling for reform within their societies.

Since the end of the Cold War, the United States has been able to move beyond its focus on defeating the Soviet Union and increasingly has made the establishment of democracy around the world a foreign policy priority. As part of this strategy, the United States has increasingly used foreign assistance to support the promotion of democratization. The United States now allocates a total of approximately $650 million annually to support elections and political processes; the rule of law; human rights protections; active participation by civil society; independent media; and governance, including strengthening legislatures, local governments, and anticorruption programs.[15] With the specific aim of strengthening the processes and proponents of reform that are the keys to successful democratization, democracy assistance programs primarily involve providing expertise, including sharing models and the experience of like-minded countries, and direct financial or material support to critical actors and institutions.

In the past, the Middle East has, for the most part, been left out of the overall U.S. policy of providing support to establish democratic political systems around the world. Democracy has largely been absent from the diplomatic dialogue between the United States and its allies in the region. Some assistance has been provided, but most of the projects supported have been low-risk programs that focused on reinforcing government-approved institutions and halfhearted reform processes, strengthening civil society, and reforming commercial laws and other economic issues that might indirectly affect prospects for democracy in the future. Although some of the programs were technically well designed, their impact has been negligible, given the lack of political will within the regimes to embrace political reform and the lack of political will within the U.S. government to use its diplomatic heft and foreign assistance to push Middle Eastern regimes actively toward democratization.[16] Because the threat will only increase if current political conditions continue unchanged, a new U.S. strategy that embraces robust political change in the region is clearly needed.

Switching Gears? Democracy Initiatives after September 11

The events of September 11, 2001, served as a catalyst for a new era of democracy promotion in the Middle East. Two months after the attacks, Undersecretary for Global Affairs Paula Dobriansky argued, "The advancement of human rights and democracy is ... the bedrock of our war on terrorism."[17] The administration has since taken a number of important steps that deserve to be recognized and encouraged.

- The Millennium Challenge Account (MCA), announced in March 2002 by Bush as a new, global development-assistance initiative, will provide up to $5 billion annually to countries that "rule justly, invest in their own people, and encourage economic freedom."[18] Although officials maintain that the idea originated before September 11, the MCA was reenergized and reshaped in the aftermath of the attacks as part of the administration's new connection between development assistance and U.S. efforts to fight terrorism. Bush stated, "As we wage war today to keep the world safe from terror, we must also work to make the world a better place for all its citizens."[19] Only a limited set of countries in the Middle East will meet the strict per capita income limits, but because eligibility for aid is in part determined by a country's record of "ruling justly," the program sends an important message that democratic practices will be rewarded.

- The 2002 National Security Strategy reiterated the importance of democracy to U.S. foreign policy objectives. The document proclaimed that "[t]he national security strategy of the United States must ... look outward for possibilities to expand liberty" and stated that the United States will "use [its] foreign aid to promote freedom and support those who struggle non-violently for it, ensuring that nations moving towards democracy are rewarded for the steps they take."[20] This is the strongest pro-democracy statement that has been contained in a U.S. national security strategy—a fact that largely went unnoticed in the furor over the document's call for preemptive strikes.

- The Middle East Partnership Initiative (MEPI), announced by Powell in December 2002, was designed to address the "political, economic, and educational underdevelopment" of the Middle East.[21] The program, as announced, provided $29 million in fiscal year 2003 to promote civil society, education reform, equal status for women, economic reform, and private-sector development. Although many decried the original amount of funding, the administration recently requested $200 million for the MEPI in the FY 2003 supplemental and $145 million in its FY 2004 budget request.

- Even before MEPI was announced, the Department of State's Bureau for Democracy, Human Rights, and Labor (DRL) set aside an increased portion of its worldwide funds for promising democracy-building projects in the Middle East. Moreover, in a historically unprecedented joint effort, DRL has worked with the Bureau of Near Eastern Affairs to undertake a comprehensive review of assistance efforts in Egypt—a strategically important U.S. partner in the war against terrorism. The Bush administration's denial in August 2002 of the Egyptian government's request for additional assistance as a protest against the continued imprisonment of human rights activist Saad Eddin Ibrahim was seen as an encouraging sign of a genuine change in U.S. policy toward Egypt.

- The administration has also launched initiatives beyond the Middle East, including new and comprehensive assistance programs in Afghanistan and Pakistan. Democracy programs in a number of Central Asian countries have been significantly increased in the last two years as well.

Beyond the Rhetoric

The Bush administration's strong public statements stressing the need for democratic governments and practices, and the additional resources that have been made available toward those ends, potentially mark a historic departure from past U.S. foreign policy and assistance strategies in the Middle East, and they deserve support. In addition to the steps already taken, however, the administration can and should do more to ensure the effective implementation of its stated priority.

The administration's commitment to following through to meet its goals in the Middle East remains debatable. Skeptics doubt whether policies aimed at democratization can ever be pursued fully, given the U.S. reliance in the war on terrorism on nondemocratic partners such as Saudi Arabia—to name a particularly autocratic ally.

U.S. policies and assistance in Pakistan and Afghanistan have raised doubts about how much the Bush administration may be willing to back democratization in the Middle East as part of an antiterrorist strategy. The United States restarted a large-scale assistance program in Pakistan after the events of September 11, but that program does not have democracy building as a centerpiece of its strategy, despite the evident need for political reform. The U.S. government has also been remarkably quiet in the face of a number of decidedly undemocratic actions taken by President Pervez Musharraf. Despite its promising new rhetoric on the importance of democratization, the administration has largely ignored the promotion of democracy and has given Musharraf blanket support in exchange for his cooperation with U.S. objectives.

In the case of Afghanistan, the United States badly stumbled in meeting its postwar assistance pledges. The administration's FY 2003 budget proposal contained no request for funds for Afghanistan (on the hopes that a supplemental bill would make additional funds available). When monies began to flow, democratization programs lost priority to a road project and other humanitarian and agricultural programs. An official strategy for democratization was not approved until December 2002. Meanwhile, the United States has funded a number of activities that may complicate the eventual development of democratic institutions and processes in that country, particularly if the U.S.-funded constitutional reform effort has been hijacked, as many fear, by the head of Afghanistan's Supreme Court, who is a well-known Islamist.

One country that will be widely viewed as a litmus test of the new U.S. democracy policy is Egypt. As a result of the original Camp David process, the United States has provided Egypt with a fixed level of assistance, independent of the Egyptian government's performance or commitment to political, social, or economic reforms. Moreover, the terms of the assistance relationship allow the Egyptian government to directly approve all foreign assistance projects provided to the country by the U.S. Agency for International Development (USAID)—authority that has proven particularly problematic for democracy assistance in that country. Currently, the Egyptian government can block USAID assistance to any civil society groups it finds politically unacceptable, severely limiting the effectiveness of that support and alienating human rights activists in Egypt.

Egypt is a critical case not only because it is the largest U.S. assistance recipient in the region, but also because the process of U.S. foreign assistance allocation and distribution in Egypt provides a microcosm of the problems extant in the greater U.S. foreign assistance policy toward promoting democracy in the Middle East. The underlying problem is that U.S. foreign policy has multiple, sometimes contradictory objectives in Egypt and throughout the Middle East. In the past, democracy advocates within USAID have felt constrained by the policy dictates of a State Department and a White House that were simply not interested in promoting democracy through U.S. diplomatic or assistance efforts.

The experience of Egypt and the more recent cases of Afghanistan and Pakistan demonstrate a desperate need for clear and unified policy guidance to U.S. representatives in the region that promoting democratization really is now a priority and that foreign assistance must be utilized in a direct and deliberate fashion to foster genuine democratic reform.

Getting the Most Bang for Our Buck

To increase the effectiveness of its new democratization strategy, the administration must ensure that it has adequate resources to address the challenges of a complex region and that those resources are strategically targeted and deftly implemented.

- *The U.S. government should find ways to incorporate democratization efforts better into assistance strategies, particularly in postconflict or failed states.*

As demonstrated by the experience in Afghanistan, the current approach seems to be sequential and staged, directly providing humanitarian and reconstruction aid and support for traditional health and education concerns, while political programs tend to be indirect, focusing on generating local participation and dialogue and reinforcing the capacity and authority of central governments. Early elections are not a desirable first step in many cases, but the United States should clearly back democratization efforts at the outset and provide assistance to civic groups, human rights organizations, and independent journalists who can question and conduct dialogue with new governments. If the U.S. government delays too long in introducing democracy building in its assistance strategies, those countries' government officials might become established and unwilling to introduce processes, including elections, that might diminish their own political power.

- *If promoting democracy is as high a priority as the administration maintains, the White House needs to request, and work to ensure that Congress allocates, adequate funds for democracy assistance.*

Without a congressional earmark for democracy assistance and with mobilized constituencies inside and the outside the administration aggressively lobbying to protect other areas, funds for democracy-building programs in the past have been seen as discretionary and are the first to be cut when budget choices have to be made. The latest MEPI requests are promising, but the administration must remain focused on providing adequate resources for democracy far into the future and not let short-term, postconflict reconstruction needs squeeze out support for democracy.

- *Funds that are available must be used strategically.*

It is troubling that the U.S. government as a whole largely ignored the Middle East as a priority for democracy assistance over the last 10 years. The State Department and USAID must have an overall strategic vision—and a budget allocation process—that ensures that funds for democracy assistance are allocated according to global democracy needs and priorities, and are not driven primarily by the preferences of particular regional bureau officials. The distribution of MEPI funds should be governed by an overall strategy that guides which countries and sectors are the most critical and promising.

- *USAID should be involved.*
Ensuring strategic use of assistance also means bringing resource experts to the table. USAID is always the favorite target of criticism around Washington, but along with its arcane procurement and management processes, the agency has a wealth of experts who know how to craft programs to meet policy objectives. For the last 10 years, USAID has recruited and trained a cadre of democracy officers who form a talent base that the administration should task with designing innovative democratization programs in the Middle East and other key regions.

- *The government should tap the expertise of the U.S. nongovernmental sector.*
Civil society organizations have enormous institutional knowledge, insights, and expertise that can be brought to bear on the challenge of democratization in the Middle East. The U.S. government should provide overall strategic guidance but not try to produce detailed blueprints outlining mandatory approaches. Such micromanagement restricts the ability of nongovernmental actors to contribute new, creative ideas and approaches to the difficult task of promoting democracy in a region where no one either inside or outside the government has the "silver bullet" to promote change. Democracy programs are unavoidably politically sensitive, but U.S. ambassadors and USAID personnel should be careful to resist the urge to maximize their control through the use of contracts and elaborate reporting procedures. Insisting on such rigorous procedures simply dilutes the impact of those programs and wastes the talents of members of U.S. civil society, arguably the U.S. government's greatest asset in promoting democracy.

- *The U.S. government needs to convince democracy and human rights activists in the region that the United States is genuinely interested in promoting democratization—even if it produces short-term setbacks for other U.S. policy objectives.*

Regional perceptions of the United States are at an all-time low, which has led to initial negative reactions to the most recent U.S. initiatives. Changing those perceptions will require more than simply a slick public relations effort; it will require consistent advocacy of democracy and human rights concerns. Recognizing that democracy will not always prevail among competing policy objectives, the administration needs to evaluate more carefully the negative consequences of its short-term actions—including those taken in the war against terror—for its long-term interests in pursuing democracy in the region. In the assistance area, the United States understandably wants credit for the support it is providing for democracy and human rights in the region, but the current emphasis on branding all projects as U.S. government–supported may backfire and thus undermine the effectiveness of that support.

Patience and Diligence Required

The Bush administration deserves recognition for the emphasis it has placed on democratization as part of its long-term national security strategy and for the increased resources it has been willing to commit to pursuing this policy in the Middle East. Democratization is not without risks, but it is essential to address many of the underlying conditions that have fueled the current wave of political extremism and terrorist violence in the region. In the end, political change in the Middle East, as elsewhere, will be driven by individuals within those societies who are committed to bringing forth a new political reality in their own countries. Nevertheless, the administration can help support those reformers through a strategic allocation and implementation of democracy assistance directly to them and through clear, consistent diplomatic messages about the importance of democracy and human rights. Given the realities of the region, we should not expect immediate results, nor for regimes to emerge that are automatically pro-American. In the long term, however, it is in the overall interests of the United States that the least-democratic region of the world become a part of the emerging global community of democracies.

Notes

1. Colin Powell, speech before the Heritage Foundation, Washington, D.C., December 12, 2002 (hereinafter Powell speech).

2. See "Freedom in the World 2002: Liberty's Expansion in a Turbulent World," http://freedomhouse.org/research/freeworld/2002/web.pdf (accessed April 10, 2003) (hereinafter Freedom House survey results). Burma, Cuba, North Korea, Sudan, and Turkmenistan are the other five countries considered the "worst of the worst" by Freedom House.

3. Fareed Zakaria, *The Future of Freedom* (New York: W. W. Norton, 2003), p. 136.

4. United Nations Development Program (UNDP), *Arab Human Development Report 2002* (New York: UNDP, 2002), pp. 88, 92, and 87.

5. See Marina Ottaway, "Promoting Democracy in the Middle East: The Problem of U.S. Credibility," *Carnegie Endowment Working Papers* (Washington, D.C.: March 2003).

6. See Amartya Sen, *Development as Freedom* (New York: Random House, Anchor Books, 1999), pp. 180–186.

7. George W. Bush, *The National Security Strategy of the United States of America* (Washington, D.C.: U.S. Government Printing Office, September 2002), preface.

8. UNDP, *Human Development Report 2002* (New York: UNDP, 2003), p. 3.

9. Sen, *Development as Freedom*, p. 19.

10. George W. Bush, speech at the American Enterprise Institute, February 28, 2003.

11. See Jack L. Snyder, *From Voting to Violence: Democratization and Nationalist Conflict* (New York: W. W. Norton, 2000). See also Sharon Morris, "Mitigating and Managing Conflict," in U.S. Agency for International Development (USAID), *Foreign Aid in National Interest* (Washington, D.C.: USAID, 2003).

12. Zakaria, *The Future of Freedom*, p. 19.

13. Freedom House survey results.

14. See Samuel Huntington, *The Third Wave: Democratization in the Late Twentieth Century* (Norman, Okla.: University of Oklahoma Press, 1991).

15. Office of Democracy and Governance, USAID, "FY 2002 Democracy Assistance," Washington, D.C. Fiscal year 2002 data is estimated as of October 23, 2002.

16. Amy Hawthorne, "Can the U.S. Promote Democracy in the Middle East?" *Current History* (January 2003): 21, www.ceip.org/files/pdf/2002-HawthorneCurrentHist.pdf (accessed April 10, 2003).

17. Paula Dobriansky, speech before the Heritage Foundation, Washington, D.C., December 21, 2001.

18. George W. Bush, remarks on global development, Inter-American Development Bank, Washington, D.C., March 14, 2002.

19. Ibid.

20. *National Security Strategy of the United States of America*, Section 2 (citing President Bush).

21. Powell speech.

The Battle for Hearts and Minds

Lessons and New Directions for Foreign Assistance

The tragedy of September 11 and growing U.S. commitments around the world have forced the United States to confront escalating public expenditures for homeland defense, new private-sector costs to help protect critical infrastructure, and numerous trade-offs as security has come to overshadow other priorities. In the public mind, U.S. foreign policy post–September 11 carries a sense of urgency we have not seen in a decade. Americans feel a new sense of vulnerability; nevertheless, as we wrestle, debate, and implement programs to meet those pre– and post–September 11 challenges, our underlying foreign policy, national security, and international economic policy objectives remain constant.

U.S. policy is shaped by and encourages personal liberty and respect for human rights, democracy, pluralism, the rule of law, and broad-based capitalism as the mode of economic development. Free markets, entrepreneurial opportunity, and a withdrawal from large, state-central planning is embraced, in varying degrees, as the chief means by which nations can improve the quality of life for their citizens. Democratic choice and individual opportunity have succeeded over Communist and central-planning ideologies precisely because such systems have proven incapable of meeting urgent citizen needs.

Jim Kolbe is a Republican representative from Arizona and chairman of the House Appropriations Foreign Operations subcommittee. This article is derived from an October 2002 speech at the National Press Club.

The Washington Quarterly • 26:2 pp. 189–198.

Several months ago, Brent Scowcroft, National Security Council adviser to former president George H. W. Bush, commented that future U.S. security and prosperity in the world depends on how well we can change underlying trends in parts of the world post–September 11. In his view, problems transcend the fault lines between Islam and the West and result from a more complex, fractured state of affairs. The expansion of the United Nations from 51 member nations at its birth in 1945 to its current membership of 191 reflects this heightened fragmentation over the last half-century. For some 20 or 30 of these countries, the prospect of globalization offers a great promise of development. For the rest, it offers only a growing divide from the developed world. Simple statistics illustrate this trend: 40 years ago, the world's 20 richest nations had per capita incomes that were 20 times greater than the per capita incomes of the world's 20 poorest nations. Now, that difference is 37 times greater.[1]

As the world has increasingly fractured into a kaleidoscope of nation-states, it has, at the same time, become more united along key democratic and free-market dimensions. Freedom House noted continued gains in democracy in its 2001 annual report. Measured by the degree of political and civil liberties, it found that the number of free countries has increased from 65 in 1990 to 86 in 2001. Two-and-a-half billion people—40 percent of the world's population—live in free countries, the largest percentage since the organization began its survey. Yet, this great stride still means that the remaining 60 percent of the planet suffers from limited freedom. Freedom House also notes that the number of partly free countries increased from 50 in 1990 to 59 in 2001. By definition, "partly free" describes those nations in which limited political and civil liberties exist because of corruption, a weak rule of law, and dominance by one political party. Some 1.4 billion people, or 25 percent of the world's population, live in these countries. Despite the remarkable progress, we must continue to push to expand freedom's borders.

In the minds of some, globalization—the expansion of capitalism, or of free-market principles in practice—remains an evil phenomenon. A few months ago, Washington, D.C., witnessed another round of protests at the World Bank and International Monetary Fund (IMF) meetings. Young, mostly peaceful protesters marched through the corridors of power in our nation's capital, criticizing capitalism. Although the passions expressed by these protesters stem from valid concerns, we must not lose sight of the fact that the United States and the international community have an overriding foreign policy interest in sustainable global integration. Moving toward this goal will help generate the benefits that can allow the United States to attain its development and foreign policy objectives.

"Is globalization here to stay?" is not, in my view, a question that is still in doubt in either the United States or the developing world. For example, the General Agreement on Tariffs and Trade (GATT) at its inception in 1947 had 23 nations as original signers. Now, the World Trade Organization (WTO), its successor organization, has more than 140 members, of which developing nations, surprisingly enough, comprise 80 percent. Furthermore, the WTO reports that international trade has increased from $1.8 trillion in 1983 to more than $6 trillion in 2000.[2] The widespread commitment among nations to the principles of capitalism and global trade is apparent.

Aid, Trade, and Development

Over these last two sessions of Congress, I have worked hard with my colleagues to make strides in U.S. foreign assistance. Although the appropriations process for fiscal year 2003 has stalled, when the dust settles, total foreign assistance levels will not be reduced from the increases contained within the foreign operations bill passed by the House Appropriations Committee. If we assume the levels contained in the bill are enacted, U.S. assistance programs to improve child survival will have increased from a little more than $1 billion in 2001 to $1.7 billion in 2003, an increase of $700 million, or 60 percent. In addition, over the past two years, we have worked to increase funding levels to combat global health diseases.

For example, HIV/AIDS funding has more than doubled, growing from $315 million in 2001 to $786 million in 2002. Over the 2002–2003 period, Congress plans to set aside $250 million—plus an expected $100 million from the FY 2003 labor, health, and human services appropriations bill—to bring the total U.S. contribution to $650 million for the Global Fund to Fight AIDS, Tuberculosis & Malaria—the largest contribution from a single nation. Certainly, these are significant investments in fighting the pandemic, but it is clear that much more will be necessary. The Joint United Nations Program on HIV/AIDS (UNAIDS) estimates that programs in developing countries and countries in transition will need to have about $10 billion annually to fight the pandemic by 2005—just three years from now. All governments, including and specifically the United States, must increase the resources they commit to fighting this disease.

Although I take some satisfaction in these and other foreign assistance accomplishments, their impact pales in comparison to a single vote for and efforts to ultimately enact Trade Promotion Authority (TPA). That accomplishment of the 107th Congress was almost 10 years in the making. In my 18 years of Congress, it was the most dramatic bill on which I have ever worked. When first considered on the House floor on December 6, 2001, the vote was open for 48 minutes. It passed on two occasions by a single vote. In my opinion, the passage of TPA was the most important development-assistance vote in Congress in the last 10 years. It gave the president the authority to lead international trade negotiations and gave this country an indispensable tool to meet the challenge of globalization. TPA will make a dramatic difference in the developing world if used as a powerful lever to generate free trade among developed and developing countries.

That TPA vote, in my opinion, will have far greater impact than any investment the United States can make in foreign aid. Most U.S. development-assistance investments will fall far short of their objectives, if they are not completely wasted, unless economic and political systems exist to sustain them and generate economic growth as a result. With foreign assistance alone, we may positively touch a few lives, but we will see little long-term improvement in the quality of life for the people of the developing world. The traditional forms of assistance may make us feel good, but they will not last unless other economic tools work.

Lessons Learned in Development Assistance

As public officials and people of influence in development policy, it is our responsibility to continuously seek to improve our aid delivery as well as ensure that our overall development policy benefits from lessons learned over the last several decades.

LESSON #1: IT IS NOT THE QUANTITY OF FOREIGN ASSISTANCE THAT IS INTEGRAL TO SUCCESSFUL DEVELOPMENT.

The United States has given more than $167 billion (in constant 1999 U.S. dollars) in official development assistance (ODA) to 156 countries, regions, and territories since 1980. Of that number, 97 entities for which data is available received more than $144 billion in inflation-adjusted ODA since 1980; yet that group's median-inflation-adjusted per capita gross domestic product (GDP) declined from $1,076 in 1980 to $994 in 2000[3]—a decline in real terms.

No solid relationship is apparent between economic growth and ODA levels. Another study noted that, between 1980 and 2000, 23 recipients of U.S. ODA received amounts equivalent to one quarter of their entire GDP in 2000. This is just U.S. assistance; it does not include aid from other nations or the World Bank. Growth in per capita GDP for these countries averaged -0.16 percent, with 12 countries experiencing negative growth, and only 4 countries experiencing growth of more than 1 percent.[4] In another study, a former World Bank development economist found a similar noncorrelation. Bill Easterly noted that, between 1950 and 1995, Western countries gave $1 trillion in aid in constant 1985 dollars. He concluded, after studying investment and growth patterns in more than 80 countries in a similar time frame, that "[a]mong all low-income countries, there is not a clear relationship between aid and growth."[5] The time frames of these studies—20 years and 45 years, respectively—should be noted because the long duration provided sufficient time for positive progress to be achieved.

Simply put, the focus on the amount of aid is misplaced. Tax policy, regulatory policy, anticorruption practices, transparency, and the rule of law matter far more in a developing country than the amount of development assistance.

LESSON #2: IT'S ALL ABOUT ECONOMIC GROWTH.

Recent success has occurred in poverty reduction, among other key areas of development. In 1990, 29 percent of the world's population lived on an income of less than a dollar per day. In 2000 it was 23 percent, a 6-point drop. The absolute number of people living on less than a dollar per day has declined even as the world population has increased.[6] Yet, simultaneously, the ODA level has been reduced by 30 percent.[7]

Other measures confirm this progress. During 1990–2000, adult illiteracy rates for males aged 15 and older in low-income nations decreased from 35 percent to 28 percent; for females aged 15 and older, the figure declined from 56 percent to 47 percent.[8] Although only 30 percent of people in the developing world had access to clean drinking water in 1970, that figure has increased to about 80 percent today.[9] Wages and conditions have improved as economies have grown. In 1970, 35 percent of all people in developing countries were severely malnourished. In 1990 the figure had fallen to 20 percent.[10]

Why have we seen this success? Increased personal incomes enable nations to achieve their aspirations and go hand in hand with broad-based economic growth. Success stories around the globe, mostly in countries that did not receive U.S. aid, prove it. China's growth has been consistent at 7 percent, reaching 10 percent over the last decade. Indonesia, Vietnam, Brazil, and Mozambique have sustained significant economic growth. Some countries have even managed to double GDP per capita, including Botswana, Chile, Thailand, and Korea. None are major aid recipients.

Such sustained growth is only possible with capitalism, investment, and trade. The World Bank's empirical research shows that, during the last decade, income per capita in developing countries that were focused on capitalism and participation in the global trading system grew more than three times faster than in those countries that chose not to participate. Moreover, the World Bank found that the benefits of that economic growth were evenly distributed throughout the population strata of those countries. As a result, the absolute poverty rates for trading nations have also fallen sharply over the last 10 years. History has indeed shown that nations that have embraced democracy combined with capitalism and participation in the global trading system have experienced the highest economic growth and generated the highest quality of life for their citizens.

LESSON #3: GOOD GOVERNANCE MATTERS.

Yet, free markets and trade are not sufficient. For instance, several Latin American countries have been moving toward a free market for the last decade, but economic growth remains elusive. Some experts suggest that the growth of the early 1990s appears to have been an aberration—a few years sandwiched between the lost decade of the 1980s and the lost second-half of the 1990s. As a result, popular acceptance of free markets and democracy across Latin America is less certain.

The power of free markets as a tool of development cannot be exercised without the correct policy environment. Thomas Friedman, the Pulitzer Prize-winning diplomatic columnist, explains that nations must have a good governance "plug" to integrate into the global economy. A poor-quality plug simply will not meet the expectations of a global capitalist economy. Good governance is dependent on the creation of a corruption-free environment, supported by functional rule of law.

This is the case in Latin America. Historically, gross inequities of wealth and income in the region have created political environments that allow bureaucracies to manipulate the economy to benefit the power elite. As a result, pockets of both political and economic instability stretch from Haiti to Argentina. We should not be surprised that incentives exist for the traditional authoritarian Left or Right to stall growth toward free markets and more effective democratic governance.

LESSON #4: WE NEED TO REMAIN FOCUSED.

At both the multilateral and bilateral level, we have been ensnared in a cycle of "do-everything development," as Bill Easterly stated in his article, "The Cartel of Good Intentions."[11] Easterly uses the example of the IMF requirement for low-income countries to submit a Poverty Reduction Strategy Paper (PRSP). Niger's recently completed PRSP is 187 pages long, took 15 months to develop, and sets out spending for a five-year, poverty-reduction plan. The PRSP, in turn, must be compliant with the World Bank's Comprehensive Development Framework, a 14-point checklist covering everything from lumber policy to labor practices. This framework covers clean government, property rights, finance, social safety nets, education, water, arts, roads, cities, and tax policy. Policymakers seeking aid must complete a litany of reports, often duplicates or similar reports for multiple institutions—an incredibly inefficient process.

Foreign Assistance: One Leg of a Three-Legged Stool

With those four lessons in mind, we should evaluate carefully what we think the role of our development assistance should be. But before addressing that question, it is important to articulate how U.S. foreign assistance is an integral component of our overall foreign and national security policy. I often relate our total foreign assistance—the entire foreign operations bill—as one leg of a three-legged stool providing a sturdy U.S. foreign policy. Each leg is essential for the stool to carry the weight of the policies projected and coming together at the top. One leg is that of our diplomatic corps and intelligence services; another relates to national defense and security strategy; and the third has, as its core, our foreign assistance.

Our foreign assistance in a macro sense plays multiple roles within our foreign policy process. At its first level, the foreign assistance leg can be used as a vital tool to ease the suffering of people around the world. At a more nuanced level, it can enhance health, education, and national infrastructure. In light of security challenges to the United States, we can also link the foreign assistance leg of the stool to the national security leg by using it in the form of Foreign Military Financing. Of even more importance, it can and should nurture the structures of capitalism and the rule of law, making it possible for the poor to participate in market economies and for poor countries to participate in the global economy.

I believe this is the role we should want development assistance to play. If experience shows that successful development is driven by a country's ability to access and use all its available resources for economic growth—particularly those that relate to integration in the global economy—then we must strategically align development assistance to that end. Our development assistance should serve as a catalyst to help countries prepare for greater participation in the global economy.

Where Do We Go from Here?

It is time to move beyond the debate on the quantity of foreign assistance to a focus on economic growth and helping countries maximize the benefits of participating in the global economy.

We must be sure that our expectations and definition of success are aligned with our development experience. All too often, advocates for development assistance argue that success is only a matter of additional resources. Experience tells us otherwise. Decades of development experience have demonstrated that resource transfers—without the environment of an effective political economy—will generate poor results. Our policy development and our advocacy must place an emphasis on those policies that will generate success—not simply the addition of more resources.

The United States must generate a development policy that is more holistic in outlook. Two pillars must be elevated in importance. First,

U.S. policy must recognize trade and foreign direct investment as development tools. Second, economic growth must become its own objective and be strongly integrated into the fabric of our development programs. This is particularly true for many African countries where HIV/AIDS is actually projected to reduce GDP growth rates, making the situation of responding to the pandemic even more challenging.

Historically, we have focused exclusively on increases in foreign assistance and debt relief as the chief drivers of development. I would argue that giving developing countries access to the markets of the United States, Europe, and Japan creates a self-reliant path while aid is a donor-development path. For instance, if sub-Saharan Africa had an additional 1 percent of international markets in the form of exports, the region would have $60 billion more in resources derived from revenue earned through international trade.[12]

Our domestic discussion on development must consider the potential cost of failure in the new round of trade talks that were launched in Doha, Qatar, in November 2001 or of failure in negotiations for U.S. free-trade agreements (FTAs) with Central America or the countries of southern Africa. The World Bank has calculated that a successful round of global trade negotiations, coupled with related market reforms, could add a whopping $2.8 trillion to global income by 2015—much of it in developing countries.[13]

Knowing that we have a tendency to ask developing countries to accomplish all of our bilateral objectives at the same time, it is imperative that we remain focused. That should result from a reflection on our need to break out of the trap of "do-everything development."

These messages of trade and focus are not ones that we—and many in the development or advocacy communities—are accustomed to hearing. In fact, some do not wish to hear it. We have become so devoted to the assistance programs or causes we each represent. Moreover, if we are serious about development, we have to be serious about trade. As a representative of Oxfam International has said, however, the "playing field is not level."[14] It slopes downhill from developed countries.

As the Bush administration continues to work on the Millennium Challenge Account (MCA), I would offer these suggestions. It should consider offering MCA recipient countries special consideration for expedited bilateral trade preferences (such as those offered in conjunction with the African Growth and Opportunity Act or the Andean Trade Preferences Act) or the option of negotiating an FTA with the United States. The administration should offer developing countries the prospect of ownership of their development strategies with U.S. assistance. In exchange for ownership, developing countries should be willing to accept the fact that MCA resources may be withdrawn if criteria for eligibility are not maintained or results not achieved. The MCA should aim to build and reinforce the governmental capacity of recipient countries to manage their own development. In establishing the MCA, we must minimize the administrative bureaucracy and bureaucratic requirements in assistance delivery. Once countries qualify, the MCA should complement current assistance efforts but, most importantly, generate a focus on economic growth and self-sufficiency.

Finally, the administration should aim to make sure development and economic opportunity is extended to those currently outside the formal economy. By this, I mean that the rule of law, property rights, and the ideas of Hernando DeSoto should be incorporated into our programs as a development goal.[15] The promise of capitalism as a tool for economic development and poverty reduction can never fully be achieved as long as large populations have no stake in the capitalist mode of development.

In conclusion, I firmly believe that we are going to have to think outside the box in our development-assistance programs. The reality is that what we have tried in the past has not worked. We must learn from our prior experiences, and in light of the challenges we face, we must be open to new ideas and tools that will help us prioritize our efforts when helping countries achieve broad-based economic growth and integration into the global economy.

Notes

1. See Gerald F. Seib, "World Disorder: Can the U.S. Thrive If It's the Norm?" *Wall Street Journal*, February 27, 2002.

2. International Monetary Fund (IMF), *International Financial Statistics Yearbook 2002* (Washington, D.C.: International Monetary Fund, 2002), pp. 127, 133 (measured as world merchandise).

3. Brett D. Schaefer, testimony before the Foreign Operations subcommittee of the Appropriations Committee, U.S. House of Representatives, June 27, 2002.

4. Ibid.

5. William Easterly, *The Elusive Quest for Growth* (Boston: The Massachusetts Institute of Technology, 2001), pp. 25–45.

6. Data taken from statistics shared by Dr. Frances Rischard, World Bank.

7. Ibid.

8. World Bank, *World Development Indicators 2002* (Washington, D.C.: World Bank, 2002), table 2.14.

9. "Moore Welcomes Oxfam Report But Cites Ommissions and Errors," World Trade Organization press release no. 285, April 2002.

10. Ibid.

11. William Easterly, "The Cartel of Good Intentions," *Foreign Policy* (July/August 2002): 40–49.

12. One percent of world merchandise exports as reported in IMF, *International Financial Statistics Yearbook 2002*, p. 133.

13. World Bank, *Global Economic Prospects: Making Trade Work for the World's Poor* (Washington, D.C.: World Bank, 2001), p. xiii.

14. Kevin Watkins, comments during "Fair Trade and the Fight Against Poverty," forum sponsored by the Carnegie Endowment for International Peace, July 2, 2002.

15. See Hernando De Soto, *The Mystery of Capital: Why Capitalism Triumphs in the West and Fails Everywhere Else* (New York: Basic Books, 2000).